INDIVIDUALISM AND
ITS DISCONTENTS

Individualism and Its Discontents

APPROPRIATIONS OF EMERSON, 1880–1950

Charles E. Mitchell

University of Massachusetts Press

AMHERST

Copyright © 1997 by
The University of Massachusetts Press
All rights reserved
Printed in the United States of America
LC 96-39859
ISBN 1-55849-073-6
Set in Adobe Garamond by Keystone Typesetting, Inc.
Printed and bound by Braun-Brumfield, Inc.
Library of Congress Cataloging-in-Publication Data
Mitchell, Charles E., 1962–
Individualism and its discontents : appropriations of Emerson,
1880–1950 / Charles E. Mitchell.
p. cm.
Includes bibliographical references (p.) and index.
ISBN 1-55849-073-6 (alk. paper)
1. Emerson, Ralph Waldo, 1803–1882—Political and social views.
2. American literature—20th century—History and criticism.
3. American literature—19th century—History and criticism.
4. Emerson, Ralph Waldo, 1803–1882—Influence.
5. United States—Civilization—1865–1918.
6. United States—Civilization—1918–1945.
7. Individualism—United States—History.
8. Individualism in literature.   I. Title.
PS1642.S58M58   1997
810.9'005—dc21   96-39859
                                         CIP
British Library Cataloguing in Publication data are available.

Grateful acknowledgment is given to New Directions Publishing Corporation and Carcanet Press Ltd. for permission to quote from the following copyrighted works of William Carlos Williams: *The Autobiography of William Carlos Williams,* © 1948, 1951 by William Carlos Williams; *Collected Poems: Volume 2: 1939–1961,* © 1944, 1953, 1962, by William Carlos Williams, © 1988 by William Eric Williams and Paul H. Williams; *The Embodiment of Knowledge,* © 1974 by Florence H. Williams; *Imaginations,* © 1970 by Florence H. Williams; *In the American Grain,* © 1925 by James Laughlin; © 1933 by William Carlos Williams; *Paterson,* © 1946, 1948, 1949, 1958 by William Carlos Williams; *Selected Essays,* © 1954 by William Carlos Williams; *Selected Letters of William Carlos Williams,* © 1957 by William Carlos Williams.

For my parents, Charles E. and Margaret T. Mitchell

The best read naturalist who lends an entire and devout attention to truth, will see that there remains much to learn of his relation to the world, and that it is not to be learned by any addition or subtraction or other comparison of known quantities, but is arrived at by untaught sallies of the spirit, by a continual self-recovery, and by entire humility.

RALPH WALDO EMERSON, *Nature*

CONTENTS

꧁꧂

ACKNOWLEDGMENTS

As with all first books, mine has accrued more than its fair share of debt. I begin with those at the Claremont Graduate School whose compassion, encouragement, and plain decency disproved all of my worst fears about life in graduate school. Robert Dawidoff guided this project from its inception, and his example continues to inspire my own teaching and scholarship. Rena Fraden read the first version of each chapter with undeserved care, and her insightful comments contributed greatly to the final product. Michael Roth graciously loaned me the subtitle, and helped to convince me that I actually knew what I was talking about. LeeAnn Meyer read early parts of the manuscript and did her best to keep me honest and clear in my thinking. I am grateful to the John Randolph Haynes and Dora Haynes Foundation for its generous support during an early stage of this project.

Michael Kiskis, John McLaughlin, and Scott Minar, colleagues at Elmira College, offered many helpful comments, some of which pertained to the book; they also helped to create the atmosphere of refined madness that has spurred me on to completion. Bryan Reddick, Elmira's dean, provided various kinds of support, and for that and other things I thank him. Karen Sue Bishop assisted in the proofreading and exhibited skill and effort in compiling the index.

Clark Dougan and the staff at the University of Massachusetts Press offered me more encouragement than I deserved, and made this experience a downright enjoyable one. Two readers for the press gave detailed criticism that has considerably improved the book; its lingering weaknesses no doubt result from my stubborn refusal to follow all of their suggestions.

I owe a particular debt of gratitude to Mike Weiner and Diane Margolin, who provided me with something of a writer's retreat during a crucial stage of this project. Their chief contribution, however, came through their daughter, Margie Lynn Weiner, who would toddle into my room, see me staring helplessly out the window, and urge me to "Sit sit, read read, work work." If I hesitated, she would climb up on my chair and attack the keyboard herself. Without her insistence, and her useful editorial contributions, I would still be staring.

I have been graced with parents and grandparents who selflessly encouraged and supported my education, despite their never having enjoyed similar opportunities. This book is but a small measure of my appreciation. Finally, I thank my wife, Brooke Newell, for her companionship over the course of this project. In particular, I am grateful for the consideration she showed in allowing me to continue to do all the cooking, dishwashing, and household chores, each, she assured me, a valuable form of therapy. I look forward to providing her with similar assistance someday.

INTRODUCTION

"An Individualism of Vaporous Spirituality"

"Can I teach a course on American individualism without including Emerson?" I confronted this seemingly heretical question a few years ago as I undertook the revision of a lower-level American Studies course I had inherited from a colleague. The absence of Emerson from the original syllabus both troubled and relieved me: while it offended my hard-won appreciation of the centrality of Emerson to the discourses of individualism in America, it also eased the anxiety I felt at the prospect of eliciting that same appreciation from nineteen-year-olds. If my own undergraduate encounter with the Sage of Concord was any indication, the best I could hope for would be to break even: once we finished with Emerson, the students might come back to class. Fortunately, as it turned out, my sense of propriety got the better of my instinctive search for low resistance, and I decided to devote a week to "Self-Reliance," "The Divinity School Address," and selections from *Nature*.

This decision was fortunate not simply because it would have been irresponsible to exclude Emerson from such a course, but because the inclusion of Emerson helped to ground the lively debate that the course promoted. I was pleased to discover that my students were intensely interested in the various manifestations of "individualism" in American life. They located within the cultural history of individualism sources for many of the social, cultural, and political issues that pervade their own world. Of course, their attitudes toward these issues and toward the varieties of individualism associated with them differed. Nonetheless, each student was able to come up with lengthy catalogues in response to two questions: What are some contemporary problems that you associate with a too-strong devotion to individualism? What are some contemporary problems that you associate with a too-weak devotion to individualism? What emerged from these discussions was a clear sense that the contemporary rhetoric of individualism is rife with paradox, contradiction, and a remarkable flexibility. Where better to root this confusion than in the work of Emerson?

The discussions of Emerson turned out to be a microcosm of the course. Self-described conservative students admired the tough love of "Self-Reliance," feared the anarchy implicit in "The Divinity School Address," and were suspicious of the New-Ageism that reverberated throughout *Nature*. These same students warmed to the echoes of Emerson in the Social Darwinist William Graham Sumner, condemned Edna Pontellier (in Kate Chopin's *The Awakening*) for abandoning her family responsibilities, and thought that there was no room for the "expressive individualism" of the Beats and Dennis Rodman. Libertarian-leaning students admired Emerson's tough-love *and* his attack on established religion, but were less than impressed with his mysticism. These students considered Charlotte Perkins Gilman to be a whiner for complaining about the corrosive effects of individualism on women, and affirmed Huck Finn's decision to "light out for the territory." Finally, liberal students tended to reject Emerson's anti-society views, but were quick to embrace his ecumenical approach to religion. They respected Edward Bellamy's attempt to articulate an alternative to individualism, John Dewey's attempt to define a new individualism, and the anticonformity of Jack Kerouac's *On the Road*. They also appreciated the connection between Emerson's anti-establishment religious sentiments and those of Martin Luther King's "Letter from Birmingham Jail."

While these alignments are, in themselves, rather unsurprising, they nonetheless reveal the degree of confusion that accompanies contemporary discussions of individualism in American life. Few people want to be seen as opposing the most dominant trait in our national character, but even fewer can deny that American society is currently plagued by some form of individualism run amok. Indeed, our confrontation with Emerson prompted a good deal of critical reappraisal: religious liberals struggled to distinguish David Koresh from Emerson's plea for a private relationship with the Divine, while conservatives questioned the equity of a legal system that sees no difference between individual human beings and individual corporations. I found my students' healthy debate of these questions to be refreshingly sincere when compared with the pronouncements emanating from various public officials and social commentators—of all political stripes—who, while paying fealty to some vague notion of individualism, simultaneously argue that some other vague notion of individualism is the source of all our ills.

It should come as no surprise to students of Emerson that the discourse of individualism in America is marked by such contradiction and paradox. If, as I believe, Emerson is the most articulate and representative expounder of American individualism, it is because his own work so clearly reflects the contradictions and paradoxes inherent in democratic individuality. In the over one hundred years since his death, Emerson has been claimed by back-to-the-landers and industrial capitalists, Nietzsche and Nike footwear. All such claims of Emerson, and indeed all commentary on him, are ultimately based on some understanding of his treatment of individualism: his observations on the relationship between the individual and the universe, or the individual and social institutions; his reflections on the place of individuals of genius within a democracy; his consideration of the value of history and tradition in shaping the lives of individuals in the present. In short, Emerson confronted in his own work the issues that were and remain at the core of American democracy.[1]

That the legacy of Emersonian individualism remains contested terrain can be seen in two recent and very different assessments. George Kateb's study of democratic individuality places Emerson, along with Thoreau and Whitman, at the head of a tradition of rights-based individualism that is the *sine qua non* of American democracy.[2] While Kateb offers much of his analysis as a response to communitarian critics of individualism, he is careful to distinguish democratic individuality from the oft-remarked excesses of other individualisms:

> The theory of democratic individuality rejects or attenuates or does no more than flirt with such individualist self-conceptions as the Byronic (to be at total war with one's society in behalf of one's transgressive uniqueness), the vulgar Nietzschean (to define oneself by reference to one's ability to look down on others or impose oneself on them), the Napoleonic (to use people as one's artistic medium), and the idealist (to imagine that oneself is alone real and the world is either one's effluence or only shadows and images). (I simplify.) None of these self-conceptions suits the theory of a democratic society of individuality: each is built on unending antagonism or a refusal of moral or existential equality. (31)

The moral implications of democratic individuality are crucial for Kateb, in that it is the lack of such a moral basis that the critics of individualism—liberals and conservatives—decry most loudly. Kateb's liberal individualism ensures a respect for others because "one must be a democratic individual to individuate one's sympathy and perception. . . . One becomes an individual above one's normal level by breaking up the world into individuals equally worthy of attention and response." Ultimately, democratic individuality differs from other types of individualism because it carries with it the "conviction that one can make the sense of one's infinitude a bridge to other human beings and perhaps to the rest of nature" (34).

Kateb locates the key to this form of individualism in Emerson's notion of self-abandonment, his move "away from egoism" and effort to "encourage a more intense awareness of everything outside oneself" (236). More recently, Christopher Newfield has argued that this same notion of self-abandonment places Emerson at the head of a tradition that inculcates "a habit of submission to authority that weakens autonomy and democracy alike."[3] For Newfield, Emerson's is a "corporate individualism," a "halfway democracy [that] defines freedom as individual movement and personal growth, but accompanies these with the pleasurable loss of self-governance" (5, 13). In such a scheme, corporate individualism, democratic individualism, liberal authoritarianism, and corporate liberalism become interchangeable, and the source of this pernicious confusion is Emerson himself. While Kateb tries to reconcile Emerson with his own understanding of liberal individualism, Newfield rejects liberalism and Emerson's affiliation with it outright. For Newfield, Emerson's and liberalism's effort to reconcile opposites—freedom and order, liberty and union, the self and society—is the problem rather than the solution, and liberalism itself must be transcended in the move toward a purer form of democracy characterized by a less restrained individualism (2, 214–18).[4]

It is my argument in this book that the meaning of Emerson's individualism has always been contested, and that the positions taken in this debate have invariably colored more general appraisals of Emerson and his work. Since the publication of *Nature* in 1836, critics have evaluated Emerson on the basis of the perceived appropriateness of his individualism. During the fifty or so years after his death in 1882, the cumulative force of these evaluations was singularly dismissive. Indeed, the wealth of scholarship devoted to Emerson over the past fifty years has obscured the fact that he did not always command such a prominent position in America's literary and intellectual tradition. In the decades before F. O. Matthiessen, Perry Miller, Sherman Paul, and Stephen Whicher revitalized Emerson scholarship, few poets or philosophers, critics or historians, claimed any significant allegiance to Emerson or cared to argue that his legacy held any relevance for American intellectual and cultural life.[5] Even Emerson's open admirers, like William James (who once described him as "really a critter to be thankful for"), were reluctant to claim any affinity for his ideas. Emerson occupied, at best, a peripheral place on the critical scene in the

1920s and 1930s, occasionally resurrected for whatever feeble authority he might still bestow, but more often held up as the symbol of a no longer usable past.

I begin my study with the period between Emerson's death in 1882 and the celebration of the centennial of his birth in 1903. During this time Emerson enjoyed something of an apotheosis. The eulogies overflowed with enthusiastic tributes to his personal characteristics, and successive commentators strove to surpass each other in praising his nobility of mind and purity of spirit. At the same time, these tributes effectively preempted any serious attention to his writings: after an obligatory summary of a few key ideas from the *Essays,* the typical observer proceeded to claim that Emerson's writings, however elegant, were simply too obscure to be of interest to future generations. Rather, his true significance and the source of his future reputation would rest on the timeless qualities of character and temperament that Emerson possessed in such abundance.

This focus on Emerson's exemplary personal character at the expense of the ideas contained in his writings was characteristic of the "genteel" criticism of the late nineteenth century. Writers like Oliver Wendell Holmes, Edmund Clarence Stedman, and Henry Van Dyke portrayed an Emerson who reflected their own expectations for American culture—that it be well-mannered, polite, and politically united—a set of criteria that left little room for Emerson's enigmatic and potentially volatile writings. As I will suggest, the genteel critics diverted attention from Emerson's writings while enshrining him as a cultural icon, leaving the impression that he was someone who demanded reverence but not necessarily a careful reading. By the time of the centennial this genteel image dominated discussion of Emerson's life and influence, and his greatness was accepted uncritically, as a historical fact, with only uneasy allusions to the substance of his work.

In short, chapter 1 sketches the creation and institutionalization of "Emersonianism," a broad collection of pithy sayings and motivational sentiments that quickly came to displace any direct confrontation with their putative source. Emerson, as a writer and lecturer who sought to challenge his audience more than to soothe it, was lost within the sickly sweetness of his afterglow. Chapter 2 details a series of encounters with Emersonianism by critics who had set out with at least the intention of engaging Emerson himself. While some were partially successful in peeling away the layers that concealed Emerson from view, most pointed to the all-too-obvious flaws of Emersonianism as sufficient evidence that Emerson himself was a liability. This rejection of Emerson—accomplished through a rejection of Emersonianism—was the most widely shared characteristic among the diverse figures working in the heyday of American cultural criticism between 1910 and 1940. From H. L. Mencken to Van Wyck Brooks and Irving Babbitt to Granville Hicks, the major critics of this period found Emerson to be an obstacle, someone who occupied a good deal of space in the literary canon but who ultimately had nothing important to say. Many of these critics read him as affirming an empty idealism and corrosive individualism that had no constructive role to play in modern experience, and dismissed him as the shopworn relic of an outdated and bankrupt tradition. In T. S. Eliot's revealing and frequently cited phrase, the Emerson that the modern critics had inherited from their genteel predecessors was "already an encumbrance," and most of the younger generation was content to shed itself of the burden.

Eliot's remarks are worth considering in their fuller context since they are representative of the stance many critics adopted toward Emerson. Making a case for Nathaniel Hawthorne's preeminence among the major American literary figures of the nineteenth century, Eliot concludes: "Neither Emerson nor any of the others was a real observer of the moral life. Hawthorne was, and was a realist. . . . In consequence, [his] observation of moral life . . . has solidity, has permanence, the permanence of art. It will always be of use; the essays of Emerson are already an encumbrance."[6] Eliot and the modern critics I discuss considered Emerson to be an encumbrance because there was no place for him in their search for a "usable past"; whatever significance he may have attained was rooted in the values and ideals of the nineteenth century, and he had neither the "solidity" nor the "permanence" necessary to be of other than passing interest to later generations. Of course, these critics pursued very different objectives in their work, and the uses for which they found Emerson unsuited were varied as well. Nonetheless, they did share a sense of Emerson's having overstayed his welcome, and they responded to him as if he were the product of cultural featherbedding: though his stature ensured that he was still a figure to be reckoned with, his skills were simply obsolete.

In an ironic twist, these younger critics effectively endorsed the genteel version of Emerson by accepting it largely at face value. Mencken, Brooks, and the others responded not so much to an original encounter with Emerson's work as to the Emerson who emerged from the pages of Holmes, Stedman, and Van Dyke. Such men were the avatars of the very tradition these younger critics sought to renounce, and as Emerson was so clearly their favored son, it was perhaps inevitable that the younger critics came to condemn him as guilty by association. If the genteel critics praised Emerson for his noble character, the modern critics saw this character as evidence of his irrelevance; if the genteel critics considered Emerson's detachment from the seedy details of everyday life to be his most commendable trait, the modern critics found his detachment from the experience of real life deplorable. In short, the major critics of this period were concerned primarily with discrediting the Emerson whom their forebears had enshrined and showed little interest in exploring the possibility that he might support alternate readings.

The example of Irving Howe helps to illustrate this point. In his autobiography Howe notes that, among his circle of New York critics in the 1930s and 1940s, the "whole complex of Emersonianism seemed pale, disabling, genteel, an individualism of vaporous spirituality." He goes on to observe: "we abandoned Emerson even before encountering him." While Howe eventually revised this judgment—coming to recognize that "every major American writer bears the stamp of Emerson"—his initial disdain suggests how much impact the genteel appropriation had on Emerson's subsequent reception. Howe elaborated on this in an interview with William Cain: "[We] tended to take a rather simplistic view of the whole Emersonian tradition. The idea of the paleness, the thinness, of the Emersonian tradition was one that [Philip] Rahv had picked up from various earlier critics, and it was by and large taken for granted."[7] Like Howe, many of the critics whom I discuss in chapter 2 took the genteel Emerson's "vaporous spirituality" for granted, and their rejection of that Emersonian tradition as thin and disabling was in many ways a foregone conclusion.

While the professional literary and cultural critics came to exclude Emerson from their canon of usable forebears, a number of key figures picked up strands of Emerson's thought and wove it intricately, if subtly, into their own work. The second part of this study aims to uncover this process in the work of William James, John Dewey, W.E.B. Du Bois, and William Carlos Williams. Though some discussion of Emerson's "influence" on these writers is inevitable, I am primarily interested in locating their work within a tradition that has its roots in Emerson. This tradition is defined by a common interest in such issues as the competing demands of the individual and the community, the public role of intellectual and artistic endeavor, and the meaning and value of the American past. Each of the writers I consider shares with Emerson a deep respect for individual experience and expression, and a distrust of inherited forms of tradition and authority. As I suggested above, it was the perceived simplicity of Emerson's individualism and antinomianism that led many critics to dismiss him as irrelevant. James, Dewey, Du Bois, and Williams, on the other hand, seized on these elements of Emerson's thought and built them into the foundation of their own work. Taking Emerson's radical individualism and his charge to cultivate an original relation to the universe as their starting point, they provided the context for these "rootless" ideas that others claimed was lacking.[8]

This is what I mean when I speak of these writers as working within an Emersonian tradition. Though each of them was familiar with Emerson's ideas and responded to them in some form, I am concerned less with these direct responses than with the question of shared interests and approaches, the way in which these writers echoed each other's work, and the work of Emerson, when confronting similar problems. This use of "tradition" is suggested most succinctly by Richard Brodhead, who details the various guises Hawthorne's work assumes in the novels of Herman Melville, William Dean Howells, Henry James, and William Faulkner. While these encounters are not always direct—and in Faulkner's case they tend to be elusive—Brodhead makes a convincing case for Hawthorne's place at the head of a tradition in which these other writers worked. The point is not their direct response to Hawthorne as a teacher, but their pursuit of shared interests and confrontation with similar problems. Such a study avoids the temptation of reductionism that might accompany a more narrow discussion of "influence," and illuminates the way in which the participants in a tradition both work within its boundaries and forge their own paths.[9]

The effort to define Emerson's contributions to American culture has resulted in a bountiful and richly varied body of scholarship, and I will now turn to a few of these as a means of situating my own work. My sense of how to envision an Emersonian tradition has benefited from Sherman Paul's exploration of the "green American tradition," a "branch of Emersonian thought emphasizing organic process, vital expression, cultural and political democracy, and the cultivation of an indigenous art."[10] Paul roots this tradition in Emerson and extends it to include such figures as Randolph Bourne, Edmund Wilson, Louis Sullivan, and Gary Snyder, each of whom "taught us to reattach ourselves to life and to renew ourselves in vital experiences."[11] Though my focus differs from his, Paul's work exemplifies the broad yet perceptive strokes with which such a tradition might be traced, and his cast of characters might readily join mine in a fuller portrait of the "tribe of Waldo." Similarly, Christopher Lasch has informed my efforts to understand Emerson as someone who shunned the easy optimism and empty assertions of individual boundlessness that so many other critics have assigned to him. In Lasch's reading, as in my own, Emerson was poignantly aware of human suffering and the tyranny of fate and he affirmed the dignity of the individual in spite of these limits rather than in ignorance of them.[12]

While Lasch and Paul suggest readings of Emerson that complement my own, David Marr's *American Worlds since Emerson* advances an argument against which my own work is almost entirely arranged.[13] Marr argues that Emerson's powerful notion of the "infinitude of the private man" founded an American intellectual tradition that has been both politically and socially corrosive. By subordinating social existence to the spiritual claims of the private individual and advancing a notion of a republic of letters rather than a body politic, Emerson paved the way for others—including, by Marr's account, William James and W.E.B. Du Bois—to deny not only the significance of community but the relevance of social and political action altogether. Though Marr's analysis is provocative, it rests on what I think is a narrow reading not only of Emerson but of the other figures in his tradition.

Two other studies have a more direct bearing on my own. Cornel West gathers most of the figures I discuss—including James, Dewey, and Du Bois—and places them in a "genealogy of pragmatism" that runs from Emerson through Richard Rorty.[14] Emerson sets the tone for West's examination of the later thinkers, for it was he who most forcefully articulated American pragmatism's evasion of epistemology-centered philosophy by refusing its quest for certainty and fixed standards. American pragmatism aims to "unsettle all things" and offers an ongoing cultural criticism that is "unashamedly moral" and "unequivocally ameliorative" (4–5). West argues, however, that the liberating and democratic potential of this evasion has never been fully realized because the elite, bourgeois status enjoyed by each of the pragmatists—including Du Bois—rendered the political and social implications of their work largely impotent. The final section of the book contains West's call for a "prophetic pragmatism" which would endow the legacy of Emerson, James, and Dewey, with an explicitly political mode of criticism, thereby making it more responsive to the "wretched of the earth."[15]

I find much of West's account to be stimulating, particularly his effort to locate Du Bois within this broader intellectual context. I also share West's appreciation of Dewey's ability to focus on political and social institutions without "surrendering his allegiance to Emersonian and Jamesian concerns with individuality and personality" (70). Indeed, Dewey's effort to hold these conflicting forces in balance represents for West the best that pragmatism has to offer, and I can only concur. Behind this admiration for Dewey, however, lies West's argument that both Emerson and James failed to comprehend that such a balance might ever be desirable. Drawing on their Emersonian heritage, West claims, subsequent figures in the pragmatic mode have similarly promoted separateness, detachment, and the individual at the expense of, and in opposition to, solidarity, association, and the community (18–20). Though a suitable frame of reference for the turn of the century, West finds that the persistence of this model has suppressed pragmatism's political implications and contributed to a legacy of self-indulgence and superfluousness in American intellectual life.

This claim is part of a familiar and, I believe, not especially convincing argument about the corrosive nature of Emerson's individualism. In restating it, West ignores the far more compelling argument that Emerson and James shared a deep conviction of the complex and necessary interrelationship between the individual's quest for self-fulfillment and the community's offer of structure and recognition. West also avoids confronting the argument that, far from shunning political commitment, Emerson and James steadfastly maintained that personal and cultural regeneration must accompany the struggle for social change if that struggle is to achieve any meaningful success. While West and I are obviously working with similar materials, what we construct with them is ultimately quite different; my departure from his analyses will be evident throughout.

Beginning with almost the same premise as West, the rejection by certain philosophers of an epistemology based on the notion of fixed truths, James Kloppenberg develops what amounts to an opposing argument. Kloppenberg focuses on a number of European and American philosophers—including James and Dewey—who promoted a radical theory of knowledge that substituted the acceptance of contingency for the quest after certainty. These "philosophers of the *via media*" held that knowledge, like any human endeavor, was imperfect and open-ended, and they "sought to understand knowledge as the individual's continuous breathing in and out of the environment on which he depends for life, a steady, rhythmic process of interaction instead of a mirroring by mind of a world outside it."[16] From here, Kloppenberg goes on to argue that this seemingly detached intellectual stance was intimately related with emerging theories of progressivism and social democracy. In West's terms, though contra West's argument, Kloppenberg asserts that pragmatism necessarily preceded political progressivism and was most surely not a diversion from social action.

Given the striking confluence of their work, it is disappointing that West, writing three years later, never responds to Kloppenberg's arguments.

In particular, Kloppenberg portrays William James as keenly aware of the role community and social institutions play in giving the necessary structure and meaning to individual experience, and he looks beyond James's "bourgeois" status to the deeper political implications of his work.[17] This understanding of James, along with Kloppenberg's general conception of the nature of intellectual endeavor in the years he examines, is richly instructive. Though he touches only briefly on Emerson, his invigorating analysis of the intellectual and political dimensions of pragmatism and his focus on James and Dewey as key figures suggests the power and expansiveness of Emerson himself as an originator of the tradition I examine, one which incorporates but is not limited to pragmatism.

More eloquently than any other figure, Emerson articulated the paradoxes at the heart of American intellectual and cultural life: a respect for tradition coupled with an appreciation of innovation and change; a belief in first principles accompanied by a fierce resistance to absolutism; a willingness to accept "truth" as an evolving concept; and a commitment to a cooperative democratic community that is built on a faith in the inherent worth of each individual soul. The work of James, Dewey, Du Bois, and Williams exhibits a coherence around these principles that deserves further examination. To be sure, many other figures might rightfully be included in my catalogue, and I suggest some of these extensions in the epilogue. My choice to focus on these four derives primarily from my belief that they represent the most powerful and most important appropriations of Emersonian individualism during the first half of this century, a period when Emerson's place in American culture was by no means assured.[18] James, Dewey, Du Bois, and Williams serve as transition figures, or perhaps transmission figures. In recasting Emerson for themselves, they made him available, even essential, for those who would follow. The contemporary debate over the meaning of individualism in America is, in effect, a debate over the meaning of Emerson. This debate is made more healthy, and more hopeful, by the Emerson they have bequeathed us.

CHAPTER ONE

The Aroma of Personality
and the Dignity of Clean Living

When Ralph Waldo Emerson died on April 27, 1882, his reputation had not so much been made as assumed. He had produced little new work in the years following the Civil War, and the tone of his finished work was increasingly deemed irrelevant to the intellectual discourse of the late nineteenth century. For some years the New England literary culture with which he was so closely associated had been in decline, and while Emerson's lofty personal stature remained largely intact, the response to his work had grown increasingly superficial and perfunctory.[1] Indeed, comments on Emerson, both public and private, suggested an elderly grandfather in the sitting room: a man respected still, but one who was the subject of condescending nostalgia and whose presence was recognized only fleetingly and on special occasions.

Representative of this attitude was Charles Eliot Norton, professor of classics at Harvard, prominent Brahmin, and an admirer of Emerson. In a letter of September 13, 1870, Norton wrote:

> No best man with us has done more to influence the nation than Emerson,—but the country has in a sense outgrown him. He was the friend and helper of its youth; but for the difficulties and struggles of its manhood we need the wisdom of the reflective and rational understanding, not that of the intuitions. Emerson . . . belongs to the pure and innocent age of the Presidency of Monroe or J. Q. Adams. . . . he is as remote almost from us as Plato himself.[2]

Norton's assessment of Emerson's atrophied relevance anticipated his actual demise by twelve years, yet it is typical of the tributes that would gush forth in the wake of Emerson's death. Whether in brief obituaries in the newspapers or extended retrospectives in the journals and magazines, Emerson was simultaneously mourned as a great man whose death diminished the whole nation and lamented as a vague and undisciplined thinker who left behind no meaningful legacy of ideas. H. L. Kleinfield examined the various testimonials published after Emerson's death and concluded that their cumulative effect was to transform Emerson into a "grand, towering, but insubstantial" figure on the intellectual and cultural landscape.[3] Kleinfield goes on to suggest that in the ensuing twenty years Emerson was praised in "a continually mounting crescendo" for such wonderfully vague qualities as his "purity of life" and "profundity of thought" (191). At the same time, the demands of praising Emerson while burying him increasingly overshadowed the task of assessing, in any serious way, his relevance to contemporary or future generations. Thus the image of Emerson bequeathed to the twentieth century was that of a glorified cultural icon, demanding reverence but dissociated from the experience and priorities of a newer generation of readers.[4]

In fact, the process of transforming Emerson into such a figure had begun before his death. Norton, for one, often repeated the substance of his charge. Writing in his journal for May 15, 1873, as he accompanied Emerson home from Europe aboard the steamer *Olympus,* Norton admitted that Emerson's "serene sweetness, the pure whiteness of his soul, the reflections of his soul in his face, were never more apparent to me; but never before in intercourse with him had I been so impressed with the limits of his mind" (*Letters,* 1:503). This dichotomy between the sweetness and purity of Emerson's personality and the limitations of his mind was a staple ingredient of commentary on Emerson after the Civil War, when most observers agreed that his mental powers were gradually slipping away. However, as the ambiguity of Norton's comment suggests, such commentary could very easily slip into a retroactive mood, implying that Emerson had all along been valued more for the serenity of his spirit than the always evident softness of his head. Such an attitude would prove irresistible to those who, eager to show the proper respect for the Great American Seer but lacking the time, desire, or ability to make coherent sense of his work, opted to minimize that work in favor of the personality. The result was the gradual condensation of his published volumes into a few pithy maxims about self-reliance and the moral law, leaving an Emerson who was increasingly less compelling to those who might otherwise have looked to him for intellectual sustenance.

Norton was not alone among Emerson's contemporaries in suggesting the conflicting forces upon which his growing reputation as icon rested. Henry James Sr. admired Emerson and considered him a close friend; he even had him "bless" his newborn son William. Still, the elder James was often frustrated by what he saw as Emerson's lack of intellectual foundation. He once referred to him in exasperation as "you man without a handle!" and his subsequent attempts to come to terms with Emerson reveal just how slippery the grip could be. Late in his life James recalled that "at first I was greatly disappointed in him, because his intellect never kept the promise which his lovely face and manners held out to me."[5] And yet, like so many critics to follow, James would resolve this difficulty, and contain his disappointment, by asserting that Emerson's personality alone accounted for his enduring appeal.

To be sure, James remained convinced that Emerson's indifference to the discipline of intellect was a serious flaw. In "Mr. Emerson," written between Emerson's death in May 1882 and his own death in December of the same year, James declared that Emerson's indifference to the role that the conscience and institutions like the church and the state played in controlling man's evil nature made him "fundamentally treacherous to civilization" (437). For James, concepts like "intellect," "conscience," and "society" were interchangeable, each relating to the way civilized people controlled their base instincts in the interest of harmonious living. What perplexed James was that Emerson could so thoroughly ignore the need for these restraints and yet remain so innocent and good. It was not surprising, then, that James came to value Emerson almost exclusively for his angelic presence.

In an earlier treatment James had elaborated on his appreciation for Emerson's character, noting that "it was utterly impossible to listen to Mr. Emerson's lectures without being perpetually haunted . . . by the subtlest and most searching aroma of personality."[6] It was this aroma that James came to single out as the defining characteristic of Emerson, assuring his own audience that he would have failed in his task if he had not convinced them that "Mr. Emerson's authority . . . consists, not in his ideas, not in his intellect, not in his culture, not in his science, but all simply in himself, in the form of his natural personality" (744). Earlier in the essay James made the same point with even more finality, emphasizing that "the influence exerted by Mr. Emerson over the minds of his contemporaries is not in the least of a dogmatic or intellectual, but of a purely personal quality" (742). That is, the only thing distinguishing Emerson from the common lot was his character; his ideas need not even be considered.

A second theme emerges from James's struggle with Emerson, and this too would have a secure, if subdued place in subsequent Emerson criticism. James argues that men "instinctively do . . . homage" to Emerson, despite his intellectual frailty, because he has so successfully sublimated his masculine force of will into the feminine "force of spontaneity": "It is as if the spotless feminine heart of the race had suddenly shot its ruby tide into your veins, and made you feel as never before the dignity of clean living" ("Emerson," 745, 741). In feminizing Emerson, James not only accounts for his weak intellect but makes it into something of a virtue: Emerson doesn't need a strong system of ideas because he represents the feminine side of the race, a side that is to be honored simply for its beauty and character.[7] And that, of course, was the precise nature of the tributes that Emerson would receive.

James's effort to understand and explain Emerson's appeal by discarding his ideas as inconsequential would be repeated again and again. Perhaps the most influential rendering of this theme came from James Russell Lowell, one of the more prominent literary figures of Emerson's generation.[8] In "Emerson the Lecturer," Lowell assured his audience that "we do not go to hear what Emerson says so much as to hear Emerson," a theme that would echo through many popular anecdotes about Emerson's appeal as a lecturer.[9] Indeed, Lowell himself seemed to despair of making sense of Emerson's message, content instead to bask in the glow of the medium. Regarding his reluctance to engage in any lengthy commentary upon Emerson, Lowell explains that "I will only say that one may find grandeur and consolation on a starlit night without caring to ask what it means, save grandeur and consolation" (44). By elevating Emerson to the heavens Lowell is simultaneously cutting him off from the earth, thereby justifying his own failure to engage Emerson's work directly by implying that he transcends such analysis.

In one rhetorical motion, Lowell not only rationalizes his inattention to Emerson's ideas by speaking in unassailable tones of "grandeur and consolation," but he suggests that no discussion should hope to achieve more. In fact, the force of Lowell's suggestion, that one ought not to ask what Emerson means, was borne out in his own feeble attempts at specificity. The nearest he was able to come to defining Emerson's significance, which he naturally assumed to be great, was to praise him "not so much for any direct teachings as for that inspiring lift which only genius can give," a genius which Lowell defined as the "masculine faculty of fecundating other minds" (44, 48).[10] Confronted with the daunting task of making sense of Emerson's work, Lowell chooses instead the easy and soon to be well-traveled route of reverent but shallow praise.

At the time of Emerson's death, then, there had already been established a tradition of extolling his personal virtues while ignoring or, at best, politely evading his ideas. This context informed those who took the occasion of his death as an opportunity to pose the question, "In losing Emerson, what have we lost?" The *Boston Evening Transcript,* in announcing the grave condition of "the man who has been studied, honored, and loved . . . more than any other American scholar" set the tone for all the obituaries to follow when it asserted that "the occasion does not seem one for literary critique . . . but rather for the most reverent and affectionate expression of personal feeling."[11] This expression of affection was the *sine qua non* of Emerson criticism and would continue to overshadow discussion of his work for years after his death. Thus, while the late Emerson was held up as someone who demanded attention, the terms of this attention remained almost hopelessly vague.

While the *Transcript* merely suggested that it was not the appropriate time for a discussion of Emerson's literary and intellectual accomplishments, other accounts readily admitted an inability or unwillingness to make sense of his work. The *San Francisco Chronicle* reprinted a verse from Emerson's poem "Brahma" as typical of his efforts, with the observation that "to those who can read him, they are words of sublime truth; to the majority of readers they are 'trash and nonsense,' verging on insanity." The New Orleans *Daily Picayune* was even less reticent in proclaiming that "all but the initiated devotees found him to be moonshine . . . his works [are] rather a confused pile of thought germs than an orderly array of principles."[12] Such comments, however, were not intended to pass as final judgment on Emerson's career but rather to establish the context for a keener appreciation of his superior character. As the article in the *Chronicle* concluded, "his private life was so pure, his intellectuality so exalted, and his humanity so glowing" that the obscurity of his thought was of little matter.

It was nonetheless difficult to eulogize Emerson without taking some measure of his considerable body of work, at the very least to balance the comments, vaguely imputed to the "uninitiated," that he was all moonshine and incipient madness. Groping for the right words to communicate its deep awareness of his significance, the *Chronicle* settles on the observation that while "[Emerson's] themes cover all subjects . . . mediocrity of thought is not a fault of his treatment of any of them." Similar interpretations appear in the *Chicago Tribune,* which defines Emerson as being "especially characterized by his acute sense of beauty, joined to an equally acute sense of truth," and the *Atlanta Constitution,* which assures that "none can read him without benefit, *if* they do not mistake his fancies for sober truth instead of brilliant illustrations of certain phases of that truth."[13] The conditional clause in this passage is crucial. As long as Emerson's uninitiated readers focused on his character while giving only perfunctory attention to his ideas, all would be fine. However, if they endeavored to take his ideas seriously, danger loomed. This dual message—that Emerson must be incomprehensible because to endeavor to comprehend him was dangerous—would resurface in later critics who deeply feared the effect Emerson might have on the initiated and uninitiated alike. The excessive praise of Emerson's purity and nobility was driven, in part, by the desire to compensate for the unsettling nature of his ideas, even when these ideas were at best only vaguely understood.

Other themes emerge from the notices published in the days following Emerson's death, each contributing to the subordination of his ideas to his character. Some attempted to deal with the problem of assessing Emerson's work by claiming that "his place among great men is not yet assigned. He belongs . . . not so much to his own as to future times." This effectively made it the task of those future critics to uncover the deeper significance of the thoroughly personable Emerson they inherited.[14] The *New York Times,* in a detailed and otherwise appreciative obituary, begged the question of Emerson's intellectual contributions by averring that he was more accessible to the "imaginative, intuitive minds of girls" than to the "mature and learned men of exalted position and extended reputation" whom he puzzled.[15] Recalling the comments of Henry James Sr. concerning Emerson's feminine side, this remark continues the notion that Emerson's intellect was unimportant because it was insufficiently masculine. Of course, the *Times* explicitly acknowledged that anyone pure enough to appeal to the minds of girls deserved honor and respect. Victorian America could safely entrust the simple minds of its daughters to Emersonian pabulum.[16]

Tributes published by the leading monthly magazines were somewhat more successful in presenting a measured portrait of Emerson, toning down the hyperbolic praise of his character and focusing, however briefly, on actual selections from the writings. In the *Atlantic,* William T. Harris set forth a rather involved definition of Emerson as "seer." Taking as his first task the need to refute those who would reject Emerson's writing as so much illogical rambling, Harris argued that "in Emerson's poetry we find a quite natural adherence to the requirements of organic unity": each element of Emerson's poetry (each poem, as well as each idea within those poems) was "alike means and end of all the others." On the whole, Emerson's poetry offered a consistent and coherent vision of "the revelation of the mind in nature."[17]

Harris's attention to individual poems like "The Sphinx," "Woodnotes," and "Merlin," and his effort to incorporate these into a unified account of Emerson's achievement, stands as a refreshing alternative to the more resounding but vapid tributes that had come before. Still, Harris was primarily interested in demonstrating that Emerson's work adhered to some unifying principle. As such, his discussion of the poems is somewhat wooden and reductive, and he approaches the prose with trepidation. Indeed, the essays positively stymied Harris's search for this unifying principle. After suggesting that the material in *Nature* and *English Traits* was "wisely arranged," Harris is forced to admit that, given the "ideal" nature of Emerson's essays, no unity can be found because no progress can be made within that which is ideal (247). For the remainder of the article Harris avoids any broad treatment of the essays, content to sum them all up as Emerson's translation of "the ethical code of the world" (250).

Having apparently gotten in over his head Harris quickly retreats, and in the last two pages of the article he gives Emerson the chance to enlighten or confound readers on his own through a lengthy series of quoted passages. Then, with the unity of his own essay beginning to dissolve, Harris cannot resist the temptation to shore up his effort by resorting to this familiar conclusion:

> After one has discussed his books, only half of the subject has been treated. The personal life of Emerson is as remarkable as his literary work. Never in modern times do we hear of a personality so serene and august, so sweet and sane, as that of Emerson. . . . The presence of the man did more to educate the people than the substance of his lectures. All who saw him were inspired to live more ideal lives. (252)

This said, Harris could rest assured that even if his discussion of "organic unity" and the "ethical code of the world" proved inadequate as assessments of Emerson's literary achievements, he would still have contributed to the more salient tradition of turning Emerson into a secular saint.

In the years following his death testimonials to Emerson's greatness grew in number and variety, ranging from nostalgic recollections of brief encounters to formal biographies and critical overviews. Yet despite offering, on the whole, a more precise consideration of his work, these new efforts did far more to confirm than to challenge the interpretive paradigm that held Emerson to be a beautiful and noble soul, but one whose writings were either inconsequential or, if taken too seriously, dangerous. Though it is not surprising that the numerous personal reminiscences dealt almost exclusively with Emerson's nobility and the way in which his mere presence elevated the spirit of those around him, it is surprising to see this approach figure so prominently in the accounts of critics who approached Emerson from a personal distance.[18]

Among the earliest and most influential of the full-length biographies of Emerson was Oliver Wendell Holmes's volume for the American Men of Letters series.[19] Holmes proceeded methodically through Emerson's life, pausing over each essay and the important lectures to remark upon their significance. Throughout, however, he was more interested in establishing what Emerson did not mean than in giving any clear picture of what he did. Much of this had to do with Holmes's evident desire to separate Emerson from the excesses of some of his unidentified followers, those who foolishly took Emerson at his word when he spoke of nonconformity and self-reliance but who lacked his natural inner restraint. Thus, Holmes dismissed any idea of Emerson as a radical, asserting instead that his apparent antinomian sympathies resulted from undisciplined syntax and careless diction (394–95).

Holmes had warmed up for his biography when he delivered an address before the Massachusetts Historical Society in May 1882, at a memorial meeting honoring Emerson and Longfellow. Though brief, Holmes's address anticipated the tone of his later, more sustained treatment when he concluded: "Give [Emerson] whatever place belongs to him in our literature . . . but remember this: the end and aim of his being was to make truth lovely and manhood valorous, and to bring our daily life nearer and nearer to the eternal, immortal, invisible."[20]

While in the biography Holmes strove to be more specific about the place Emerson *did* hold in American literature, he consistently interjected similar refrains affirming in vague terms Emerson's superiority of temperament and character. Holmes clearly found much of Emerson's written work to be beyond critical appraisal, and his method amounted to linking together lengthy quotes with brief editorial comments to convey the essence of the piece under discussion. He considered "The American Scholar" to be Emerson's most truthful and most readable effort, but found *Nature* mostly dangerous and the "Over-Soul" a failed attempt at the impossible task of "describing the infinite in terms of the finite" (108–15, 101, 172–73).

And, while examining the poetry, Holmes echoed Lowell's line about grandeur and consolation: "We have to recognize that there is a charm in Emerson's poems which cannot be defined any more than the fragrance of a rose or a hyacinth" (340).

The bulk of Holmes's biography follows this model, in many cases picking up on the grand generalizations that pervaded the earlier commentaries and passing them on with more authority to a subsequent generation of readers.[21] Thus, in concluding his estimate of Emerson's poetry, Holmes writes that

> We may not be able to assign the reason of the fascination the poet we have been considering exercises over us. But this we can say, that he lives in the highest atmosphere of thought; that he is always in the presence of the infinite . . . and that through all he sings as in all he says for us we recognize the same serene, high, pure intelligence and moral nature. (341–42)

In his final chapter, "Emerson: A Retrospect," Holmes similarly admits that "Emerson's place as a thinker is somewhat difficult to fix," due primarily to his tendency to mysticism which "renders him sometimes obscure, and once in a while almost, if not quite, unintelligible" (390). Yet Holmes assures his readers that Emerson's mysticism was intellectual rather than emotional, and that he "never let go the string of his balloon" (396). Then, as if this solved the issue of Emerson's place as a thinker, Holmes proceeds to evade any further consideration of that place through a remarkable sequence of equivocations:

> His perfect amiability was one of his most striking characteristics. . . . The natural purity and elevation of Emerson's character show themselves in all that he writes. His life corresponded to the ideal we form of him from his writings. . . . Whether [Emerson's prose and verse] live or fade from memory, the influence of his great and noble life . . . blends, indestructible, with the enduring elements of civilization. . . . His writings are worthy of admiration, but his manhood was the underlying quality which gave them their true value. (408–9, 419–20)

Holmes thus avoids attributing any significance to Emerson's work—the lectures he delivered and the essays he wrote—pointing instead to his "great and noble life" as the true legacy. Finally, eager to demonstrate his certainty on at least this point, Holmes ends the book with his observation that if Jesus Christ had wandered nineteenth-century New England as he had old Palestine, then he would surely have crossed the threshold of Emerson's home "to hallow and receive its blessing" (421). Elsewhere, Holmes explicitly compares Emerson to Christ in his patience, his appeal to little children, and his "pure and virtuous life"; he even compliments Emerson for being able, when necessary, to rise to "the feeling which showed itself of old in the doom pronounced on the barren fig-tree" (367, 372, 419). With Emerson keeping such company, it would verge on the blasphemous to subject his written work to any rigorous analysis, and Oliver Wendell Holmes clearly rejected the role of blasphemer.

The tradition of Emerson worship received something of a jolt in late 1883 when Matthew Arnold delivered his discourse on Emerson at the start of his American lecture tour. In fact, the tenacity of this tradition can be gauged by the controversy Arnold provoked when he dared to question some cherished but largely unexamined assumptions about the significance of Emerson's work.[22] Arnold argued, in short, that the fact that Emerson was so obviously a Great Man was by itself insufficient to warrant his elevation to the rank of Great Writer. Instead, his work as a writer and thinker should be judged by the standards of poetry and philosophy, while the inspirational and spiritual side of his work should be separated and evaluated independently.

Though Arnold's essay was by any measure sympathetic, even reverent, many observers reacted as if he had blasphemed.[23] The *Boston Daily Advertiser* took particular umbrage at Arnold's "attack" and found his piece lacking in "sympathetic knowledge of his subject." A few days later it repeated the charge, noting that "to deny Emerson superior intelligence . . . is a blindness and ignorance quite strange."[24] While most reviews shared the *Advertiser*'s resentment of Arnold's transgression, a few admitted that he might in fact have struck the more honest and accurate note. Thus, the *Boston Evening Transcript* cautiously proposed that Arnold "wove a brighter garland for the illustrious dead man than though he had lauded him with cheap and easy generalities of eulogy,"[25] an interesting comment given the *Transcript*'s use of those same "cheap and easy generalities" in its obituary twenty months previous. And, when Arnold's essay was published two years later, the *Literary World* observed that "the truth of his utterances . . . is now more generally acknowledged than was the case when we heard them for the first time."[26] Charles Eliot Norton neatly captured the mood when he wrote to Lowell that Arnold's lecture was "a piece of large, liberal, genuine criticism; but, being criticism, [it] has aroused the provincial ire of the pure disciples. On the whole Howells was right when he said that as he was listening to it he was constantly thinking, 'Ah! that is just what I should have liked to say!' " (*Letters,* 2:167).

What Arnold did in his lecture was to examine systematically the claims that Emerson's supporters might make for his prominence as a literary and intellectual figure. In each case he firmly rejected those claims, concluding that, by commonly accepted standards of form and style, Emerson was neither a legitimate poet, nor a great writer, nor a great man of letters, nor a proper philosopher.[27] Yet Arnold's tone is not that of a debunker, and he is quick to stress his deep admiration for Emerson. Moreover, he assures his audience that his judgment does not diminish Emerson's moral and spiritual force, but rather gives that force greater prominence. Finally, Arnold observes that even Emerson himself had admitted his limitations as a poet and a philosopher. What harm could there be in agreeing with that self-evaluation? On the whole, Arnold does little more than say explicitly what had been already implied by Lowell, Harris, Holmes, Edwin Percy Whipple, Edmund Clarence Stedman, and others: Emerson's work is so inscrutable that to describe him as a great poet or a great philosopher is to do all parties a disservice.[28]

After summarily dismissing Emerson from the ranks of great poets and philosophers, Arnold proceeded to argue that Emerson was best understood as a "friend and aider of those who would live in the spirit." He offers two pages of selections culled from Emerson's essays, passages that stress "character" and "self-reliance" as the guiding principles of the well-lived life (177–79). This chain of Emersonianisms nicely illustrates the Sage of Concord's peculiar inspirational power, and Arnold happily avoids the hyperbole and equivocation characteristic of so many other accounts. However, the very process of arguing for Emerson's importance by patching together selections from scattered sources quickly gives Arnold pause. Abandoning this effort, he turns instead to address the standard objection that Emerson's writing was too obscure, blindly optimistic, and often incoherent. To transcend Emerson's obscurity and see his points as true, Arnold suggests, one must understand them in a "certain high sense," and realize that "the work which Emerson did was the right work to be done then" (180). He goes on to qualify that though "his insight is admirable [and] his truth precious . . . the secret of his effect is not even these; it is in his temper. It is in the hopeful, serene, beautiful temper wherewith these, in Emerson, are indissolubly joined" (181). Thus the "truth" of Emerson's work, the inspirational power which Arnold has taken some care to distill and defend, has become subordinated once again to his serene temper. In the end, Arnold concludes, what Emerson has to offer America are "his dignity, delicacy, serenity, elevation" (186).

Despite the impression at the time that Arnold's piece marked a decisive shift toward a more formal evaluation of Emerson, it ultimately did little to challenge the prevailing critical view. Though Arnold respected Emerson's work, he found it too uncertain a foundation on which to build a lasting tradition. Rather, like Holmes, Harris, and others, Arnold adopted the position that the true significance of Emerson's work, its very meaning, rested on the serenity of his temperament and the "elevation" of his thoughts. To say that Emerson was a "friend and aider of those who would live in the spirit" was to deny, as many would, that he had anything to say to those who would live on the earth. Inevitably, since Emerson's temper lent itself more readily to discussion, his thoughts were lost in concentration on the heights from which they issued. To be sure, such criticism was inevitable in the immediate wake of Emerson's death, and there is nothing to suggest that the expressions of reverence were insincere or perfunctory. Indeed, for those who knew him personally or had attended his many lectures, the tone of these tributes no doubt captured the essence of the Emerson they knew. Still, as time passed and personal familiarity with Emerson's dignity and serenity faded, this apotheosis rang more and more hollow. An Emerson who resided in the ether became an increasingly less compelling figure to a later generation of writers.

This image of Emerson was reinforced by the stream of formal histories of American literature that appeared in the last fifteen years of the nineteenth century. Driven by the conviction that American literature had begun to come of age as a field of study, these works initiated the first wave of canonization of America's literary giants. In turn, they would exert a tremendous influence on the way those writers and their works would be viewed in subsequent decades.[29] For their accounts of Emerson, the authors of these histories relied heavily on the previously published material, including Lowell, Conway, Holmes, and Arnold, thereby helping to enshrine this earlier criticism as the foundation for subsequent study.

Among the first of these new histories was Charles F. Richardson's two-volume *American Literature,* consisting of *The Development of American Thought* and *American Poetry and Fiction.*[30] In the first volume, Richardson presented Emerson as the ardent promoter of the "idea of intellectual independence," and went on to suggest that this idea was well served by Emerson's remarkable independence of form: like nature, it was "fluctuating, spontaneous and apparently wild" (331, 360). This said, Richardson moves on to his main point, his fear that Emerson's "vagueness of thought and utterance" had the dangerous effect of "retarding [the] habits of close and orderly thought" (367–68). What is the source of this danger? How might it be avoided? Richardson doesn't say. Instead he quickly shifts gears, unwilling to court accusations of cultural patricide. He concludes:

> [O]n the general estimate, the work of Emerson is of great importance to America and to the world. His name . . . must ever stand in honor. The ideal, the beautiful, the true, the right, the godlike, he set in burning words over against the merely material, the utilitarian, the false, the politic, the animal, the worldly. (368)

While Emerson's opposition to the "merely material" might have been a useful place to start a discussion of his work, Richardson leaves it as a simple statement of fact. Without revealing just what these truths and ideals might be, Richardson compounds Emerson's purported "vagueness of thought" with an elusiveness of his own, basing his estimate of Emerson's great importance to the world on a set of criteria only minimally defined.

Other assessments follow a similar pattern.[31] Richard Burton places Emerson at the center of "the remarkable little group of New England writers who stood for God and country," and concludes, after brief references to the essays and poems, that "among [men of thought and character] Emerson must forever stand, a central figure of calm benignity, of beneficent influence, of unassailable elevation."[32] Walter Bronson takes Matthew Arnold's essay as his model, pointing perhaps even more determinedly to Emerson's limitations as a poet and a thinker, and faulting him particularly for his "defective sense of evil and sin." Yet Bronson fails to elaborate on the significance of these defects, and goes on to conclude, like Arnold before him, that Emerson's most essential characteristic is his place among the world's "great and high souls."[33]

The most striking account of Emerson in these histories comes from Barrett Wendell, professor of literature at Harvard. After a brief biographical summary, Wendell sets out to explain that the problem with Emerson is that he needs to be "read deeply" in order to be understood, a process which runs the risk of repelling readers as well as attracting them. Yet despite his urging that the serious student must "force himself to the task," Wendell assiduously avoids this deep reading himself. All he can offer as motivation for this "strenuous act of will" is the observation that "as time goes on . . . [Emerson] seems more and more sure of survival. America produced him; and whether you like him or not, he is bound to live."[34] Wendell goes on to amplify this comment:

> As one grows familiar with his work, its most characteristic trait begins to seem one which in a certain sense is not individual at all, but rather is

common to all phases of lasting literature . . . something so broadly, pervasively, lastingly human, that generation after generation will read it on with no sense of the changing epochs which have passed. . . . Though his work may lack something of true greatness, it surely seems alive with such unconditioned freedom of temper as makes great literature so inevitably lasting. (315–16)

While all this might serve as a fine *description* of the characteristic trait of Emerson's work, Wendell fails to reveal just what that trait is, unless he means to be content with the notion of "unconditioned freedom of temper." Rather than elaborate, Wendell almost gleefully proceeds to bury Emerson under a deeper blanket of obscurity. He prints the poem prefacing Emerson's essay on "Spiritual Laws" and follows it with this explication:

What this means we may admit ourselves unable to understand; but with all due vexation or humility, we can hardly help feeling that here is not a word or even a lurking mood which might not have emerged from eldest human time, or might not as well emerge from the most remote human future our imagination can conceive. (316–17)

Presumably, Wendell leaves it to his readers' imaginations whether someone in that distant past or remote future might be better able to understand the meaning of Emerson's timeless words, just as he seems content to let others engage in the strenuous study that he deems so necessary. As for Emerson's meaning in the present, Wendell has little else to say.

Wendell closes his chapter on Emerson with a few standard plaudits about his everlasting search for truth and stalwart defense of intellectual freedom, thereby fulfilling what had come to be the minimum requirements for Emerson criticism. Still, his account stands out in its meticulously crafted evasion of Emerson's writings. In a letter to Harvard colleague William James written shortly after the *Literary History* had been published, Wendell describes the book as "Tory, pro-slavery, and imperialistic; all of which I fear I am myself. I love the memory of Cotton Mather; and should be happier in a world that hadn't been graced by Channing or Emerson."[35] While there is a dose of irony in Wendell's comment there is also an element of truth, which helps to explain why he wrapped Emerson's writings in such a cloud of obscurity. As a confirmed aristocrat Wendell may have welcomed Emerson's call for intellectual self-reliance, but he could not accept that this call went out to everyone.[36] Furthermore, he was so suspicious of Emerson's lack of intellectual restraint that he found much of his writing downright dangerous when not filtered through Emerson's serene temperament. To give any prominence to these ideas, then, even simply to summarize them, would be not only distasteful but reckless. Wendell's extravagant effort to deny that Emerson's work had any recognizable meaning at all was thus, in part, an attempt to minimize the impact his ideas might have had on less well-tempered minds.

This fear of the misappropriation and misapplication of Emerson's ideas, of the potential for antinomian and anarchic abuse embedded in his apparent devotion to self-reliance and nonconformity, was a common theme. It was a force behind Holmes's decidedly conservative portrait in the biography, and it guided the elder Henry James's conviction that Emerson was "fundamentally treacherous to civilization" because of his supposed indifference to conscience. Richardson, Burton, and Bronson each admit that what was beautiful and noble in Emerson often appeared crazed and grotesque in those who accepted his inspiration without first developing his moderation. Again, Charles Eliot Norton captures the essence of the issue. In the same journal entry in which he refers to the limits of Emerson's mind, Norton muses upon Emerson's "inveterate and persistent optimism":

> [T]hough it may show only its pleasant side in such a character as Emerson's, [it] is dangerous doctrine for a people. It degenerates into fatalistic indifference to moral considerations, and to personal responsibilities; it is at the root of much of the irrational sentimentalism in our American politics . . . of much of our unwillingness to accept hard truths, and of much of the common tendency to disregard the distinctions between right and wrong, and to erase guilt on the plea of good intentions or good nature. (*Letters*, 1:506–7)

If this represents the practical effects of some of Emerson's ideas, as many were ready to believe, then it is not surprising that critics determined to uphold his high place in the American pantheon were drawn more to his elevated spirit and serene temperament. Indeed, Emerson's decency and purity emerge not only as easy generalities useful in circumventing his enigmatic ideas, but as necessary counterweights to the potential for abuse in those ideas. This is evident in E. C. Stedman's essay on Emerson in *Poets of America*. For the most part, Stedman simply reiterates the familiar tributes to Emerson as "the most serene of men," but his context is one in which Emerson's serenity plays a more urgent role. Specifically, Stedman is aware that Emerson's "transcendental and self-reliant laws of conduct," while safe for "noble minds," run the risk of corrupting a "weaker class that cannot follow where he leads" (145–46). To combat this risk, Stedman suggests, an appreciation of Emerson's "lofty nature" must be cultivated before any consideration can be given to his deep insights.

Henry Van Dyke makes a similar argument in his introduction to a volume of Emerson's essays published in 1907. A well-travelled minister and professor of English at Princeton, Van Dyke shared Stedman's admiration for Emerson as an inspirational force, but was aware that "such a philosophy, with its assertion of the right and duty of each man to discover and measure the truth for himself, without waiting to reason it or prove it, might lead to all kinds of wild and queer and extravagant views and practices."[37] According to Van Dyke, however, this extravagance was as much a product of the fragile constitutions of some of Emerson's readers as of any incipient weakness in Emerson's doctrine. As Emerson himself demonstrated, this tendency toward "practical eccentricity and irregular ways" could be effectively countered by an "orderly nature [and] strong common sense," and Van Dyke joins Stedman in arguing that these qualities must form the background of any study of Emerson's ideas.[38]

By the time of Emerson's centennial in 1903 it would be a matter of course for commentators to stress his innocence of the more alarming "misrepresentations" of his writings. Though few culprits would be identified by name, it would seem that Emerson had been invoked to justify everything from brutal capitalist exploitation to violent protests against the political, social, and economic order. In turn, literate defenders of the social order sought both to deny Emerson's complicity in the attack and claim him for their own side. Clearly, an Emerson who could be made to speak for such conflicting interests was a threat to each and needed to be approached with caution; the evasion of any serious discussion of his ideas was one measure of that caution.

Brander Matthews followed an interesting variation on this theme. Rather than circumvent discussion of Emerson's ideas by focusing on his benign temperament, Matthews responded to the threats implied in Emersonian self-reliance and nonconformity by essentially recasting those ideas, thus making Emerson safe for the masses.[39] Matthews praised Emerson for being the "foremost representative of the powerful influence which New England has exerted on American life," an influence which amounted to emphasizing the "value of labor" (93, 98). Indeed, Matthews claimed that Emerson detested slavery not primarily on moral grounds but because the system denied some white men the "duty and the dignity of labor," obviously a key ingredient in the "sturdy and wholesome Americanism" to which Matthews was committed (105, 98). In the opening pages of his

Introduction to American Literature, Matthews observed that "literature is likely to be strong and great in proportion as the people who speak the language are strong and great" (10), and his encounter with Emerson is an effort to accommodate the work of the great seer to his own devotion to literary nationalism: a strong American literature needs a strong Emerson, a prophet of hard work and the dignity of labor, rather than a friend and aider of those who would live in the spirit.[40]

Matthews manages to praise Emerson's accomplishments without once alluding to his temperament. At the same time, his portrait of Emerson as the guiding light of cultural nationalism and plain living through hard work is narrow and forced. Matthews simply asserts his reading of Emerson without referring to specific writings for support, even anecdotal support, and in this sense his evocation of Emerson's inspirational force differs little from those who lauded his serenity. Whether his writings are treated as merely secondary outgrowths of his elevated spirit or are dubiously prompted as the source of wholesome Americanism, Emerson's work remains enigmatic, and untouched.

Just as Emerson's death offered commentators a chance to reflect on what he left behind, the occasion of his centennial provided an opportunity to sort through that legacy and reexamine Emerson's significance. Kleinfield argues that the numerous testimonials of 1903 served to consummate the process of beatification that had begun in 1882 (191). While this is true for much of the commentary, a number of observers joined Brander Matthews in appropriating Emerson for particular literary, political or social ends, muting their reverence for his person in favor of an explication of selected ideas. This approach, rather than building on the established pattern of hagiography, promoted it in spite of itself. As Emerson emerged as the preferred spokesman for an increasingly varied, and often contradictory set of causes, his noble spirit became the only attribute on which all could agree.

Most of the expressions of praise are familiar enough to require only summary comment. The Society of American Authors reminded readers of its journal that "Emerson's greatest legacy to his countrymen is not his work, wonderful and enduring though it is, but the recollection of a life devoted to the loftiest ideals enshrined in the temple of pure thought."[41] This attitude was shared by Le Baron Russell Briggs, dean of Harvard College, who, commencing the festivities in Concord on May 25, declared that Emerson's greatness was "not as a philosopher, poet or patriot, but as a helper of men. He made men better by simply walking among them."[42] Later that day Charles Eliot Norton, honoring the spirit of the occasion by suppressing his conviction that Emerson's intellect was deficient, again served as a barometer of the critical atmosphere:

> If I were to describe Emerson in a single phrase, I should say that of all the men I have known he made the strongest impression of consistent loftiness of character. . . . His superiority was evident in the natural simplicity of his manners and demeanor. Affectation, self-consciousness, parade, were impossible to him. His habitual bearing was of sweet gravity and reserve, in which was no aloofness, but a ready responsiveness to every claim of thought or word of another.[43]

While it is so far clear that the method of appraising Emerson by asserting his superior temperament remained essentially unchanged at the time of the centennial, Kleinfield is on less certain ground when he suggests that the appreciative acknowledgments of Emerson's devotion to "democracy" were merely addenda to these ritualistic tributes (192). To be sure, a number of the centennial tributes introduced this theme of Emerson's commitment to the spirit of democracy and went on to argue that this commitment was the key to understanding his greatness.[44] However, Kleinfield does not address the fact that each writer had in mind a different set of values, attitudes, and practices when referring to "democracy," and that the subsequent identification of Emerson with democracy would mean something different in each case. In this sense, Kleinfield fails to see that promoting Emerson as the champion of democracy was not necessarily analogous to promoting him as the champion of good manners.

Of the articles Kleinfield cites, George Willis Cooke, Hamilton Wright Mabie and the piece in *Outlook* each see Emerson as embodying a democracy vaguely defined as the application of love and justice to human affairs in pursuit of "the complete emancipation of the individual spirit" (Mabie, 907). Such happy generalizations, about both Emerson and democracy, certainly correspond to the imprecise way in which Emerson had long been discussed: Emerson himself is thoroughly inoffensive in his person, and the democracy he represents must be equally free of controversy and conflict, that is, firmly apolitical. Insofar as Emerson is the incarnation of this conception of democracy, George Cooke's assertion that he "was of no party nor sect, but belonged to mankind" would stand as a reliable measure of the breadth, if not the depth, of his appeal (257).

When we turn to the *Nation,* however, the democracy that Emerson purportedly represents is of a decidedly different type, and Emerson himself assumes a different posture. Reacting to a climate still in turmoil over the "insurrection" in the Philippines and a nascent American imperialism, the *Nation* strives to supplement the stock tributes to his accomplishments as poet, seer and philosopher by recalling his contributions as a concerned citizen: At a time when "the right and duty of free, full, independent criticism of governmental and national policy and action are challenged," when "we have seen the opposition of many right-thinking men muffled because they feel it will be of no use" or because their protests have been "hissed at as disloyalty," it is well to be reminded of and reinvigorated with Emerson's spirit of proclamation and protest (428). This portrait of Emerson as the prophet of active dissent and rebellion stands in marked contrast to the mild-mannered intellectual skeptic portrayed by everyone from Oliver Wendell Holmes to Hamilton Wright Mabie. In fact, it is just this kind of reading of Emerson that Holmes, Wendell, and Matthews sought to suppress, either by emphasizing the nobility of his mind, which would not tolerate such excesses, or by appropriating him for the unassailable forces of social order. In claiming him for an activist definition of "democracy," the *Nation* is doing more than simply mimicking the tradition of Emerson worship.

Bliss Carman follows the *Nation* in looking to Emerson for a response to the Philippines issue:

> We never needed Emerson's radiant faith in ideas and ideals more than we do today, and such a faith never seemed further from our thoughts. . . . To tell the truth, we need the Philippines much less than we need another Emerson; but since we have got the Philippines, we need an original Emerson all the more. (120)

While pleas for a resurgent Emersonian faith in ideas and ideals had been a standard component of Emerson criticism since his death, Carman diverges from that path in suggesting a specific application of that faith. Though the *Nation* is more direct in aligning Emerson with actual protest, Carman's claim on Emerson as a potential ally of the anti-imperialists, made in the name of his commitment to "democracy," challenges the prevailing notion of Emerson as being elevated above earthly affairs.

No one found Emerson more responsive to practical and worldly issues than Charles William Eliot, the president of Harvard and a tireless campaigner for educational reform. Speaking at the celebration in Boston on May 24, Eliot argued that Emerson had provided the intellectual foundations for every single positive development in "education, social organization, and religion" in the years since his death. Matching each of his points with a passage from Emerson's works, Eliot demonstrated Emerson's responsibility for the elective system, the arts and crafts movement, landscape architecture, and the symphony orchestra (845–47, 852). He was even, it seems, posthumously responsible for the construction of Harvard Stadium (848). As for Emerson's sense of American democracy, Eliot provides a rather intriguing portrait. While Emerson had warned against the potential excesses of industrialism, he had also been firmly opposed to organized labor and fixed wages, convinced that poor and rich alike must be protected from the temptations of selfishness and greed. Indeed, in Eliot's careful construction from scattered passages in the journals and essays, Emerson clearly favored a democratic nobility that would "guide and adorn life for the multitude" and protect all from the "evil intellectual effects of democracy" (850).[45]

In portraying Emerson as the advocate of a benevolent aristocratic democracy, Eliot was able to apply him to other contemporary issues. A member of the Anti-Imperialist League, Eliot opposed the American military presence in Cuba and the Philippines. However, since America already *had* the Philippines, as Bliss Carman noted, Eliot turned to Emerson for comfort. Referring to Emerson's "prophetic teaching" that "We shall one day learn to supersede politics by education," Eliot argues that American involvement in Cuba and the Philippines had in fact come to fulfill this prediction, becoming a noble effort to extend higher education to those less developed races: "The Cubans are to be raised in the scale of civilization and public happiness; so both they and we think they must have better schools. The Filipinos, too, are to be developed after the American fashion; so we send them a thousand teachers of English" (846). Rather than calling for dissent or protest, Emerson can be seen as providing the inspiration for one important facet of the white man's burden.

Of course, the question of whether or not Emerson would have approved of the annexation of the Philippines is moot; the important point here is that he could be claimed as spokesman for many disparate and often conflicting positions. In addition to his support for both aristocratic democracy and popular dissent, he was appropriated for the "strong" literary nationalism of Brander Matthews and the "weak" aestheticism of E. C. Stedman and Henry Van Dyke. And, while most observers held Emerson above the crass materialism of the business world, W. Robertson Nicoll spoke for another view when he suggested that "from his works a book might be compiled on the conduct of life, which hard-headed business men would distribute among their employees," a book from which they would learn to "give mind, soul, heart and body to business."[46]

Though certainly not unique to Emerson, the nature of his writings made him especially susceptible to this selective plucking, a fact that Holmes, Arnold, Richardson, and others noted with apprehension. Even John Albee, a self-described disciple of Emerson, found that "it must be admitted that Emerson's sentences separated from their fellows readily lend themselves to every sort of propaganda."[47] Most commentators avoided this sticky problem by restricting themselves to enumerating his gifts of manner and temper. Even Bliss Carman and the *Nation* based their challenge to the prevailing hagiography not on an extended treatment of Emerson's writings but by invoking another side of his spirit, a democratic side. Ironically, efforts like Eliot's that sought to claim Emerson for specific programs may simply have enhanced the appeal of these vague tributes, since an Emerson who meant very little was less threatening than an Emerson who could be made to mean almost anything.

Emerson's observations on religion provoked the most careful and, of course, most contentious discussions. Earlier commentators, including Holmes, Richardson, and Whipple, had attempted a revision of Emerson's position on doctrinal Christianity, arguing in short that such a pure and noble spirit must inevitably have been a good, church-going Christian. On the other hand, religiously liberal organs like the *Unitarian Review* and *Unity* not only asserted Emerson's opposition to doctrine but praised it, claiming that he had permanently liberated religious faith from doctrinal constraints and confidently predicting that every pulpit would soon preach its own Emersonian gospel.[48] By the time of the centennial this discussion had reached something of an apogee, and the question of Emerson's influence on religion enjoyed much interesting debate.

George Gordon surveyed Emerson's religious writings and concluded that the "Deity of Emerson is too vague, too uncertain," and his attitude toward Jesus an "embarrassment" to anyone who still takes their religion seriously. Of course, since "serious" religion had been in a decline, Gordon grants that Emerson enjoyed a rather wide influence among those who had patched together their spiritual lives from various denominations and who were not bothered by doctrinal inconsistency.[49] James Mudge arrived at a similar conclusion about Emerson's defects as a religious teacher, arguing that Emerson was in fact a "pagan . . . modified by Christian influences." Mudge even turns the tables on Emerson by suggesting that "what is sound and vital and lasting in his teachings" came to him "more or less directly" through the intercession of the "great Master."[50]

Both Gordon and Mudge were concerned that the outpouring of sentimental tributes to Emerson on the occasion of his centennial would conceal his unconventional thoughts on religion. This concern was shared by D. S. Gregory, who worried that the "phenomenal eclat" with which the centennial was celebrated might corrupt those in the "unliterary public" who were unaware of Emerson's serious and persistent doctrinal heresies. Gregory was clearly more disturbed than Gordon and Mudge by Emerson's apostasy, and argued that all of the ruinous qualities of "the new theology and spiritualism and Christian Science" had received their completest expression in his work. In rejecting Christianity, Gregory concludes, Emerson and those in his school had rejected "the only thing that has ever been any good."[51]

In striving to set the record straight on the issue of Emerson's religiosity, these critics devoted more careful attention to his work than was to be found in any of the refined tributes to Emerson the Poet, Emerson the Seer, or Emerson the Spiritual Guide. At the same time that they challenged readers to be aware of the full scope of Emerson's ideas, then, they challenged the prevailing critical approach that had consistently obscured those ideas through the rhetoric of hero worship. An unsigned article in the *Ethical Record* also sought to counterpoise the shallowness of standard Emerson criticism with an explication of his religious teachings, but where Gordon, Gregory, and Mudge each believed that Emerson's attitude toward religion was in some way unhealthy, this article argued that his religious apostasy was the main reason he should be remembered.[52]

"The Emasculation of Emerson" singles out the tradition of genteel tributes as being responsible for the "lack of sturdiness and reality, the evasiveness and thinness" that characterized discussion of Emerson's religious ideas. Rather than describing the "vigorous and uncompromising emancipator" that he truly was, this tradition had transformed Emerson into a "respectable Christian parson and apologist" and stripped away what was truly "distinctive and epochal in his message." In discarding the Christianity of his time, Emerson had discarded something that was diseased and dying and had replaced it with a "new revelation" of a life of "greater idealism, greater consistency, greater courage." This, concludes the *Ethical Record,* is the Emerson who should be celebrated and whose lessons should be applied.[53]

Though essentially in agreement on the substance of Emerson's religious ideas, these accounts differ significantly on whether those ideas should be approached with gratitude or caution. This implicit challenge to the established pattern of avoiding Emerson's ideas by exalting his character was complemented by the explicit argument of Gregory and the *Ethical Record* that hagiography was inadequate to the task of interpreting Emerson's lesson. John Jay Chapman had come to a similar conclusion six years before the centennial when he observed that the consistent reduction of "the living soul of Emerson to mere dead attributes like 'moral courage' " would inevitably curtail any wide appreciation of Emerson's achievement. Nevertheless, Chapman reluctantly agreed that this manner of discussing Emerson was "necessary . . . in order that we might talk about him at all," since Emerson was important not as a poet or philosopher or thinker but "solely as a character."[54] Thus, while convinced that this method of discussing Emerson was inadequate, Chapman despaired of any suitable alternative.

Chapman's despair was rooted in his sense that Emerson's ideas were of limited significance, a conviction that placed Chapman at the center of the critical tradition he deplored. Indeed, Chapman's dilemma points to the dominance this tradition achieved in the twenty years following Emerson's death: not only was it the preferred way to discuss Emerson, it was essentially the only way. While a few critics offered assessments of Emerson's work that went beyond the "easy generalities of eulogy," they were among a minority, and publications like the *Ethical Record* and *Homiletic Review* could not compete with *Harper's, Atlantic,* or the daily papers in circulation or influence. Indeed, even the relatively minor debate that took place over Emerson's relationship to religion and democracy was a sign of precisely the kind of cultural disharmony that the mainstream critics sought to avoid. Thus, the cumulative portrait of Emerson by 1903 combined effusive tributes to the purity and nobility of his soul with stern caution against taking his ideas too seriously. This ultimately worked to separate Emerson's personal legacy from his work until each existed almost independently of the other: Emerson the Man garnered the accolades while Emerson the writer and thinker was dismissed as vague, undisciplined, and dangerous.

This idealization of Emerson in the late nineteenth century was a reflection of the cultural and intellectual forces of the "Gilded Age," variously termed Victorianism or, after George Santayana, the genteel tradition. Stow Persons, Larzer Ziff, Alan Trachtenberg, Henry May, and others have suggested the role played by self-styled "custodians of culture" who, through their powerful positions in education and journalism, influenced the teaching of cultural values in the schools and the discussion of those values in the leading magazines.[55] As college teachers, textbook authors, and contributors to and editors of *Century, Harper's, Scribner's,* and the *Atlantic,* men like Norton, Eliot, Van Dyke, Mabie, and Stedman promoted a cultural ideal that served to buttress their threatened sense of moral and political order. Faced with the "impossibly unaesthetic whirl of social conditions" occasioned by the economic and demographic changes after the Civil War, the custodians of the genteel tradition relied on the "static idealization of the human condition" to preserve the illusion that American culture, at least, remained unified and harmonious.[56]

Both Trachtenberg and Persons consider the dilemma confronting these defenders of a culture that was becoming increasingly irrelevant to social and economic experience. Trachtenberg notes:

> [C]ulture seemed increasingly the sphere of women. . . . The rise to power of culture was at once the rise of a powerful idea of the feminine, of woman's role: the dispensing of values nonmaterial, nonaggressive, nonexploitative. As culture came to seem the repository of elevating thoughts and cleansing emotions, it seemed all the more as if the rough world of masculine enterprise had called into being its redemptive opposite. (145)

This division between the male and female spheres, between the world of business and the realm of culture, resulted in a sort of schizophrenia, with male critics articulating and defending a cultural tradition that they knew had little to do with the "real" world, yet which they intended to serve as a corrective for the disintegrating forces at work in that world. In promoting an idealized, feminized culture that secured the necessary illusion of harmony and unity, these critics simultaneously undercut their own relevance, and the relevance of the cultural ideals they cherished. They could not enshrine their culture and wield it, too.

This context illuminates the collective portrait of Emerson that took shape in this period. He was valued precisely because of the elevation and purity of his thought and his high moral tone, for his manner more than for anything he actually wrote. These attributes raised him above the sordid details of everyday life and represented the timeless and universal values that the genteel critics counted on to preserve the unity and order of American culture. In this way Emerson served to smooth over difference and dissension: he embodied what American culture needed to balance the aggressive, masculine, and dispersing tendencies of the social and economic order. Thus, at the same time that Emerson's transcendence of the real world was celebrated as his most distinguishing mark, his potential for correcting that world remained the key to his relevance.

Ultimately, Emerson was made over by the genteel tradition in its own image. The terms of his greatness remained sufficiently vague that they could stand for the eternal values so dear to the genteel critics, while at the same time this vagueness was all those critics could offer in response to the very real social and economic dislocations they confronted. This made Emerson an awkward figure for the generation of writers and critics coming to prominence in the early twentieth century. If his significance resided in the elevated detachment of his ideas, then there was little to recommend him to those whose understanding of culture demanded more than a sweet-tempered New England moralist. When Mark Twain committed his infamous transgression in lampooning Emerson, Longfellow, and Holmes at the Whittier birthday dinner in 1877, William Dean Howells observed that Twain should have been aware of the "species of religious veneration" in which those men were held.[57] By 1903, the veneration of Emerson had become part of a cultural tradition. As this tradition came under increasing attack, the Emerson that it had preserved and cherished would be vulnerable as well.

CHAPTER TWO

The Undersexed Valetudinarian:
Emerson and Modern Criticism

Critics and historians have long written the history of modern American literature and criticism as the story of the revolt against the genteel tradition of the late nineteenth century. Though the exact beginning of this revolt is variously associated with the publication of the first volume of Paul Elmer More's *Shelburne Essays* in 1904, with John Macy's *Spirit of American Literature* in 1913, or with Van Wyck Brooks's *America's Coming of Age* in 1915, the consensus is clear that the early twentieth century saw a dramatic growth in the scope and intensity of American criticism, a growth which fed off of a rejection of the tradition inherited from the genteel critics.[1] Though these modern critics—who wielded a variety of political, economic, psychological, and ethical presumptions—were primarily concerned with refuting or correcting one another, they were nonetheless united in the task of overturning the work of "the minions of gentility" (Aaron, 24). Even Alfred Kazin, who warned in 1942 that such a model was deceptively simplistic, acknowledged that it did tell much of the story.[2]

Kazin's monumental *On Native Grounds* remains an invaluable guide to the literary and critical currents of the first forty years of the twentieth century. In contrast with the literary idealism of the older school, Kazin detailed the revolution in realism accomplished by a younger generation of writers and critics. This generation was marked by a regional diversity that effectively broke through the New England provincialism that had dominated previous discussion of the "national" literature. In establishing their own terms these critics—from the New Humanists to the Marxists—repudiated their predecessors on the grounds that their regional bias and vaguely idealistic conception of the function of culture failed to reflect the realities of American experience.

This situation suggests the difficulty Emerson presented for modern critics: as the very embodiment of the genteel ideal and as a potent symbol of New England parochialism, he was doubly implicated in the tradition that they repudiated. Indeed, the appropriation of Emerson by the genteel critics was so thorough that few modern critics endeavored to question it: whatever his possible virtues, Emerson "became a kind of John the Baptist whose severed head modern American critics often exhibit as an awful example of the 'Genteel Tradition.'"[3] In staking out their own critical territory, self-styled liberal critics like Van Wyck Brooks, Waldo Frank, and Ludwig Lewishon, conservative New Humanists like Irving Babbitt and Paul Elmer More, Marxists like Granville Hicks and V. F. Calverton, for-malists like Yvor Winters and Allen Tate, and *sui generis* critics like H. L. Mencken each rejected outright the genteel Emerson and, if they reformu-lated him at all, did so in a way that underlined his virtual irrelevance to modern experience.[4] Henry May has noted that these younger critics, looking for strong, inspiring, and liberating figures, had little use for an Emerson who was "hidden behind a thick veil of platitude" (48). In their shared quest for new variations on a usable past, the moderns found that "Emerson was scarcely usable and hardly acceptable" (Hoffman, 125).

Among the earliest challenges to the genteel version of Emerson was Paul Elmer More's centennial appreciation for the *Independent* in 1903. Al-though quick to declare his reverence, More was concerned that Emerson had perhaps been too much a presence of late: "Emerson cannot escape his own condemnation of the wise: 'Though in our lonely hours we draw a new strength out of their memory, yet, pressed on our attention, as they are by the thoughtless and customary, they fatigue and invade.'"[5] As he de-velops the essay, More leaves little doubt that he considers Emerson the worse off for this overabundance of attention, a focus that has cast his limitations in a clearer and less-forgiving light.

More values Emerson chiefly for what he calls dualism, an articulation of the double consciousness that recognizes both the forces of nature and the yearning of the soul, the potential for individual freedom and the power of fate, private integrity, and public responsibility (74–75). Indeed, More locates Emerson's strength precisely in his refusal to attempt any spurious reconciliation of these opposing poles. Almost immediately, however, More notes that this unreconciled dualism also holds the key to Emerson's limitations. When adopted by individuals with "weak minds," Emerson's message becomes "a snare to mankind," permitting and even encouraging all sorts of philosophical and political absurdities, from Christian Science to "that unformed creature called Anti-imperialism" which "wantonly closes the eyes to distinctions and would see a Washington in every Aguinaldo" (81–82).[6]

The question of Emerson's responsibility for the alleged excesses of his weak-minded followers was an old one. More initially suggests that Emerson should not be held directly accountable, and in this he follows Van Dyke, Stedman, Holmes, and others who sought to turn attention away from Emerson's ideas—which were the source of the trouble—and toward the reverence of his character. More soon comes to reconsider his position, however, suggesting that while "it would be indiscriminating to lay at Emerson's door" the full blame for the excesses of his doctrine, nevertheless "we are justified in holding him mainly responsible for the harm that flowed from it" (78). Though equivocal in his final judgment, More is clearly rejecting the easy and well-trodden path of evading Emerson's ideas by praising his character.

"The Influence of Emerson" is essentially a record of More's struggle with his suspicion that the man whose standing as a cultural icon he is celebrating may, in fact, no longer be relevant. Since Emerson's ideas are so dangerously imprecise and his exalted personality little more than a charming cultural artifact, More finds the task of assessing his significance on the one hundredth anniversary of his birth distinctly uncomfortable. After suggesting the damage Emerson's influence had done to certain aspects of American political and intellectual life, More stops short, as if he were caught desecrating a temple:

> I feel already something of that shame which must have fallen upon the *advocatus diaboli* constrained by his office to utter a protest against the saints. Yet I trust my words will not be taken as directed against the sweet spirit of Emerson, whom I reverence this side of idolatry. (83)

As Mark Twain and Matthew Arnold had learned, to criticize Emerson in any way might elicit charges of diabolical intentions, so More wished to tread carefully. Not yet ready to declare the emperor's apparent nakedness, he is nonetheless caught in the process of a double-take. While Emerson's "sweet spirit" certainly seems to merit the reverence it is shown, More begins to wonder whether a closer look might expose the emptiness at the center of this kind of idolatry.

More came back to the subject of Emerson fourteen years later with his contribution to the *Cambridge History of American Literature*.[7] Here again, he begins with an assertion that Emerson is "the outstanding figure of

American letters," one who "has obtained a recognition such as no other of his countrymen can claim" (173). However, after the obligatory biographical sketch, More quickly moves on to an account of Emerson's weaknesses: his failure to realize the "full meaning and fateful seriousness" of the double nature of experience and his being "sometimes too ready to wave aside its consequences" (173, 185–86). Unlike the earlier essay, where More struggled with the problem of whether to blame Emerson for the more serious manifestations of these faults in his followers, he here moves right into an account of Emerson's harmful influence on those who were "divested of the common sense and strong character which were ballast to the master's shining optimism" (188).

While earlier critics had admitted that Emerson was at least in part to blame for the absurdities unleashed by the vagaries of his thought, they resolved the problem by pointing to his character and temperament as the necessary context for that thought. That is, they encouraged the cultivation of an Emersonian character as prerequisite to the consideration of Emersonian ideas. More refuses to follow this line for he is apparently unwilling to turn his essay into another panegyric on Emerson's purity and nobility. Where other critics had excused the apparently dangerous implications of Emerson's ideas by declaring them irrelevant in comparison to his character, More is firm in holding that Emerson's significance rests precisely on the relevance of what he thought and wrote.

The implications of this assertion are inescapable, and More is less hesitant in this later essay to state what he implied in the earlier one: "Emerson saw the good and radiated spiritual light as few other men of his century did; but his blindness to the reality of evil was not of his strength, it was of his weakness. Hence it is that he often loses value for his admirers in proportion to their maturity and experience" (188). Though not an outright rejection of Emerson as the standard-bearer of a no-longer-usable past, More's treatment leaves little doubt as to Emerson's declining relevance to those whose maturity and experience demand sterner stuff.

More's claim about Emerson's declining value recalls Charles Eliot Norton's remark about the country's having outgrown Emerson's youthful optimism; it also anticipates a similar observation by More's teacher and fellow New Humanist, Irving Babbitt. Warner Rice relates the following story:

> On one occasion, when Emerson's name had come into the conversation, Mrs. Babbitt reminded [Babbitt] that he showed little interest in the set of this writer's works which she had given him, volume by volume, as holiday and anniversary gifts. At once the floodgates of his mind were opened on the

subject of Emerson. Emerson had stimulated him in his youth, long ago. . . .
Emerson had made much of God as the "inner check." All this was good. But
re-readings of Emerson had proved disappointing. The driving force of the
man was an expansive—and really a shallow—optimism.[8]

Like More, Babbitt was interested in Emerson's expression of dualism, the
interplay between impulse and restraint, desire and the inner check; and,
again like More, Babbitt was ultimately frustrated by Emerson's refusal to
strike a balance between these two poles, and his too eager willingness to
dismiss the reality of evil.[9]

Babbitt's most extensive treatment of Emerson is found in *The Masters of
Modern French Criticism*, a desperate, at times vitriolic attack on the "Rousseauist venom" that had poisoned modern criticism by "eliminating the
aristocratic and selective element from the standard of taste."[10] The result,
as Babbitt painstakingly details, has been a dramatic descent into flux,
relativity, and a glorification of "unchecked spontaneity" (45). While he
admits that the rigid demands of informed judgment might have exerted a
tyranny over the legitimate claims of spontaneity in the past, Babbitt sees
the contemporary situation, in which impulse reigns supreme, as clearly
unacceptable.[11] At this point he turns to Emerson and devotes considerable
effort toward making him useful as an antidote for this condition, suggesting that only he can restore the balance between "vital impulses and vital
control" (252).

Babbitt is at pains to assure his readers that he seeks a fair balance
between these forces, and he explains his emphasis on the need for order by
pointing to the rampant excesses of unrestrained impulse. It is not surprising then that his reliance on Emerson soon proves troublesome. Indeed, his
attempt to make Emerson over as the defender of absolute critical standards of judgment seems doomed from the start. In one of a number of
similar maneuvers, Babbitt first acknowledges Emerson's apparent apostasy, his claim that a "true man belongs to no other time and place, but is
the centre of things." Babbitt then goes on to assert, however, that Emerson
"has not therefore succumbed . . . to the doctrine of relativity and the
feeling of universal illusion that accompanies it; on the contrary, he has
attained to a new sense of the unity of human nature—a unity founded, not
on tradition, but on insight" (344–45). This process of explaining away
Emerson's all too obvious faults will become increasingly difficult for Babbitt to pull off as he advances through his argument.

At this point, Babbitt could have argued that in such essays as "The
Over-Soul" and "Circles," Emerson had articulated a "higher" vision of

what bound men together, a vision of unity based not on a stale tradition but invigorated by an ever-unfolding sense of divine purpose; he could have pointed to this as the key to the balance Emerson had struck between the whimsy of the impressionist and the rigidity of the traditionalist. He did neither. Instead, Babbitt returned immediately to the task of castigating the impressionist—by implication Emerson's opposite—who "denies the element of absolute judgment and so feels free to indulge his temperament with epicurean indolence" (346). It becomes clear, indeed, that for Babbitt the "insight" upon which Emerson based his "new sense of the unity of human nature" was nothing less than an insight into the transcendent nature of traditional standards of judgment and taste. That is, for Babbitt, Emerson suggests that we can sustain what are essentially the same standards without relying on "tradition" for their authority: critical standards are a permanent part of God's "inner check."

Babbitt's chief task is to ensure that the forces of impulse never achieve the kind of tyranny over the field that the forces of order inevitably seem to command. He may speak of balance, but what he seeks is redress. The more Babbitt warms to this task the less Emerson has to contribute. In moving toward his conclusion, Babbitt repeats his concern about the "Rousseauist" or "the pseudo-democrat" who "would eliminate from the norm the humanistic or aristocratic element." He then ruefully admits that

> Emerson, who has been our guide thus far, can be of little service to us here. He had humanitarian illusions of his own—illusions that he shared with his whole generation. . . . We also have to face the fact that Emerson, who has emphasized more happily perhaps than any other recent writer the need of selectiveness in the individual, and also the wisdom of the selections embodied in tradition, nevertheless gave undue encouragement to the ordinary man, to the man who is undisciplined and unselective and untraditional. (352–54)

In spite of his happy emphasis on the need for selectivity, Emerson fails Babbitt because of the "humanitarian illusions" he harbors about ordinary, undisciplined, untraditional men. Rather than encouragement, Babbitt suggests that such men need a few hard lessons in the wisdom of traditional standards of taste. Despite his lingering hope that Emerson might have provided those lessons, Babbitt is forced to "face the fact" that Emerson is not the man he needs him to be. Emerson is useful for Babbitt insofar as Babbitt wishes to appear responsive to the need to resist the tyranny of tradition; it is as if the mere act of invoking Emerson's name might direct attention away from his otherwise rigid agenda. When it comes to pressing on with that agenda, Babbitt must reluctantly cast Emerson aside.

Babbitt's use of Emerson in this book, like the book itself, is at times tortuous. On the one hand the tone is superior and confident, and Babbitt pursues his attack on Rousseauist excesses as if the battle had long been decided in his favor. On the other hand, he concedes the "all-pervading impressionism of contemporary literature and life," and cultivates the image of one crying in the wilderness. Indeed, Babbitt's vision of an acceptable balance between impulse and order is so limited that he cannot help but conclude that "the full attainment of our standard should prove impossible" (392). This makes his use of Emerson so intriguing, for even as he desperately strives to make Emerson speak for the forces of order, Babbitt knows that in calling on Emerson he has already descended fatefully into the enemy's camp.

In trying to make Emerson useful in his attack on modern literature, Babbitt was in effect attempting to reclaim Emerson from the vague, idealized image perpetuated by the genteel critics. These earlier critics had quickly realized that Emerson could be used to say many things and they largely avoided making any specific claims for his ideas. Babbitt makes such claims, and in the process shoots himself in the foot. Like More, Babbitt demanded more from Emerson than that he radiate a lovely character, and, also like More, he was frustrated in his attempt to use Emerson as a buttress for his New Humanism. Indeed, given the cultural program they promoted, their disappointment with Emerson was inevitable.[12] The genteel critics revealed their essential conservatism by elevating Emerson above the details of everyday life to a position as guardian of truth and beauty, ideals that all could appreciate with proper guidance; the Humanists wrenched Emerson from this pinnacle and used him as a cudgel in their reactionary attempt to restore a culture that made insight into such ideals the domain of a privileged few.[13]

The New Humanism of More and Babbitt was never a particularly potent force on the critical scene in the teens and twenties, and each was characterized more by the stridency of his arguments than the extent of his influence. Another student of Babbitt's, Stuart Sherman, achieved more in the way of respectability—he served as one of the four editors of the *Cambridge History of American Literature*—and enjoyed significantly more notoriety as the favorite target of H. L. Mencken's campaign against the "Professor Doctors." Though an avowed disciple of Babbitt early in his brief career (he died in 1926 at the age of forty-five), Sherman came to reject, if politely, much of his teacher's illiberal biases.[14] Interestingly, this diversion can be gauged by their differing views on Emerson. In 1922, Sherman edited and wrote an introduction to a selection of Emerson's essays and in a letter to Babbitt wrote: "If it had been a volume really of my own, I should have asked permission to inscribe your name in it." Babbitt's response suggests that it was just as well that Sherman had not sought that permission, for he found the introduction "very nearly a pure panegyric" and observed that "I fancy that the reservations I am for making in regard to Emerson and above all in regard to Emersonian influence are of a much more fundamental character than you deem needful."[15]

At first glance, Sherman's treatment of Emerson differs little from that of either Babbitt or More. Like them he is interested in making Emerson useful for modern criticism, noting that "what it most concerns us to enquire about him is what he can do for us."[16] Sherman also echoes Babbitt and More in locating Emerson's significance in his dualism, his forging a middle path between the vital forces of tradition and the "cramping and lifeless part" of the past (74). This image of Emerson striking a balance between two extremes recurs throughout the essay and in a variety of aspects: Emerson reconciles conformity and individualism, liberty and responsibility, romantic idealism and scientific positivism. For Sherman, he is the "true emancipator" because, even as he "strikes off the old shackles" he "immediately . . . suggests new service" (78).

To this point, Sherman's Emerson closely resembles Babbitt's depiction of the man who might teach modern critics the enduring value of restraint in a world given over to impulse. Yet where both Babbitt and More ultimately stumbled over just how useful Emerson could be as a minister of restraint, Sherman had no such trouble. Even though he praises Emerson for perceiving that "a decent conformity is the very secret of freedom," Sherman's idea of conformity is far more generous than Babbitt's. Babbitt needed Emerson to defend traditional standards of taste and had to give him up when he proved unsuited to the task; Sherman, clearly attracted to the encouragement Emerson offered to individual insight, was willing to go along with him a little further. This was the fundamental difference to which Babbitt alluded in his reply: his own notion of an acceptable balance between the forces of order and the forces of liberation privileged order; Sherman seemed content to give liberation more room.

This is not to say that Sherman was blind to the potential for excess in Emerson's ideas, or that he looked on that potential with equanimity. Sherman, too, constructed a set of limits around Emerson's liberating impulses, insuring that they were safe for anyone who might want to draw inspiration from them. Where the genteel critics turned to Emerson's exemplary personal characteristics as a defense against the murkiness of his ideas, Sherman surrounds Emerson's ideas with a discipline that is explicitly Christian. He observes that "Emerson's is the radicalism of a conservative," a fact made obvious by his "many references to the character and teaching of Jesus, to whom he returns again and again." Sherman proceeds through the rest of the essay to emphasize Emerson's fundamentally Christian nature (84).

The suggestion that Emerson returned "again and again" to the character and teachings of Jesus, or that he was in any but the most indirect way to be considered a Christian, would have stunned those who had detailed his frustrating *lack* of attention to the historical person and teachings of Christ. Even Oliver Wendell Holmes, who felt free to compare Emerson to Christ, regretted the fact that Emerson devoted more attention to Shakespeare, Napoleon, Plato, Plutarch, and Goethe (382). Still, Sherman persists in joining Emerson with Christianity, and it is clear that his admiration for Emerson's task of liberation is rooted firmly in his conviction that Emerson was at the same time bound by the Christian teaching of self-restraint (93).

Sherman's argument for Emerson's commitment to the teachings of Christ is rather thin; he is content simply to say it is so and move on. Without this element, however, Emerson might have proved as useless for Sherman as he was for Babbitt. In "The Point of View in American Criticism," Sherman defines his project as demonstrating that democracy and standards can coexist, that men living in a democracy do not forfeit all means of discriminating between what is and what is not desirable. To this end he advocates the reintegration of religion with democracy, but is quick to point out that he has in mind a religion that is spiritual rather than moralistic, one that is no more a "principle of repression . . . than it is a principle of release."[17] It is, in short, a religion of balance, and Emerson is Sherman's favored prophet.

Sherman crafts Emerson in his own image, as someone who is devoted to popular democracy but aware of its faults, sensitive to repression but suspicious of unrestrained release. While this sounds much like the disingenuous protestations of Babbitt, Sherman seems to mean what he says. In a letter to William C. Brownell, Sherman explained the goal of his criticism:

The line I have taken and intend to follow is the encouragement of the native tradition, with all its imperfections on its head, the Puritan, the pioneer, the

Jacksonian strain, the adventurous, daring, exploring, spirit, democracy—
whatever it can be made to mean, and including, at any rate, a growing
fraternity. . . . I want to get the Emersons and the Jacksons together, and
their offspring to intermarry. I believe the American breed will profit by the
misalliance.[18]

Sherman never had the chance to demonstrate how far he was willing to go
in encouraging this daring and exploring spirit in literature, and critics
point to his pronounced Anglo-Saxon bias as evidence of his refusal to
venture too far.[19] Still, his was one of the few sustained attempts at the time
to appropriate Emerson as the foundation of a critical project, and it is
unfortunate that his early death prevented him from pursuing his experiments in cross-breeding.

The New Humanists, particularly Sherman, were frequent targets of H. L.
Mencken's relentless attacks on the softness, pretension, and narrowness
he perceived in American criticism. For Mencken, the Humanists and
the genteel critics—the professors and the literary journalists—were essentially interchangeable: More, Sherman, and Babbitt, along with Hamilton
Wright Mabie, Henry Van Dyke, Fred Lewis Pattee, and others, he either
relegated to the role of "honorary pallbearers of literature" or dismissed
as the "pathetic spokesmen of the artistic faith that lies in suburban pas-
tors, fresh-water college professors and directors of the Y.M.C.A."[20] More's
"staggeringly ignorant 'criticism'" and Mabie's "pious prattle for high-
school girls" were manifestations of the same disease, and Mencken saw no
reason to consider fine points of discrimination in administering the cure.[21]

Mencken's bombastic denunciation of most of the critics of his day was
based in part on his intense interest in the work of men like Nietzsche,
Theodore Dreiser, and George Bernard Shaw, writers whom the "Professor
Doctors" either ignored or condemned. Given his disgust with such critics'
demonstrated preference for the works of writers long since dead, it is not
surprising that Mencken found little use for Emerson. Emerson was, after
all, the darling of those whom Mencken abhorred, the warmed-over relic of
a New England tradition that ought finally to be put to rest. There could be
little in Emerson that Mencken would find useful, short of a neatly pack-
aged representation of all that was wrong with modern critical thought.

Mencken approached Emerson warily. At times, he faulted Emerson's
critics and followers for having misinterpreted his thought and, in the
process, denying Emerson his rightful legacy. In his final contribution to

the *Smart Set* in 1923, Mencken offers the following observations on Emerson's peculiar place in the history of American literature:

> It was obviously Emerson's central aim in life to liberate the American mind—to set it free from the crippling ethical obsessions of Puritanism, to break down herd thinking, to make liberty more real on the intellectual plane than it could ever be on the political plane. It is his tragic fate to be mouthed and admired today chiefly by persons who have entirely misunderstood his position—in brief, by the heirs and assigns of the very prigs and dullards he spent his whole life opposing.[22]

Mencken here assigns Emerson exactly the same task that Mencken took on himself: freeing the American mind from puritanical repression, promoting intellectual liberty, and exposing dullards and prigs. It is easy to hear the bitterness in his tone when he goes on to observe that "Emerson paved the way for every intellectual revolt that has occurred since his time, and yet he has always been brought into court, not as a witness for the rebels, but as a witness for the militia and the police" (334). Mencken elsewhere remarks on Emerson's "extraordinary mental equipment," and rues the fact that his influence has been limited to "half educated dolts whose thinking is all mellow and witless booziness."[23] This Emerson is very much Mencken's man, and Mencken's sympathetic identification with him suggests the potential for a broader appropriation. However, Mencken was less interested in recovering a usable Emerson than in attacking those who had so egregiously misunderstood him; he displayed Emerson as evidence in his prosecution of prigs and dullards without any corresponding effort to restore the victim.

Mencken did not always treat Emerson quite so sympathetically. While holding him up as a wronged prophet provided him with a way of going after the dolts who had gotten him wrong, Mencken at other times wavered on the question of whether there was, in fact, a right way to apprehend Emerson. In "An Unheeded Law-Giver," he reveals a keen awareness of the state of Emerson criticism:

> One discerns in all right-thinking American criticism, the doctrine that Ralph Waldo Emerson was a great man, but the specifications supporting that doctrine are seldom displayed with any clarity. . . . [P]ractically all the existing criticism of him is marked by his own mellifluous obscurity.[24]

Here, Mencken suggests that Emerson's own "mellifluous obscurity" is at least in part to blame for the dullness of his critics: Emerson was not a revolutionary but "imitative and cautious . . . he stated his own [ideas] so warily and so muggily that they were ratified on the one hand by Nietzsche and on the other hand by the messiahs of the New Thought" (191). Though Mencken appreciates the irony of Emerson's being so warmly received by opposing camps, he suspects that this is as much a reflection of Emerson's inherent weakness as of his critics' lack of perceptiveness. Indeed, Mencken is wary of Emerson's being so easily appropriated, and while he respects Nietzsche's admiration for Emerson he regrets the influence Emerson has had on American thought:

> What remains of him at home . . . is no more than, on the one hand, a somewhat absurd affectation of intellectual fastidiousness . . . and, on the other hand, a debased Transcendentalism rolled into pills for fat women with vague pains and inattentive husbands—in brief, the New Thought—in brief, imbecility. This New Thought, a decadent end-product of American super-ficiality, now almost monopolizes him. (194)

That Emerson could have inspired such absurdities, however unwittingly, is enough for Mencken to question his usefulness. In another piece, Mencken explains that Emerson failed "both as a great teacher and as a great artist because of his remoteness from the active, exigent life that he was a part of. . . . [H]e carried on his inquiries in the manner of a medieval monk, and his conclusions showed all the nebulousness that one associates with the monkish character."[25] Mencken's complaint is thus not simply that Emerson was misinterpreted by fools and dullards, but that he invited such misinterpretation by failing to root his work in the concrete details of real life.

Mencken's suspicion of Emerson deepened in later years. In a review of Regis Michaud's *Emerson: The Enraptured Yankee,* he quips that Emerson's philosophy "seems to be made precisely for the lunch-table idealists," men who would be all too easily satisfied by its

> almost incomparable sweep of soothing generalities [and] vast marshaling of sugary and not too specific words . . . I can imagine nothing better suited to the spiritual needs of used-car dealers, trust company vice-presidents, bath fixture magnates, and the like, gathered together in the sight of God to take cheer from one another and shove the Republic along its rocky road.[26]

The derisive rhetoric was Mencken's trademark; within it lay the author's studied conclusion that, whatever merits Emerson may have possessed on his own, he had come to represent everything contemptible about American culture. Commenting on his recent translation of Nietzsche's *Anti-*

Christ, Mencken admitted: "I probably failed, but nevertheless I came considerably closer to success than the other translators of the book, all of whom converted it into an essay by Emerson, with corrections by Bruce Barton."[27] Mencken respected brutal honesty, the naturalism of Dreiser and the nihilism of Nietzsche; he championed writers who were firmly rooted in the gritty details of everyday life, who defied convention and resisted softness. The Emerson he inherited from the genteel critics and whom he found everywhere evident in the shallowness of popular thought, was so lacking in vitality, so thoroughly anathema to his purpose, that Mencken found it more expedient to reject him than attempt to recover his latent revolutionary potential.[28] Misunderstood by his critics or not, Emerson was at base "moony, hollow and sterile."[29]

Mencken's discarding of Emerson was rooted in his inability to make Emerson useful, just as Irving Babbitt and T. S. Eliot ultimately rejected Emerson as irrelevant to their own critical projects. This conscious search for a usable tradition in the American past is a defining characteristic of the criticism of this period, and the evaluations of Emerson explicitly turn on the degree to which he is found useful. Van Wyck Brooks made this search the central aim of his early work, and his "On Creating a Usable Past" served as something of a founding document.[30] Brooks found American culture burdened with an understanding of the past that was passive and fixed. Rather than uncovering elements in that past which would "contribute to some common understanding in the present," most writers and critics followed the lead of the professors who revelled in the "vicarious world of the dead" and maintained that the past was an ideal by which the present could only measure its failures (337–38). As a result, American culture had become a "travesty of a civilization," lacking the vitality that accompanies an active connection with the past: "The present is a void, and the American writer floats in that void because the past that survives in the common mind of the present is a past without living value" (339).

Brooks addresses this crisis by urging writers and critics to identify and rejuvenate that which is usable in the American literary tradition. The questions to ask are: "*What is important for us?* What, out of all the multifarious achievements and desires of the American literary mind, ought we to elect to remember?" (340). In answering these questions modern writers will carry the past into the present and enrich that present by locating it in an ever-evolving tradition. No longer an ideal to which modern writers can only vainly aspire, the literature of the past can become a living force interacting with the literature of the present, guiding it rather than limiting it. Ultimately, the creation of a usable past will lead to a culture that is more intimately related to the experience of the people it purports to represent.

Brooks had addressed similar issues in an earlier volume, *America's Coming-of-Age*. Here, he argued that the stagnant condition of American culture resulted from the simultaneous devotion to two irreconcilable sets of values: on the one hand the assumption of "transcendent theory" and "high ideals," and on the other hand the "catchpenny realities" of business life.[31] This division afforded American culture no middle ground between a highbrow faith in "vaporous idealism" and a lowbrow worship of "self-interested practicality" (34). For Brooks, this situation forced the artist and critic to wander aimlessly in a vacuum while condemning American society in general to a kind of nihilism, trapped between unrealizable ideals and meaningless activity.

Brooks's argument about the division between ideals and practice corresponded to a deeper division between culture and experience: American culture was thoroughly disassociated from American experience, while the daily activity of American life was pursued in the absence of any higher meaning, a meaning that culture should ordinarily provide. By creating a usable past, Brooks suggests, the modern writer can begin to bridge this gap by bringing culture and experience closer together. In the ensuing dialectic, the "vaporous ideals" would be made to speak more directly to the real experience of living Americans, and that experience would be endowed with a higher purpose than the mere pursuit of material self-interest.

While Brooks developed his argument with some confidence, he was not at all optimistic that his project would be realized. Indeed, his sense of the sterility of American culture was so deep that he despaired of any successful rejuvenation. This despair is evident in Brooks's discussion of university professors, whose standing as cultural authorities he deems largely responsible for the pervasiveness of this rootless idealism. The university such professors inhabit is

> a place, one can fairly say, where ideals are cherished precisely because they are ineffectual, because they are ineptly and mournfully beautiful . . . because they make life progressively uninteresting, because, practically and in effect, they are illusions and frauds and infinitely charming lies. (24)

Brooks is here anticipating the tenor of Mencken's attacks on the genteel professors and their overly idealized version of the literary past. Like Mencken, Brooks rejected the genteel critics' transformation of culture into a realm of the beautiful and the true, and considered the version of the American literary tradition these critics handed down to be devoid of any lasting significance. In creating a usable past to replace this stale tradition Brooks would have to discard much of what this tradition preserved. One of the most representative products of this tradition was Emerson.

In *America's Coming-of-Age,* Brooks declared Emerson to be the very embodiment of the division between ideals and practice that had rendered American literature so ineffective. According to Brooks, Emerson's style irritated so many modern writers "because he has so little natural sense of the relation between the abstract and the concrete." In fact, "the truth is that Emerson was not interested in human life; he cared nothing for experience or emotion, possessing so little himself" (75, 77–78). Emerson's refusal to wed the abstract to the concrete was a crucial failure for Brooks, who considered a firm relation between the concrete and the abstract, between experience and culture, essential if American literature were to emerge from its condition of lethargic ineptitude. Emerson's perceived deficiency in this area led Brooks and other like-minded critics to view him as expendable.

Throughout his discussion of Emerson, Brooks asks the simple questions that he would propose as the starting point for all criticism: Why should we remember Emerson? What does he mean for us, today? The answers Brooks arrives at indicate the degree to which he found Emerson singularly unusable: rather than encouraging a culture of common understanding, Emerson "presided over and gave its tone to this world of infinite social fragmentation and unlimited free will," thereby evading any common ground between ideals and experience; instead of promoting his idealism as a restraint on the pursuit of self-interest, he unleashed a "thoroughgoing, self-reliant individualism." In his final judgment, Brooks considers Emerson to be "incapable of an effective social ideal" and no longer a figure worthy of attention (79–82).

Brooks was looking for a literary tradition that nurtured social consciousness, one that tempered the individualistic pursuit of business success with a commitment to social responsibility and cultural community. What he found in Emerson was someone whose work

> has all the qualities of the typical baccalaureate sermon [which] has never been found inconveniently inconsistent with the facts and requirements of business life. . . . Since the day of Emerson's address on "The American Scholar" the whole of American literature has had the semblance of one vast, all-embracing baccalaureate sermon, addressed to the private virtues of young men. It has been one shining deluge of righteousness, purity, practical mysticism. (84–85)

Brooks here confronts and rejects the version of Emerson promoted by the genteel critics. This Emerson, whose purity and nobility of mind transcended more worldly concerns and imbued American literature with a tradition of "high ideals," fell far short of Brooks's goal for an active, socially engaged tradition. Other than indirectly sanctifying the pursuit of wealth, Emerson had nothing to contribute to modern life.

Brooks concludes his discussion of Emerson with an illustration of the typical "personal and social effects" that Emerson had engendered in contemporary American society. In a rented cottage in California surrounded by "an aroma of delicate futility," Brooks had encountered the work of George William Curtis, a man who "had that pale, earnest cast of mind which always comes from thinking more about what Sir Galahad didn't do than about the object of his quest." For Brooks, Curtis was the epitome of Emerson's influence. Driven by the "superannuated boyishness of the Emersonian tradition," Curtis's understanding of society could be "fairly well summed up in his energetic though perfectly well-mannered invective against smoking cigarettes in the presence of ladies" (86–87). Whatever their noble intentions, Emerson and the men and women he inspired were "like high-minded weather-cocks on a windless day" (89). Brooks sought a tradition that would give direction to society rather than simply indicate the direction society had already taken.

Brooks would return to Emerson later in his career when, with *The Life of Emerson* and his series on New England, he attempted to place Emerson at the center of a tradition of vibrant optimism and hope, a tradition he felt America then needed to recapture. As Christopher Lasch has pointed out, however, Brooks's new-found appreciation of Emerson "left it unclear why a more sophisticated and disillusioned generation should take any but a nostalgic interest in the 'Orpheus' of the nation's infancy."[32] Indeed, the *Life* was little more than a rearrangement of Emerson's own words, loosely connected by Brooks's often vapid commentary and lacking even the most subtle attempt to explain why Emerson was now so important.[33] Brooks's critics have also pointed to the fact that his later work on Emerson coincided with the onset of his emotional breakdown and marked a division in his career where he discarded his "serious work of criticism" in favor of the anonymity available in a collection of "stylized paraphrases" of his subject's own words.[34] However explained, Brooks's strained efforts to make Emerson usable for the 1930s and beyond paled in comparison with his thorough, clearly reasoned rejection of Emerson at the start of his career.

Waldo Frank shared Brooks's interest in uncovering a usable past and held similar beliefs about the crisis that confronted American culture. As a founder and editor—along with Brooks, Randolph Bourne, and Paul Rosenfeld—of *The Seven Arts* and a frequent contributor to *The Dial,* Frank sought to make modern literature an active participant in the struggle against acquisitiveness and materialism.[35] *Our America* was his attempt to construct a tradition in which that struggle might flourish, a usable past that would guide modern writers in their effort to restore the reformative power of literature and rejuvenate American culture.[36] And just as Frank took his cue from Brooks concerning the need for a usable past, so too did he follow Brooks in finding Emerson poorly suited to contributing to this tradition.

Frank approached Emerson in a manner reminiscent of Mencken, finding him to be a "sensitive and aspiring scholar" who was crushed by the obtuseness of his social world and misappropriated by his followers. Though at first sympathetic to Emerson's plight, Frank was evidently not interested in rescuing Emerson's reputation from this misuse. Instead, like both Brooks and Mencken, Frank ultimately faults Emerson for inviting misinterpretation by failing to make himself plain. Though Emerson had "vision," "considerable mental power," and "the genius of aspiration," in short, all "the equipment of a cultural leader," his "books are vague, his instances remote . . . his works are essentially discards from weakness," and his potential for leadership is thereby compromised (69).

Frank identified the fundamental source of Emerson's weakness as his withdrawing from the "actual world of men," a retreat from society that isolated him from all that was "mortal-human" (69–70). This was a crucial point for Frank, who shared Brooks's commitment to a socially engaged literature. Since Emerson "abhorred American affairs and was repugned by the traffic of reality," he had little to contribute to Frank's search for a usable past (71). When he later takes up Henry Thoreau, Frank's stance toward Emerson becomes explicit: "The words of Emerson who flanked empires by air-route are become vague and impalpable and abstract: the words of Thoreau who faced reality . . . ring solid and full of virile beauty. Emerson wrote pleasant sentences over the dead body of Thoreau. But Thoreau's sentences are helping to bury Emerson today" (151). Emerson, whose very significance had been rooted in his supposed divorce from the demands of vulgar experience, gets swept aside because he refused to confront those demands.

Frank is aware that he is rejecting not only Emerson but the tradition that had grown up around him and had come to define so much of American culture. Emerson "ruled supreme in thoughtful circles. His philosophy supplied the norm for our poetry and fiction, his manner became the manners of the cultured." In fact, Frank comes to see Emerson as more of a founder of the genteel tradition than its prized creation. Confronted with a society that was "wholly measured by materialistic standards," writers and critics in the Emersonian tradition sought to transcend these standards rather than challenge them. They "concocted air-brews" as substitutes for the experience of real life, and "could not face the truth that the 'spirit' and the 'splendor' that they desired were to be found alone in the 'details and prose' which they rejected. And to be found nowhere else" (70–71). By ignoring the details of the "actual world of men," Emerson and the genteel critics and writers who followed him unwittingly acquiesced in the separation of culture from experience and condemned that culture to irrelevance.

For Frank, the culture that Emerson supposedly founded was easily appropriated by the material world it sought to transcend, and Frank is quick to point to the irony of the fact that Emerson was "delivered up into the patronage of the material world he hated . . . he did his share of feeding it, easing it, giving it strength." By helping to cement the division between culture and experience, Emerson "gave to a material American world the very dualism it required," providing a distant, nonthreatening, but high-minded idealism that would ease the conscience of the business-man and soothe his pursuit of wealth with the serenity of beautiful poetry: "The hypocrisy of the American who goes to church on Sunday and bleeds his brother Monday . . . found support by a bitter irony in the books of this pure spirit" (71–72, 75). Frank found Emersonian culture to be so rootless that even its best intentions were turned against it, and the only use he could make of it was as an example of what to avoid.

Both Brooks and Frank rejected Emerson because his work failed to promote a culture that was critically engaged with what they took to be the defining experience of modern America: a frantic pursuit of material well-being carried on in the absence of any system of values that would give life meaning. In the ensuing years, when many critics came to view American experience as fundamentally determined by either class oppression or moralistic repression, the demand that culture be related to that experience grew louder and more rigorous. In the Freudian criticism of Ludwig Lewishon and the Marxist perspectives adopted by V. F. Calverton and Granville Hicks, Emerson would be judged on the basis of how well his work measured up as, respectively, an expression of the vital impulses and a weapon in the class struggle.[37]

In *Expression in America* Lewishon approached the American literary past as a storehouse of repressed emotions and sublimated sexuality. In seeking to liberate these energies, he candidly relied on what he termed the Freudian theory of art as a revolt against repression. In the American case, "the true history of literature . . . is the history of those poets and thinkers who first in mere theory, later in both theory and practice, denied the Puritan division of experience from expression, broke the moulds of the artificer, and brought their countrymen first freedom of perception and of thought, next flexibility of conduct in pursuit of each man's idea of the good life."[38] Lewishon's book is an effort to trace the denial of "Puritanism" that constituted the main line of a usable American literary past.

Lewishon's project shares much with those of Brooks and Frank, in that each sought to redress the division between the details of American experience, on the one hand, and the various elements that made up American ideals, American culture, or American expression, on the other. Lewishon also follows Brooks, Mencken, and many other modern critics in locating the origin of this division in America's Puritan heritage. Since the Puritan ethos refused to impose rules of conduct on political or business life, American society compensated for its "fierce sinning" in these areas by "bearing down with unparalleled harshness upon all the more amiable and expansive forces of human nature" (xx–xxi). It is this "unparalleled harshness" that Lewishon is out to expose, and he surpasses his colleagues in antipuritanism by consistently implying that, through their legacy of repression, the Puritans were directly responsible for the sterility of American culture.

This context may help to explain the relentlessness with which Lewishon goes after Emerson. Indeed, his discussion of Emerson is nothing less than a study in malicious dissection, for he sees Emerson as the embodiment of all that was sterile and life-denying in the Puritan tradition. Lewishon associates both Emerson and Thoreau with the "artificers," a group he has identified with an inferior stage in the development of the expressive mind.[39] The artificer can deceive his audience into "thinking him spontaneous and original" while he is, in fact, "only tricky and sentimental"; his words may have the appearance of vitality, but they merely reformulate stale ideas (xxi–xxii). In a similar way, Emerson and Thoreau suffer from a "disproportion between power and result, between intellectual intrepidity and temperamental lack of vitality" (106). Like the artificer, their "expression . . . has little to do with experience," and their influence on American culture can only be regretted.

Lewishon's problem with Emerson and Thoreau—for he discusses them as if they were essentially interchangeable—is that the radical criticism which charged their writings was so divorced from real life that they subsequently came to be honored and absorbed by the very culture they sought to change. Though intellectually daring, they instilled a false sense of vitality that failed to effectively challenge the prevailing sterility of American expressive life. Lewishon wants to explain this enigma, and he quotes a number of passages from the *Journals* in which Emerson describes his "want of animal spirits," insufficient "vital force," and lack of sympathy with "dark, turbid, mournful, passionate natures" (109). From this evidence, Lewishon immediately concludes that "there were whole ranges of experience" to which Emerson had no access—experiences that ranged from passionate vitality to dark tragedy—and that this is why Emerson's radical criticism packed so little punch.

At this point Lewishon is merely using different language to make a familiar charge, recalling suggestions of Emerson's innocence of evil and his remarkably mild temper that, in one form or another, were staples of earlier Emerson criticism. Following this, however, he asserts:

> I content myself with saying that Emerson's low vitality which he calls absence of animal spirits affected his love life from the beginning. Passionate ardor, plastic vision, high intensity of speech, the somber and triumphant glow of life as tragic and yet as infinitely precious and significant—all these things were not for him. (110)

Instead of simply pointing to Emerson's lack of grounding in experience as the reason for his irrelevance to contemporary criticism—the path followed by Brooks and Frank—Lewishon sets out an inclusive portrait of Emerson's overwhelming inadequacy, making elaborate connections between the limitations of his written work and the supposed shortcomings of his personal life: his dysfunctional love life, lack of emotional intensity, and failure to grasp the tragic significance of life are all explained by his repressed animal vitality.[40]

Lewishon rounds out his account of Emerson's inadequacies by observing that, again like Thoreau, he was a "chilled under-sexed valetudinarian, deprived of helpful and sympathetic social and intellectual atmosphere" (112). Finally, he concludes that Emerson's was

> a mind that had no commerce with deep, primordial, tragic, human things, an almost abstract, disembodied mind, fine but thin, bloodless and so unclouded, never somber, almost never troubled to its depth because it had no direct contact with the problems and conflicts—nine-tenths of human life—which spring from human passions, relations, longings, triumphs, despairs. (117)

Lewishon's primary interest through all of this was to demonstrate Emerson's deficiency as a contributor to the "true" American literary tradition, and the first half of his chapter on Emerson and Thoreau is essentially a revelation of all the ways in which they represented aspects of the past that were unusable. Insofar as Emerson can be counted among the artificers, "no sound history of literature can now or hereafter be written that does not recognize and know and exclude him and fix its attention wholly upon the products of the creative spirit" (xxii). Toward the end of the chapter, however, Lewishon turns his attention to some of Emerson's more worthy achievements and suggests that there may still be a place for him in this "sound" literary history:

> The thing to do to save Emerson is, as I have sufficiently pointed out, to strip the chief doctrines of the great essays from the mysticism and relapses into conventional modes of feeling, to gather from the other works earlier and later all that confirms and fortifies those central and saving doctrines and thus to liberate in Emerson that element of the permanent which he undoubtedly possesses. (130–31)

In short, the task at hand is to extract from Emerson's essays, poems, and journals a volume of aphorisms in which he articulates his "central and saving" doctrine: the call for a true poet, the "free creative individual" who faithfully expresses only the truth by which he lives (121–22). For Lewishon, this volume would draw heavily on "The American Scholar," "Self-Reliance," and "The Poet," and would assiduously ignore "Compensation," "The Over-Soul," and "Circles," essays that have been overrated by "a lazy and probably not always candid" critical tradition (122–23, 127). In this way, Emerson's "low vitality and lack of intensity, his consequent exclusion of both passion and the tragic—all that accounts for his too respectable status—can be gradually eliminated from his work. Into his magnificent and liberating central doctrines new American generations can pour their ardor and their hope" (131).

The details of this reclamation project reveal another dimension in Lewishon's criticism of Emerson and of his critical project in general. In the introduction, Lewishon's call for Americans to break the repressive bonds of their Puritan heritage seems intended to correct for a history of social hypocrisy and injustice, and his discussion of the nefarious division between experience and expression echoes the sentiments of Van Wyck Brooks and Waldo Frank. However, while both Brooks and Frank devoted much of their critical energy to promoting a culture based on community and cooperation, Lewishon is primarily interested in liberating creative individuals from the constraints that inevitably accompany such community. His singular commitment to *individual* creative expression as an end in itself contrasts sharply with Brooks's call for American writers to give purpose to the lives of their less articulate compatriots.

Lewishon reveals something of this attitude as he assembles his anthology of Emerson's more worthy passages. *Nature* and some of the early essays are "too entangled in idealistic metaphysics" and contain too many "strictly clerical vestiges" to be of much use. Emerson "dragged his feeble teleology along with him to the end," and he is far too often guilty of such "irresponsible verbiage" as "I believe in Eternity" and "What is a farm but a mute gospel?" Rather, Emerson should be remembered for the "brilliant light" of his "central and memorable passages concerning the individual and the individual's creative function." It is important at this point to recall that Lewishon finds these passages concentrated in "Self-Reliance" and "The Poet," and that he has rejected outright "The Over-Soul," "Circles," and "Compensation" as containing little of value.

Significantly, it is in these latter essays, as a number of Emerson's earlier critics had observed, that he explicitly tempers his pleas for free individual expression with moving and not strictly metaphysical accounts of the interrelatedness of these individuals and the diverse forms that their creative expression might take. It was Emerson's task to both liberate expression and provide a context for it, a task that paved the way for Whitman to praise the "poetry" produced by shoemakers, carpenters, and sewing girls. In Lewishon's abridged version, Emerson's liberation is deprived of that context and the creative individual is liberated from puritanical repression for the sake of expression itself. By the end of his chapter on Emerson, Lewishon's implied concern with the hypocrisy and injustice resulting from the division between creative expression and social experience has been replaced by a call for the liberation of a rootless and detached class of expressive individuals whose relation to society is left ambiguous.[41]

Lewishon's account of Emerson reveals the limitations of his theoretical framework, a framework based both on a Manichaean opposition between repression and expression and a commitment to reuniting expression with social experience. That Lewishon identifies his method with the theoretical advances of Freud does little to clarify the muddled relationships he struggles to define between his three key terms. In the introduction Lewishon defends his use of Freudian methodology by declaring that "the portrayer of any aspect of human life or civilization who does not do so today will soon be like some mariner of old who, refusing to acknowledge the invention of mathematical instruments because their precision was not yet perfect, still stubbornly sailed his vessel by the stars" (vii). This revealing analogy suggests Lewishon's interest in applying the principles of modern science to the study of expressive culture, an approach that promises a truer and more reliable image of its object. Nonetheless, despite Lewishon's acknowledgment that we still must endure a measure of imprecision, the Emerson that his method serves up might well make one yearn for the days when men were guided more by their senses than their instruments.

A different kind of rigid framework drove the Marxist criticism of Emerson. As suggested in the work of Frank and Brooks, Emerson posed special problems for the critic seeking to uncover a literary tradition rooted in the details of human experience.[42] His supposedly atomistic individualism, naive optimism, and occasional lapses into mystical detachment made him even less acceptable to critics who defined "real experience" in terms of economic determinism and class conflict. V. F. Calverton's *The Liberation of American Literature* and Granville Hicks's *The Great Tradition* are among the most important of the early Marxist interpretations of American literature, and their accounts of Emerson demonstrate just how far his fortunes had fallen by the middle of the 1930s.

Calverton is quick to set out the parameters of his project:

> I have taken the aesthetic element for granted, and in almost all cases have immediately proceeded to an analysis of the philosophy, or ideology if you will, that underlay the individual author's work. . . . I have endeavored . . . to trace the development of American literature in relationship with those social forces, expressed in the form of class content, which it is necessary for us to understand first if we are to work out a sound critical method. Without such an understanding, criticism cannot found itself upon a secure social basis, and all analysis of the aesthetic element can amount to nothing more than subjective caprice.[43]

In taking for granted the "aesthetic element," Calverton candidly adopted what many critics of Marxism would come to regard as a fundamentally nonliterary stance, one that subordinated the truly literary element of a piece of writing to a narrow, predetermined ideological analysis. Of course, this was precisely what most Marxist critics in the thirties intended. Calverton set out to rewrite the history of American literature as a history of American writers' awareness of and responses to the class system, and he sought to construct a usable past around those writers who recognized the effects of that system and worked to subvert it.

For Calverton, the "basic psychological determinant in our national ideology" is the "petty bourgeois individualism of the frontier" (244). This ideology of rugged individualism promoted a false consciousness of personal independence that obscured the workings of the class system and contributed to the persistent romantic image of the individual as isolated from society. In Emerson, this "anarcho-individualism" provided the heart of his philosophy: "His optimism, his eloquent defense of democracy, his belief in the individual, his stress upon personal independence and self-reliance, were all generated in his mind by the impact of the frontier." Moreover, "those ideas of Emerson which influenced American thought and which continue to attract American intellectuals to-day, are those which were inspired by the frontier" (246). As filtered through Emerson's high-toned, transcendental lens, rugged frontier individualism came to serve as a respectable foundation for civilized society, as appropriate a guiding force in the boardroom and the statehouse as on the western plains.

Calverton appreciates that Emerson's assertion of frontier individualism was useful in its time and place. It was his "faith in man the individual, this faith in the individual isolated from society, the individual independent from society . . . that endowed his doctrine with the spirit of challenge," a spirit that helped to overthrow the vestiges of a colonial ethos and provide a theoretical grounding for a broadly conceived notion of democracy (247–48). However, Calverton finds Emerson's enduring influence on American thought to be less happy. While his panegyrics on self-reliance and independent individuals served to electrify mid-nineteenth-century America, Emerson simultaneously constructed elaborate metaphysical conceits to protect him from the implications of what he preached. In a revealing analogy, Calverton compares Emerson with the Menshevik revolutionaries in czarist Russia who, "when they saw a revolution in reality, became horrified, and who, because they were not prepared for the ruthless tasks of carrying a revolution to its inevitable conclusion, became the most bitter opponents of the Bolsheviki who put the revolution into actual practice and made it work" (247n). In Calverton's view, Emersonian individualism provided the philosophical foundation necessary for America to begin the process of social revolution; at the same time, it nurtured a stubborn resistance to the sense of social responsibility and sacrifice that would be necessary for that revolution to succeed.

For Calverton, Emerson has little to offer a Marxist tradition because he emphasized the independent individual as the primary social unit. This individualism explained Emerson's lack of sympathy for "the masses" and his general resistance to any system of identity based on group characteristics or conditions. Moreover, it was this aspect of Emerson that exerted the greatest influence on subsequent American thought, leading to a wholesale rejection of the class-based analysis that was central to Marxist criticism. Calverton observes:

> Emerson extended the petty bourgeois philosophy of the frontier to its farthest anarchical extreme, extolling at times attitudes that were as definitely antisocial in their implications as the activities of the frontiersmen who early defied every semblance of state, authority, and tradition. . . . Eternally, then, Emerson's stress is upon the self, the individual self, the personal ego. Society can take care of itself, or go hang, as the frontiersman would have put it. It is the individual who must be stressed, the individual who must learn to stand alone, and become sufficient within himself. (249)

Though at first a welcome means of liberation, Emersonian individualism inevitably deteriorated into its "anarchical extreme." Thus, "without wishing it, Emerson gave sanction by virtue of his doctrines to every type of exploitation which the frontier encouraged." Emerson thus proves to be a peculiar burden on Calverton and other Marxist critics: he cannot quite be dismissed but his influence can only be regretted.

Calverton struggles to maintain the appropriate tone of reverence toward Emerson while also making clear his conviction that Emerson has nothing to contribute to modern society. He is quick to emphasize that Emerson did not consciously intend his doctrines to support antisocial tendencies or exploitative economic policies, and assures us that Emerson's faith in the common man was "thoroughly sincere" (254, 258). Yet this faith turned out to be rooted in an abstraction, for "when that common man arose in his might . . . Emerson became alarmed, and was moved to defend caste against mass." Calverton cannot escape the conclusion that Emerson was, down deep, a prophet of the petty bourgeois, and that his whole project was aimed at protecting the status of that class.

Calverton goes on to repeat these observations in various guises. Emersonian individualism became a mass phenomenon in America rather than a class one, making all of America middle-class in its ideology. As a result, "the whole country became afflicted with the psychology of the entrepreneur. The where and how of individual advance absorbed the interest of the poor as well as the rich. Men and women of all classes became more interested in the improvement of their individual lot than in the amelioration of their social lot" (266). This was the necessary precondition for the entrenchment of predatory capitalism at the end of the nineteenth century, and persisted into 1932 as a powerful means of resisting any analysis of America as a class-based society.

In the final pages of his study Calverton returns to Emerson and attempts to make him speak to modern America: "What is needed in America to-day is a renewed faith in the masses. American literature has to find something of that faith in the potentialities of the proletariat which Emerson and Whitman possessed in the nineteenth century." Yet Calverton immediately reverses himself, observing that while this faith may have been "fitting and persuasive enough in their generation it led only to disaster in the next." Ultimately, "the faith of Emerson and Whitman belongs to the past, and not to the future. Their belief in the common man was a belief in him as a petty bourgeois individualist; our belief must be in him as proletarian collectivist" (479–80).

Emerson was so obviously unsuited to a Marxist literary program that Calverton's account of his limitations seems effortless. While many earlier critics had struggled to come to terms with Emerson, Calverton has only to lay out his critical method and watch Emerson fall neatly into place: he represents both the coming to power of the petty bourgeois on the shoulders of the proletariat and the subsequent retrenchment of that class against the further liberation of the proletariat. In like manner, Granville Hicks moves through his study of Emerson unaffected by the hesitations, doubts, and twists and turns that characterized Emerson criticism from Matthew Arnold through Ludwig Lewishon. Hicks wrote *The Great Tradition* in 1933 and revised it two years later; during these years he was a doctrinaire communist and closely associated with the League of American Writers, experiences which clearly shaped his perspective on American literature.[44] Though Emerson did not play the definitive role in Hicks's account that he did in Calverton's, he still emerges as a figure whose wide influence on American literature has been unfortunate.

Hicks begins his study with the passing away of the major figures of the "American Renaissance" and the intellectual vacuum left in their wake. Yet while he acknowledges that such men as Emerson, Thoreau, Hawthorne, and Melville made significant contributions to American literature, Hicks suspects that their significance was interred with their bones: "Far worse than the departure of these men was the silence of their work amid the clamor of the age. What, after all, had any of them to say to the new generation? What did self-reliance mean to Jay Gould and Commodore Vanderbilt? What could it mean to young girls in New York sweat shops?"[45] Like Calverton, Hicks believes that Emerson's self-reliant individualism, while perhaps a necessary and vital force in his time, became, in the age of the robber barons, the buttress of the exploiters and the opium of the masses.

Hicks found Emerson's primary deficiency to be his mystical optimism, his faith that all would be set aright by the workings of a universal, divine force. This put him fundamentally at odds with the basic assumptions of socialist critics:

> Emerson could not open his mouth without making clear his indifference to political parties and economic programs, so certain was he that the great human issues were superior to them. For him the only important activities of the race of man took place upon that level whereon the individual soul merged with the Over-Soul. Hence he believed that all considerations of social position or economic status were insignificant, since no hardships of a material sort could prevent the exercise of what he regarded as the peculiarly human functions. (8)

Instead of confronting the hard realities of politics and economics, Emerson put his faith in the Over-Soul and, Hicks suggests, simply hoped for the best: "Always the vision of realities grew dim as he came to the task of prescribing means for correcting the evils he saw, and he usually ended his discourses by abandoning himself, with rhapsodic fervor, to his faith in the beneficent laws of the universe" (9).

Having suggested the qualities in Emerson that made him unassimilable to a Marxist tradition, Hicks goes on to examine the manifestations of Emerson's thought in those whom he influenced. Hicks grudgingly acknowledges that there was "much value" in the work of Emerson, Thoreau, and Hawthorne since otherwise "we should not be reading them today," but he insists that this unspecified value was obscured as these men came to be honored "for their least admirable qualities."[46] Thus, "it was easy to canonize Emerson the optimist and the consoler, the preacher of sturdy individualism, but Emerson the rebel was better forgotten. The post-war generation not only failed to rise to the level of the heroes of the past; it brought them down upon its own plane" (11). This postwar generation, represented by men like James Russell Lowell, John Greenleaf Whittier, and Oliver Wendell Holmes, did little more than transform Emerson's legacy into the pabulum that nurtured ineffectual critics like Richard Watson Gilder and Edmund Clarence Stedman (12–17). Ultimately, Emerson's potential as an intellectual leader was subverted by the severe limitations of the genteel critics who came to adopt him.

Hicks considers Emerson's adoption by the genteel tradition to be a result of his underlying ambiguity, akin to the dualism identified by Brooks and Frank. Critics like Gilder and Stedman embodied Emerson's least admirable characteristics: his detachment from social reality and his indistinct belief in universal truth and beauty. From a Marxist perspective, however, these were not only frustratingly naive but positively dangerous positions. Hicks follows Calverton in claiming that Emerson's faith in "frontier individualism" was the source of all the damage associated with his influence. At one time a noble and liberating ideal, this faith was easily transformed into a justification for all sorts of viciousness:

> Emerson's great faith in humanity was based upon a historical reality, the emergence, especially on the frontier, of the common man. . . . After the Civil War allegiance to the common man did not mean reverence for the pioneer virtues, for the pioneer virtues, when translated into the terms of an industrial economy, were cut-throat competitiveness and ruthless exploitation. Allegiance to the common man meant loyalty to the poor farmer, at the mercy of bankers and middlemen, and to the factory hand, held under the employer's lash in a cruel slavery to the machine. Emerson's teachings, which had seemed so clear and strong at the beginning of his life, were no longer unambiguous: they could be, and they were, so interpreted as to justify the Morgans, Rockefellers, and Carnegies, or they could be restated in terms of the aspirations of the victims rather than the victors. Needless to say, the former interpretation triumphed. Few indeed were the disciples who saw that, however equivocal the letter, the message of the spirit of Emerson was clear. (29)

This lengthy passage effectively sums up the problems that Emersonian individualism posed to liberal-minded critics. Emerson failed to connect his doctrines with any concrete notion of social reality and thus invited interpretations that were not always compatible with his noble intentions. Moreover, his faith in individual men inclined him to reject the masses of common men when their clamor threatened his "petty bourgeois" security. Emerson's self-reliant individualism thus achieved its most prominent, if unintended influence in the Carnegies and the Vanderbilts, those who found it a useful justification for their own ruthless pursuit of individual gain. Ultimately, Marxist critics like Hicks and Calverton and unaffiliated liberals like Brooks and Frank rejected Emerson not so much for his ideas as for what he failed to protect himself against: the prophet of mid-nineteenth-century individualism became the posthumous author of late-nineteenth- and early-twentieth-century economic rapaciousness, and whatever place he might otherwise have enjoyed in a vital and usable literary tradition was consequently denied.

For left-leaning critics of the twenties and thirties, good literature was that which most distinctly treated such subjects as moral hypocrisy, class op-

pression, and the spiritual vacuity of modern life. While this view dominated criticism at least through the mid-thirties, conservative critics were
equally committed to gaining control over the theory and practice of their
craft. Opposed to the assumptions that social utility and the reflection of
"real life" were the defining characteristics of good literature stood a loosely
connected group of critics who focused on literary form and sought to
separate the discussion of literature from such explicit reliance on "extra-
literary" conditions. Specifically, the Southern Agrarians and their various
heirs in the New Criticism—Allen Tate, John Crowe Ransom, Robert Penn
Warren, Cleanth Brooks, R. P. Blackmur, and Yvor Winters—rejected the
social, psychological, and political bases from which many other critics
approached literature. Instead, they sought to direct attention back toward
literature as a work of art unified within itself, expressive of some value or
truth, and conforming to an acceptable structure.[47]

Of these "formalist" critics, only Yvor Winters wrote at any length on
Emerson.[48] Winters defines his theory of the "nature and function of
literature" as moralistic in purpose and absolutist in method, a theory that
frankly judges a work of literature to be good or bad insofar as it "makes a
defensible rational statement about a given human experience . . . and at
the same time communicates the emotion that ought to be motivated by
that rational understanding of that experience."[49] Literature is thus, above
all else, a product of an individual's rational faculties: a poet explores an
emotion not simply for the sake of expression, but as a means of exploring
and judging the motivation behind that emotion. Likewise, a writer describes an experience not for the purpose of affecting social policy but only
to effect an understanding of that specific experience. Finally, these ex-
ercises of the reason are supported and given meaning by a method of
judgment that Winters sees as firmly rooted in the Christian tradition of
moral propriety. Winters thus establishes two criteria for criticism: to de-
termine whether a piece of work has a clear intention and, if it does, to
subject that intention to moral judgment.

Though not a strict formalist, Winters nonetheless demanded that literature have its own internal unity. An author's personal history or social
conditions were external factors of only secondary interest to the work of
true criticism. Rather, the work of art is to be judged according to the
rational, moral environment that it contains within itself. This paradigm
put Winters at odds with the didacticism of the Marxists and the relativism
of the liberal critics who saw literature as either a weapon in the class war
or as a means of social amelioration; it also placed him in opposition to critics
like Ludwig Lewishon and poets in the "hedonistic" tradition of Whitman

who, Winters believed, promoted expression for its own sake.[50] Ultimately, Winters adopted an adversarial stance toward almost all of American literature insofar as that literature was rooted in a tradition that obscured rational process and evaded moral judgment.

Emerson, of course, is at the center of this seriously flawed tradition, and Winters is unsparing in detailing his inadequacies. In *Primitivism and Decadence,* he approaches Emerson through Allen Tate's observation that the Emersonian man is potentially perfect because Emerson admitted no possibility of tragedy or error in the human condition.[51] Winters then adds:

> To continue with extreme terms—which will give us, if not what Emerson desired, the results which his doctrine and others similar have encouraged— we arrive at these conclusions: If there is no possibility of error, the revision of judgement is meaningless; immediate inspiration is correct; but immediate inspiration amounts to the same thing as unrevised reactions to stimuli; unrevised reactions are mechanical; man in a state of perfection is an automaton; an automatic man is insane. Hence, Emerson's perfect man is a madman. (54–55)

Winters sees Emerson as encouraging a "sentimental debauchery of self-indulgence" in those who would follow him, and he cares not at all to suggest that perhaps the fault lies more in Emerson's followers than in himself. Indeed, Winters's point is that, whatever his intentions, Emerson's writings are hopelessly obscure and promulgate dangerously ill-defined ideas. As such they invite whatever interpretations his readers may make, and no degree of pleading Emerson's sweet temperament and moral character can excuse him from blame for the madness his doctrines unleashed.

Winters treats Emerson at greater length in *Maule's Curse* where he probes the "intellectual and moral significance" of the work of Hawthorne, Cooper, Poe, Emerson, Jones Very, Dickinson, Melville, and Henry James (155). These writers were marked by the same obscurity and confusion that characterized much of American thought, Winters argues, and the world they created is fraught with uncertainty and moral weakness.[52] In the novels of James, Hawthorne, and Melville in particular, characters inhabit a world that is guided by moral ambiguity: there are no clear choices to be made, no distinction between right and wrong, because there is no firm system of values on which to base such choices. Hawthorne saw the concept of sin not as an absolute but as something to be explored in an allegory; his rejection of the religious tradition that had given meaning to sin deprived him of the context necessary for a suitable treatment of the subject. For his part, Melville was so consumed by ambiguity and the lack of correspondence between motivation and action that his characters were incapable of making meaningful judgments. Finally, Henry James's preoccupation with plot exposed the limitations of his "moral sense," for his characters move through a series of choices that have no moral grounding.[53] In Winters's moralistic and absolutist criticism, literature has value only to the degree that it promotes a rational and moral response to the emotions and experiences it represents; it fails as literature if it relies on shades of meaning rather than strict moral judgment.

Emerson represented the extreme of this condition, for, Winters claims, he denied the very possibility of moral judgment: "Emerson eliminated the need of moral conviction and of moral understanding alike, by promulgating the allied doctrines of equivalence and inevitable virtue. In an Emersonian universe there is equally no need and no possibility of judgment; it is a universe of amiable but of perfectly unconscious imbeciles" (164). Populated by madmen and imbeciles, Emerson's universe is paralyzed by its creator's failure to provide clear guidelines for making choices and understanding experience. Winters returns to this theme again, arguing that Emerson's central doctrine is "inadmissible" because it "eliminates at a stroke both choice and the values that serve as a basis for choice, it substitutes for a doctrine of values a doctrine of equivalence, thus rendering man an automaton and paralyzing all genuine action" (267). In Winters's scheme, moral conviction and moral understanding are rooted in a traditional system of values, and Emerson's denial of the ultimate authority of that tradition, and indeed of any *system* of values, leaves him incapable of providing moral guidance.

Ultimately, the measure of Emerson's failure is the fact that while he "claims to speak with the authority of thought . . . he lacks that authority" (279). According to Winters, Emerson has not himself experienced the mystical detachment and transcendence upon which his faith in self-reliance, compensation and the over-soul rely; he "deals not with experience, but with his own theory of the experience." Furthermore, Emerson has scuttled the traditional moral basis of life and replaced it with an ambiguous set of doctrines that are of little use in the ongoing human endeavor of moral navigation. While such a condition might have had little impact when confined to an isolated Emerson of Concord, as the driving principle of an intellectual tradition it can only be disastrous. Winters concludes that Emerson is, at the core, a "fraud and a sentimentalist." In the guise of promoting a more meaningful way of life based on spiritual and mystical principles, Emerson had actually obscured the only true basis for moral judgment and liberated untold manifestations of insanity.

Winters's antipathy toward Emerson goes well beyond the caustic gibes of H. L. Mencken and the contempt of Ludwig Lewishon, revealing an underlying bitterness that seems entirely out of place when discussing the sweet-tempered Sage of Concord. It is only when he comes to discuss Emerson's influence on Hart Crane that Winters reveals the full context of his attitude toward Emerson. In "The Significance of the Bridge" Winters argues that Crane's failure as a poet was a direct result of his tragic reliance on Emerson and Whitman. Though he believes Crane drew most directly on Whitman, Winters focuses his withering criticism on Emerson since "nearly all of Whitman's thought was derived from Emerson, or could easily have been" (578). Crane represents Emersonianism unleashed, the realization of those "anarchic and anti-moral doctrines" no longer governed by the restraining impulses of the "New England habit": "The social restraints, the products of generations of religious discipline, which operated to minimize the influence of Romantic philosophy in the personal lives of Emerson and Whitman, were at most only slightly operative in Crane's career" (587–89). Thoroughly absorbing the lesson of Emerson as mediated by Whitman, Crane exposed himself to the madness that Emerson's temperament held at bay. The result was a misguided career and a shattered life—Crane committed suicide in 1932—for which Emerson bears ultimate responsibility.

Winters is only partially concerned in this essay with evaluating Crane's work, since he had expressed his disappointment with *The Bridge* in an earlier review:

> [These] poems illustrate the danger inherent in Mr. Crane's almost blind faith in his moment-to-moment inspiration, the danger that the author may turn himself into a kind of stylistic automaton, the danger that he may develop a sentimental leniency toward his vices and become wholly their victim, instead of understanding and eliminating them."[54]

In the later essay Winters restates these conclusions and then proceeds to demonstrate how the wreckage of Crane's poetry results from his uncritical acceptance of the obscurity and ungrounded relativism of Emerson and Whitman. Crane's poetry confirms, once and for all, the essential hollowness at the center of these men's writing and should serve to warn subsequent poets away from their perilous influence. From here, Winters moves on to his second concern: a passionate argument that Crane's suicide is the logical outcome of the influence of Emerson.

Winters himself suffers no obscurity in pursuing this argument. He describes with evident feeling how badly Crane looked the last time he had seen him, how debilitated he was from "cultivating all of his impulses." He goes on to briefly recount the last few years of Crane's life, concluding with a simple statement of his suicide. Then, as if overwhelmed with the need to assign blame, Winters immediately observes:

> The doctrine of Emerson and Whitman, if really put into practice, should naturally lead to suicide: in the first place, if the impulses are indulged systematically and passionately, they can lead only to madness; in the second place, death, according to the doctrine, is not only a release from suffering but is also and inevitably the way to beatitude. There is no question, according to the doctrine, of moral preparation for salvation; death leads automatically to salvation. (589–90)

From Emerson, Crane acquired a fascination with death, with the End rather than the Way to the End, and courted his own destruction with religious devotion. Intoxicated on the "thoroughgoing relativism" and rejection of moral judgment that were the distilled essence of Emersonianism, Crane followed the doctrines of his teacher to their inevitable, tragic conclusion:

> We have, it would seem, a poet of great genius, who ruined his life and his talent by living and writing as the two greatest religious teachers of our nation recommended. . . . The Emersonian doctrine . . . should naturally result in madness if one really lived it; it should result in literary confusion if one really wrote it. Crane accepted it; he lived it; he wrote it; and we have seen what he was and wrote. (598–99)

In short, Crane's life "had the value of a thoroughgoing demonstration" of the perils of Emersonianism (602).

Winters's striking account of Emerson's influence on Crane's suicide becomes, in the closing pages of the essay, a scathing attack on the critical tradition that had enshrined Emerson as the source of American wisdom. In the person of Professor X, his composite portrait of the genteel academician, Winters relentlessly exposes the inadequacies of genteel criticism and the absurdities of its devotion to Emerson. Professor X is an inveterate admirer and intellectual disciple of Emerson who "is able to approve of Emerson because he has never for a moment realized that literature could be more than a charming amenity." When pressed, he can neither justify his admiration nor explain the significance of his discipleship. Instead, he

> tells us that Emerson was an "idealist" but he does not tell us what kind. He tells us that Emerson taught self-reliance, but not that Emerson meant reliance on irresponsible impulse. He will cite us a dozen fragments of what

might be mistaken for wisdom, and cite Emerson as the source; but he will neither admit what these fragments mean in the Emersonian system nor go to the trouble of setting them in a new system which would give them an acceptable meaning—and which would no longer be Emersonian. (601–2)

Here, in addition to Winters's characteristic indictment of obscurity and the failure of critics to ground their work in "acceptable meaning," we can hear echoes of the positions adopted by critics as diverse as Mencken, Irving Babbitt, Van Wyck Brooks, and V. F. Calverton. Each of these critics shared in the call to reject the image of Emerson transmitted by the genteel critics, an image that canonized Emerson for an idealism that was, at best, ill-defined, while mostly ignoring the problems associated with the supposed ambiguity of his ideas. This tradition epitomized what was for Winters essentially anticriticism, in that it evaded both clarity and judgment. Ultimately, Winters's project amounts to an impassioned plea for American criticism to change its principles, to reject its Emersonian inheritance and seek out firmer ground. Emerson was not simply irrelevant to modern criticism, he was positively treacherous, and those critics who had let him through the door on account of his pure character were guilty of gross dereliction of duty.

The irony of Winters's urgent tone is that, in many ways, he was attacking a straw man. At the time he was writing hardly a critic could be found who would admit to accepting Emersonian principles as a model, and Winters thus risked apoplexy in fighting a battle that had already been won. Like Calverton, Brooks, and others, Winters found Emerson's radical individualism to be an obstacle to his construction of a usable past. However, the usable past he sought to construct also excluded Calverton and Brooks. Indeed, it excluded almost everyone. In fact, Winters seems to have grasped onto Emerson as only the most convenient brush with which to tar virtually all subsequent writing in America, writing which stubbornly refused to conform to the strict critical standards of Yvor Winters himself. Though Winters's is very much the extreme case, his account stands as a distilation of three decades of discussion of Emerson's influence on, and place in, American culture: we must reconsider the homage we pay Emerson, for we are in fact worshipping a false god.

In 1903, Emerson was all but universally hailed as the great moral teacher whose nobility of mind and purity of spirit secured him a place in the highest rank of American men of letters; by 1940, he was all but universally regarded as a failure, an honored ancestor whose doctrines proved to be insufficiently grounded in experience, naively optimistic, or socially corrosive. The earlier critics had ignored Emerson's ideas in favor of his character and temperament. Later critics, unswayed by his temperament and concerned about the implications of his ideas, found Emerson to be fundamentally unsound.

The most immediate explanation for this shift in the evaluation of Emerson is that the terms by which criticism was practiced had changed. Modern critics demanded more from their craft than idealized accounts of how a particular writer or work embodied the eternal values. The criticism of this later period was more aggressive and more explicitly ideological; it sought to provide a broader context for understanding the significance of literature, both past and present. While this shift in critical values alone would have led to a significant reevaluation of Emerson, it was compounded by the degree to which Emerson was a product of the old criticism. He had been so successfully appropriated by the genteel critics, was so readily made over by them in their own image, that modern critics were overwhelmed with that image before coming into any direct contact with Emerson himself. One of the greatest obstacles to Emerson's work enjoying a meaningful place in modern America was the apparently anarchic nature of his individualism and self-reliance, doctrines that alienated conservatives and liberals alike. The genteel critics dismissed these difficulties because, on the whole, they were not interested in making Emerson useful in any immediate way; they were content simply to praise his standing as an avatar of truth and beauty and treat his ideas as charming idiosyncrasies. Modern critics had little use for such a disembodied prophet, and focused their energies on the flaws of the genteel Emerson rather than attempting to recreate him for their own positive use.

Newton Arvin suggested something of this when he observed, in a review of Brooks's *Life of Emerson,* that Emerson had

> succeeded so well, at least superficially, in what he aimed at, that it is now almost impossible, in turning one's eyes back in his direction, to see Emerson himself: what one sees is so largely just the great "glad" glow of Emersonianism. What one sees is really President Eliot and the elective system at Harvard; or William James and the will to believe; or Elbert Hubbard and the "Message to Garcia"; or Theodore Roosevelt and the strenuous life; or Mrs Eddy and the illusions of mortal mind.[55]

Arvin goes on to argue that Emerson's reputation and influence in the twentieth century has become clouded by this appropriation: evaluation of

Emerson himself had given way to the discussion of the "Emersonian cliches" which served as the defining values of nineteenth century middle class culture. And, Arvin observed, as that culture "is on the wane, it would look as if Emerson had had his day, and were about to be eclipsed once for all" (11).

Arvin is optimistic, however, that critics will come to see the "genuine difference" between Emerson and Emersonianism. Certainly there will be readers who cannot "fail to feel that the Emersonian tradition is mainly a vulgarization of Emerson. . . . To read the essays and the journals now, amid the stench sent up by a rotten individualism, is to feel, if only confusedly, that the mountebanks of self-help and self-expression are not entitled to the whole of Emerson" (12–13). This plea to reread Emerson afresh and to get beyond the simplified version of Emersonianism offered by his idolaters and critics alike, was joined by Bliss Perry and O. W. Firkins. Perry was hopeful that Emerson could be resurrected once the extreme reaction against the literature of the nineteenth century had been spent, at which time the essays could be read as they were intended, as chapters toward a whole rather than collections of unrelated aphorisms. Similarly, Firkins maintained that "wise men to whom he is temporarily useless suspect that Emerson and the world have not cast their final reckoning together."[56] Emerson contained exhilarating, creative, and eminently usable forces that both genteel and modern critics had missed, and that only a fresh reading could recover.

This recovery would formally commence with the work of F. O. Matthiessen and Perry Miller and continue with the further investigations of Stephen Whicher and Newton Arvin. These critics explicitly sought to rescue Emerson from what they saw as decades of careless misreading, and engaged in detailed analyses of the content and context of his writings. Prior to this explicit resurrection of Emerson, however, there had evolved a powerful if subtle Emersonian tradition that offered an alternative to both the genteel apotheosis and the modernist rejection. This tradition is best represented in the work of William James, John Dewey, W.E.B. Du Bois, and William Carlos Williams, each of whom fashioned a flexible and decidedly liberal context for Emerson's problematic individualism. In the process they rehabilitated that individualism, rescuing it from the contempt and abuse to which it was so frequently subjected. While their work deepens our understanding of Emerson's enduring significance, it also, when considered as part of this Emersonian tradition, takes on a deeper meaning of its own.

CHAPTER THREE

William James and
the Varieties of Emerson

Students of American intellectual history could ask for no richer material than the supposed first encounter between William James and Ralph Waldo Emerson. In 1842, the year in which his first child, Waldo, died at the age of five, Emerson delivered a series of lectures in New York City. He soon became acquainted with Henry James Sr. and was a frequent guest at his house in Washington Square. It was on one of these visits that James brought Emerson upstairs to "bless" his newborn son William. From that first pregnant meeting it has been impossible not to see the shadow of Emerson looming over the life and work of William James, and the temptation to view Emerson as James's intellectual godfather or James as a surrogate son carrying on his father's work would presumably be irresistible.

That many critics have resisted this temptation is perhaps a result of its being so obvious, for most comments on Emerson and James stress that their connection is tenuous, indirect, even coincidental. Indeed, Emerson's active discouragement of discipleship in any form and James's maverick insistence on following his own genius present an immediate challenge to anyone attempting to squeeze them into the same niche. F. O. Matthiessen has aptly described the circumstances of the Emerson-James connection, for while he observes that the comments of the three Jameses upon Emerson "compose by themselves a chapter in American intellectual history," he admits that, in William's case, the shape this chapter might take is uncertain:

[W]ith philosophers as expansive as Emerson and W[illiam] J[ames], and as blithely unconcerned with logical consistency, it would be foolish to try to pin down too many of their correspondences. WJ owed to Emerson substantially what H[enry] J[ames] owed to Hawthorne, not an assessable sum but rather the pervasive and inescapable debt that a man owes to the largest figure in his immediate background who is devoted to the same pursuit.[1]

Matthiessen was right to eschew the narrow interest in correspondences, for as Frederic Carpenter discovered in his examination of James's private copies of Emerson's works, James drew on Emerson in a far more creative manner. James owned copies of all but a few of Emerson's published volumes—including *Nature and Addresses,* both series of the *Essays, Representative Men,* and *The Conduct of Life*—and his extensive marginalia indicate that he read aggressively almost everything Emerson wrote, most of it more than once.[2] Instead of sitting in rapt attention before the words of his master, James appears as a strong reader who culled from Emerson only what he found useful while openly dismissing all that was "against my philosophy." It is thus not so much a case of James's work corresponding to Emerson's as of James independently pursuing similar interests and using Emerson as a navigational aid.

While Carpenter and Matthiessen have covered the basic issues relating to James's use of Emerson, other critics have built on their work in exploring the significance of this connection. George Cotkin sees Emerson and James as representing successive stages of public philosophy, a secularized form of the ministry devoted to communicating lofty philosophical arguments to a general audience. This shared sense of vocation is the essential starting point for any comparative discussion of the two thinkers for it helps to explain many of their similarities, both in style and subject. Concerned more with texts than the means of delivery, Frank Lentricchia portrays James as a source of American modernist ideology and also attempts to claim him as a precursive figure in his own postmodern brand of Marxist criticism. Lentricchia considers Emerson and James as "twined ideological agencies" within these movements in American literature, and suggests some of the ways in which James revitalized Emerson's radical individualism for a time when "Emersonian nonconformity" was no longer an adequate response to social and political reality. Similarly, Richard Poirier describes James as "offer[ing] us Emerson clarified and enforced" in so far as he builds upon Emerson's faith in the supreme value of moments of transition and transformation. Poirier sees both Emerson and James as anticipating Nietzsche and Foucault in confessing this faith and questioning traditional notions of "the self."[3]

Lentricchia comes the closest to suggesting the kind of relationship between James and Emerson that I trace in the following pages, and his argument for James's enduring importance parallels mine in certain respects. He sees Emerson as the "moral and political authority behind James's pragmatism" and believes that the "Emerson/James connection may constitute the most influential enhancement of intellectual force in American literary history."[4] This pragmatism is an "emancipating critical force which would liberate the particular, the local, the secret self from intellectual, economic, and political structuralizations which would consume, control, deny all particularity, all locality, and all secret selfhood."[5] While Lentricchia is right to point to the liberating force of James's work, he incorrectly equates James's idea of pluralism with antinomianism and exaggerates the degree to which James promoted radical social change. As I will suggest, James sought to free individuals from intellectual constructions that limited their potential only as a first step toward imagining more tolerant and inclusive "structuralizations."

While these critics provide useful suggestions for thinking about James's indebtedness to and revisions of Emerson, they are primarily interested in other issues and treat this one largely in passing. My goal is to illuminate James's thought by examining his comments on Emerson and tracing the many ways in which his work parallels Emerson's own. The three major strands of James's philosophy—pragmatism, radical empiricism, and pluralism—each echo ideas that were central to Emerson. Similarly, James's attitude toward religion recalls certain aspects of Emerson's transcendental rejection of doctrinal Christianity and suggests the deeper implications of their shared intellectual presumptions. James freely incorporated his reading of Emerson into his own work, and the intellectual encounter between these two men reveals the ways in which one strong, independent mind alternately is possessed by and repossesses another.

James took full advantage of his familiarity with Emerson's writings, turning to them at various places in his work both to illustrate minor points and to provide the authoritative word in support of his larger arguments. It was not until 1903, however, when he accepted an invitation to speak at the celebration of Emerson's Centennial in Concord that he formally organized his thoughts about Emerson. James approached this task with characteristic vigor and conscientiousness, rereading virtually all of Emerson's works and striving to convey the full scope of his significance within the allotted fifteen minutes.[6] Much of the address consists of passages from Emerson's writings that James carefully selected as representative of his work, and he blends these passages into a succinct statement of his belief in

Emerson's still vital importance. It is in this brief address that we can most clearly measure James's appropriation of Emerson.

James saw Emerson's greatness residing in two general characteristics: the moral example he set by remaining within the limits of his own genius and his all-consuming faith in the inherent worth of each individual form of existence. In a letter to his brother Henry written three weeks before the Concord festivities, James observed:

> The reading of the divine Emerson, volume after volume, has done me a lot of good, and, strange to say, has thrown a strong practical light on my own path. The incorruptible way in which he followed his own vocation, of seeing such truths as the Universal Soul vouchsafed to him from day to day and month to month, and reporting them in the right literary form, and thereafter kept his limits absolutely . . . knowing both his strength and its limits . . . seems to me a moral lesson to all men who have any genius, however small, to foster.[7]

In the address itself James declared this quality of Emerson's to be more important even than his "rich mental gifts": "Rarely has a man so known the limits of his genius or so unfailingly kept within them. . . . perhaps the paramount impression one gets of his life is of his loyalty to his own type and mission."[8]

James understood Emerson's type to be that of the scholar or seer, the always active recorder of perceptions whose mission was to report his ever-unfolding vision in "worthy form." Emerson's admirable loyalty to this mission, however, came at a price, for while the "duty of spiritual seeing and reporting determined the whole tenor of his life," such a life betrayed a certain awkward detachment, a refusal of the entanglements and invasions that inevitably accompany life within a society. James recognized that Emerson must often have seemed "provokingly remote and unavailable" to those "hot-blooded moralists with more objective ideas of duty," but is sure that those who "can see things in more liberal perspective" must approve of the results: "The faultless tact with which [Emerson] kept his safe limits while he so dauntlessly asserted himself within them is an example fitted to give heart to other theorists and artists the world over" (1120–21).

That James devoted the first part of his address to defining Emerson's vocation and applauding his loyalty to it is consistent with the overwhelming consensus among James's critics and biographers that the question of vocation was of central importance to his thought.[9] Caught between his desire to forge his own path and the practical need to satisfy his father's lingering and unspecified expectations for him, James struggled throughout his career both to discover his vocation and to feel comfortable in pursuing it. His appreciation for Emerson's keen sense of purpose serves in many ways as a resolution of this struggle. Indeed, James had come to see his own vocation as quite similar to Emerson's, and is thus all the more eager to set out its inherent virtues. The majority of James's published writings were, like Emerson's, originally delivered as public lectures, and James frequently refers to his own work as the passing on of his perceptions and understandings for the audience's consideration. In the same letter to Henry in which he praised Emerson's fealty to his vocation, James writes of the "strong practical light" that Emerson's example has thrown on his own path. Thus inspired he resolves to follow this path more diligently, recording "such impression as my own intellect has received from the Universe." James clearly found in Emerson a model for the carrying out of his own work, and in affirming the dignity of Emerson's calling he is also asserting that of his own.

This is particularly evident in the defensive tone James assumes when referring to the "hot-blooded moralists" who found Emerson's sense of duty inadequate. The allusion here is to Emerson's familiar lack of sympathy with reformers and philanthropists, for James knew that Emerson must have frustrated many an activist with his stubborn resolve to remain within the limits of his seership.[10] This attitude appears throughout Emerson's early lectures, including "American Scholar," "The Conservative," and "Man the Reformer," but is expressed most fully in "Self-Reliance": "Do not tell me, as a good man did to-day, of my obligation to put all poor men in good situations. Are they *my* poor? I tell thee, thou foolish philanthropist, that I grudge the dollar, the dime, the cent, I give to such men as do not belong to me and to whom I do not belong." Emerson then goes on vigorously to disavow his responsibility for such "miscellaneous popular charities" as "the education at college of fools" and providing "aims to sots," and concludes: "What I must do is all that concerns me, not what the people think. This rule, equally arduous in actual and in intellectual life, may serve for the whole distinction between greatness and meanness. It is the harder, because you will always find those who think they know what is your duty better than you know it."[11]

James clearly had passages like this in mind as he composed his address on Emerson, and was sensitive to the fact that the task of spiritual seeing and reporting to which Emerson had dedicated his life—and which James adapted as a model for his own career—could appear to some as an evasion of responsibility rather than the performance of a worthwhile duty. Yet while recognizing this potential criticism James steadfastly maintained that

Emerson's work was important on its own terms. Indeed, he asserted not only that Emerson was right to stick to his guns rather than dissipate his energies aiding worthy causes, but implies that by so keeping within his limits Emerson made a more effective contribution to those causes than if he had acted on someone else's notion of his duty. Young reformers of the Civil War generation had attested to just this point when they identified Emerson's unswerving devotion to the dictates of his conscience as the inspiration for their own commitment to social justice.[12] To be sure, Emerson may have hesitated to join the abolitionists and might have been lukewarm in his support of the various social reforms that dominated his times, and this doubtless lowered his standing among those who were more actively committed to these causes. For James, however, Emerson's steady application to the task of revealing the individual's relationship with the universe was a crucial and positive contribution to those causes, and the most worthy contribution Emerson could have made.

It is important to note here that James is not simply defending Emerson—or attempting to immunize himself—against possible charges of political apathy. His own involvement in political and social issues was considerably more generous than Emerson's, and in pursuing *his* calling James was never accused of the detachment and coldness that critics invariably attributed to his vocational mentor. Indeed, James's interest in whether Emerson sufficiently met his social obligations is merely ancillary to his concern with the broader question of just what it meant to do the kind of intellectual "work" that both he and Emerson were committed to doing. In short, what was the use to which their efforts tended? James's entire philosophy revolved around the idea that the value of a belief or theory or way of life inhered in its practical effect: it had to be of some use. As we have seen James did not exempt Emerson from this test, for his approval of Emerson's loyalty to his own task is contingent upon his work having achieved satisfying results. James agrees with Emerson that people ought to follow the vocation to which they were called, and he expects that vocation to be useful.

In a remarkable letter written when he was barely sixteen years old, James touches on each of these issues in a way that would recur through the rest of his life. Endeavoring to "prove" to his friend Edgar Van Winkle why "everyone . . . should do in society what he would do if left to himself," James methodically examines the meaning of vocation and what it is that determines a vocation's utility.[13] He begins by raising and answering two simple questions: "What ought to be everyone's object in life? To be as much use as possible. . . . But what is use? . . . [U]se consists in some *pleasure,* mental or bodily, conferred upon humanity." James soon transforms this "object of life" into a responsibility: "It is then the duty of everyone to do as much good as possible. . . . Suppose we do nothing and die; we have swindled society. Nature, in giving us birth, had saddled us with a debt which we must pay off some time or other." The very fact that we exist, then, not only implies that we have a purpose in existing but confers upon us the responsibility to find and fulfill that purpose, to earn our place in society by doing good.

From this disarmingly simple statement of what would be the guiding faith of his life and work, James goes on to explore the, for him, crucial question of what shape the doing of good might take. He recognizes that what he calls bodily pleasure, achieved through the satisfaction of material needs, is the most evident measure of the utility of a particular vocation: one is valued to the degree that one makes access to the necessities of life more convenient. From this, James fears, it is but a small step to honoring only those vocations which serve material interests while disregarding those whose good use is subtle and less immediate. Here, as in the address on Emerson, James is struggling with a dual allegiance. On the one hand is his belief that life is meaningful only to the degree that it is useful, that it achieves some practical effect; on the other hand, James is clearly drawn to the realm of "mental" pleasure in which practical effects are difficult to assess in any precise way. He is thus intent on establishing the utility of a broader range of interests and modes of living: "True *use,* or good, does not then consist in mere brute force. For what was our mind given us if not that we should employ it?" James goes on to offer the following example:

> Poets may be laughed at for being useless, impractical people. But suppose the author of the "Psalm of Life" had attempted to invent steam engines (for which I suppose he has no genius) in the hope of being useful, how much time would he have wasted and how much would we have lost! But no, he did better, he followed his taste, and redeemed his life, by writing the "psalm" which is as useful a production as any I know. Astronomy and natural history are of little *practical* use, and as such are not all important at the present day, but they afford inexpressible pleasure to those who are interested in them and therefore are useful. And I think that a man who was urged toward them by his tastes and who, wishing to be more useful, should make discoveries of little importance in practical branches would do very wrong.

James here expands his notion of vocation to incorporate interests and passions, the various activities large and small that make up the practice of life. Whether one is poet or inventor, birdwatcher or stargazer, seer or working philanthropist, the true measure of success is how well one does whatever it is one chooses to do. There is a passage in Emerson's "The Method of Nature," an essay on which James drew heavily in composing his centenary address, that suggests what is at stake here: "Each individual soul is such, in virtue of its being a power to translate the world into some particular language of its own; if not into a picture, a statue, or a dance,— why, then, into a trade, an art, a science, a mode of living, a conversation, a character, an influence" (122–23). In his mature work James would return to the ideas he so eloquently expressed in this youthful letter and weave them into his exploration of religious experience and the pluralistic vision that he urged upon his various audiences. In particular he would maintain that the value of another person's life, his happinesses, his ideals, his beliefs, is rarely obvious even to the most disinterested observer and that we need continuously to be on guard against this blindness in conducting our relationships with others. As the young James sensed, mutual tolerance grows out of mutual respect for each other's particular ways of navigating through life.

After devoting the first third of his address to establishing the nature and worthiness of Emerson's vocation, James turns to the results of Emerson's work, the perceptions he recorded in the course of studying the spirit of the universe. Quoting extensively from such essays as "The Method of Nature" and "Spiritual Laws," James sketches Emerson's revelation as a series of variations on one fundamental truth, a truth which he finds most simply expressed in Emerson's poem "Voluntaries":

> So nigh is grandeur to our dust,
> So near is God to man!

From this verse James extracts Emerson's primary insight: "through the individual fact there ever shone for [Emerson] the effulgence of the Universal Reason. The great Cosmic Intellect terminates and houses itself in mortal men and passing hours. Each of us is an angle of its eternal vision" (1121). James then quotes a passage from "The Method of Nature": "O rich and various Man! thou palace of sight and sound, carrying in thy senses the morning and the night and the unfathomable galaxy; in thy brain, the geometry of the City of God; in thy heart the bower of love and the realms of right and wrong" (Emerson, 122).[14] For James, Emerson's simple yet powerful conviction that the experience of each individual reveals a measure of reality, however small, and must therefore be treated with respect, is the necessary starting point of any philosophical exploration worthy of our attention.

The rest of Emerson's work, as James presents it, evolves directly out of this all-embracing faith in the dignity of the individual. Given that each person is in this way a conduit for the "great Cosmic Intellect," James continues, "it follows that there is something in each and all of us, even the lowliest, that ought not to consent to borrowing traditions and living at second hand." In turn, "this faith that in a life at first hand there is something sacred is perhaps the most characteristic note in Emerson's writings" (1121). Emerson initially sounded this note in the opening paragraph of his first book, *Nature,* where he urged his retrospective age to cultivate "an original relation to the universe." This injunction would reverberate throughout his work, especially in such essays as "The American Scholar" and "History" where Emerson sought to undermine the stupefying power of tradition and replace it with an appreciation of the immediate, the momentary, and the original. And just as this validation of life at first hand grew, for James, out of Emerson's faith in the sufficiency of each individual, it in turn underwrote Emerson's belief that every individual was implicitly a necessary part of existence. James quotes from "Nominalist and Realist": "If John was perfect, why are you and I alive? As long as any man exists there is some need of him" (Emerson, 583).

There is a clear logic guiding James's unfolding of Emerson's message: since the individual is sufficient in himself as an expression of the spirit of the universe, and since every individual can achieve unique insight into that universe, it seems evident that each person has a unique and necessary contribution that they are not only called on to make but are inherently capable of making. Support for James's reading here can be found throughout Emerson's work, but a passage from "Considerations by the Way" is the most representative: "Life brings to each his task, and, whatever art you select, algebra, painting, architecture, poems, commerce, politics,—all are attainable, even to the miraculous triumph, on the same terms, of selecting that for which you are apt" (Emerson, 1095). For James, this "belief that the individual must in reason be adequate to the vocation for which the Spirit of the world has called him into being" is among Emerson's most sublime and compelling revelations (1122). James himself quotes from "Spiritual Laws" where Emerson writes: "Heaven is large and affords space for all modes of love and fortitude. . . . The fact that I am here certainly shows me that the Soul had need of an organ here, and shall I not assume the post?" (Emerson, 321).

Ultimately, then, James comes full circle to the issue of vocation, not only as he raised it at the beginning of his address on Emerson but as he had first broached the subject forty-five years earlier in the letter to Edgar Van Winkle. Emerson's task, his use, his purpose in living, was to reveal in its various guises and to the fullest degree the "sovereignty of the living individual"; in succeeding so admirably he both fulfilled his own task and, in the very nature of his accomplishment, validated the particular task of every other individual: baker, poet, astronomer, inventor, and turn-of-the-century public philosopher. Emerson not only provided the insights from which much of William James's own work progressed, he legitimized the very form James chose to pursue his task.

This is not to suggest that James's admiration for Emerson was unqualified. Frederic Carpenter observed that James indicated his firm disapproval of those passages which betrayed excessive abstractness, a monistic conception of the universe, or a transcendental doctrine of evil, by noting in the margin "against my philosophy" wherever they occurred.[15] Of these James appears to be least disturbed by the first two, for he found that Emerson sufficiently balanced his abstraction with attention to the concrete and never allowed his monism to overwhelm his far more ardent commitment to radical individualism and pluralism.[16] On the other hand, James was never comfortable with Emerson's deficient sense of evil. At various places in his work he described Emerson as the paragon of healthy-mindedness, a person of the once-born type who failed to comprehend that pain, suffering, and sadness were for many inescapable parts of reality.[17] In the letters he wrote during the weeks surrounding his address at Concord, James mingled such reservations among his more ecstatic paeans to Emerson's "divine" and "exquisite" nature: "Rereading him *in extenso,* almost *in toto,* lately, has made him loom larger than ever to me as a human being, but I feel the distinct lack in him of too little understanding of the morbid side of life" (*Letters,* 2:197). Specifically, James found that Emerson was incapable of appreciating those elements in orthodox theology that were "permanently true"—those that formed the empirical bases for such doctrines as original sin and mankind's fallen state—however right he was in rejecting the dogma that had grown up around them. Indeed, James notes that he has "been a little scandalized at the non-resisting manner in which orthodox sheets have celebrated [Emerson's] anniversary," feeling that those who profess to believe in such doctrines ought to confront Emerson more warily.

While James was thus aware that there were points on which he and Emerson disagreed, his interest in these points was largely perfunctory; he wanted to make use of Emerson, not make sense of him, and his method was to mine Emerson for the valuable insights he contained, take these along, and leave the detritus behind. Gerald Myers considers this to be characteristic of James's voracious mind: "James based his thinking on a core of steadfast convictions and tended to take from other thinkers only what harmonized with those convictions. What he found in the writers who he said had influenced his thought was less a discovery of something new than an echo of something he already believed" (xiii).[18] In Emerson James confronted a deafening crescendo of such echoes which not only confirmed his own steadfast convictions but were absorbed into them. He closes his tribute to Emerson by once again summarizing the essence of his revelation:

> The point of any pen can be an epitome of reality; the commonest person's act, if genuinely activated, can lay hold on eternity. This vision is the head-spring of all his outpourings. . . . [Emerson's] life was one long conversation with the invisible divine, expressing itself through individuals and particulars:—"So nigh is grandeur to our dust, so near is God to man!" (1125)

This insight was equally the head-spring of all of William James's outpourings, and formed a permanent part of his intellectual vocabulary.

It is difficult to categorize the many aspects of James's thought in any precise way. His two most important intellectual biographers, Ralph Barton Perry and Gerald Myers, attempt to organize his diffuse writings into manageable chapters revolving around such topics as "Knowledge," "Reality," "Consciousness," and "Social and Political Sentiments." Such divisions prove to be ephemeral, however, and the distinctions they attempt to draw between different aspects of James's thought tend at first to blur and then dissolve under the weight of his free-ranging and ever-fermenting imagination. Of course, both Perry and Myers freely admit the indeterminacy of their categorizations and rely on these distinctions only as a way of providing the necessary structure for their work. While each component of what Myers refers to as the Jamesian worldview thus blends almost imperceptibly into the whole, it is possible to identify three general ideas that James himself felt captured the essential nature of his work: pluralism, radical empiricism, and pragmatism. Each of these ideas both builds upon and is in turn built into the others, and all three find a common validation in James's reading of Emerson.

Pluralism and radical empiricism represent James's most direct appropriations of Emerson's insight into the sovereignty of the individual and they provide the subtext for virtually everything he wrote. He sketches the relationship between these two ideas in the preface to *The Will to Believe,* a selection of essays and lectures he had delivered throughout the 1880s and 1890s. Pluralism is a description of the nature of reality; it embraces and stresses the fact that there are as many distinct points of view as there are individuals to hold them, and insists that "there is no possible point of view from which the world can appear an absolutely single fact." Thus, every individual manifests a part of reality but no single individual is privy to the whole of it. Radical empiricism, in turn, is a means of interpreting and understanding such a pluralistic universe; it accepts these multiple points of view as a given and refuses the temptation either to overcome them or to interpret them away.[19] Unlike monism or determinism, which posit a single interpretation of reality by which the validity of individual perceptions and experiences may be judged, radical empiricism posits a reality that is always in flux and which, at any given moment, implicitly accommodates the wide variety of human experiences. For James, radical empiricism is the only adequate response to a universe that is gloriously and ineluctably pluralistic.

In the preface to his second collection of essays, *Talks to Teachers,* James identifies his "pluralistic or individualistic philosophy" as the fundamental principle animating his work: "The facts and worths of life need many cognizers to take them in. There is no point of view absolutely public and universal. Private and uncommunicable perceptions always remain over." Pluralism brings a moral imperative to bear on those who wish to live responsibly in such a universe, demanding that every individual be accepted as a necessary representative of reality: "The practical consequence of such a philosophy is the well-known democratic respect for the sacredness of individuality,—is, at any rate, the outward tolerance of whatever is not itself intolerant."[20] Foremost a statement of fact about the nature of the world in which people live, James's pluralism makes a distinct claim about how people ought to conduct their lives within that world, a claim that they can accept or refuse at their own risk.

James treats his idea of pluralism most directly in the well-known "On a Certain Blindness in Human Beings," a piece he himself recognized as one of his most important compositions.[21] In the preface to *Talks to Teachers* he wrote "I wish I were able to make [it] more impressive. It is more than the mere piece of sentimentalism which it may seem to some readers. It connects itself with a definite view of the world and of our moral relations to the same" (19). In a letter he wrote soon after publication of the essay James offered that it "is really the perception on which my whole individualistic philosophy is based."[22] More precisely, "On a Certain Blindness" deals with the conditions against which James's individualistic philosophy must struggle: the "blindness with which we are all afflicted in regard to the feelings of creatures and people different from ourselves" is the primary obstacle to our complete realization of the essential pluralism of the universe, and it is James's goal both to expose this blindness and suggest the way to clearer vision (149).

For James, this blindness and its consequences are in many respects inevitable:

> We are practical beings, each of us with limited functions and duties to perform. Each is bound to feel intensely the importance of his own duties and the significance of the situations that these call forth. But this feeling is in each of us a vital secret, for sympathy with which we vainly look to others. The others are too much absorbed in their own vital secrets to take an interest in ours. Hence the stupidity and injustice of our opinions, so far as they deal with the significance of alien lives. Hence the falsity of our judgements, so far as they presume to decide in an absolute way on the value of other persons' conditions or ideals. (149)

James returns to this point over and again: our inability to know the full significance of any other person's life mandates that we withhold judgment. He uses as an example his own reaction to a series of forest settlements he had encountered while traveling in the mountains of North Carolina. James describes his first impression as one of "unmitigated squalor," and he admits that he felt scorn for those who had defiled the landscape only to live under such hideous and rudimentary conditions. Upon speaking with the inhabitants, however, James learned that they placed a high value on these homesteads and derived much satisfaction from having wrested their living from the land. He reports that he immediately saw the narrowness of his judgment and recognized that he had failed to grasp the "whole inward significance of the situation," the "peculiar ideality" of the settlers' conditions. To respect that ideality and accept the inner significance of these people, however alien their sensibilities might have been to his, is for James the inescapable requirement of pluralism, and one that we must consistently struggle to meet (150–52). Emerson writes in "Fate" that "the riddle of the age has for each a private solution," to which James would hasten to add that no private individual should presume that his particular solution speaks for anyone else.[23]

In typical fashion James extends his discussion of this "certain blindness" to the subject of vocation: just as we tend to judge the inner significance of others by our own particular values and feelings, so do we evaluate the external manifestation of each individual's interests and skills according to our own limited sense of which activities are worthwhile. In this case, however, James sees the demands of pluralism running into a more intense resistance:

> [W]e are but finite, and each one of us has some single specialized vocation of his own. And it seems as if energy in the service of its particular duties might be got only by hardening the heart toward everything unlike them. Our deadness toward all but one particular kind of joy would thus be the price we inevitably have to pay for being practical creatures. (155–56)

This concern with our failure to see the pleasure and utility provided by a variety of vocations and interests both echoes James's letter to Edgar Van Winkle and foreshadows his address on Emerson. The observation here is the same: We miss the greater joy that would be ours if we but understood that each task afforded its own pleasures and fulfilled its own particular need, if, that is, we accepted the pluralistic view as descriptive of reality.

James clearly recognizes that as this blindness is endemic and rooted in the practical conditions of human life it will not easily yield to the essentially moral claims of pluralism. Indeed, it is only in rare moments of insight that the ordinary person can overcome this blindness and apprehend the "vast world of inner life" beyond his own: "This higher vision of an inner significance in what, until then, we had realized only in the dead external way, often comes over a person suddenly; and, when it does so, it makes an epoch in his history. As Emerson says, there is a depth in these moments that constrains us to ascribe more reality to them than to all other experiences" (157). From Emerson's validation of this moment of insight as the most compelling of all our experiences, James moves on to Walt Whitman's more exuberant celebration of the beauty and dignity of individual lives and commonplace experience. Quoting lengthy excerpts from "Crossing Brooklyn Ferry" and one of Whitman's letters to Peter Doyle, James observes that the "very repetition of the scene to new generations of men . . . the eternal recurrence of the common order" is the very essence of "all the excitements, joys, and meanings that ever were, or ever shall be, in this world. To be rapt with satisfied attention, like Whitman, to the mere spectacle of the world's presence, is one way, and the most fundamental way, of confessing one's sense of its unfathomable significance and importance" (163).

James uses Emerson and Whitman to convey the intense exhilaration of such moments of transcendent vision, moments when we escape the constraints of our blindness and see as we have never seen before that an individual's experiences, interests, and beliefs, however common or unheroic, are an invaluable part of the world in which each of us live. In "Circles" Emerson wrote: "The poor and the low have their way of expressing the last facts of philosophy as well as you" (410). For James, this statement entails more than a prescription for tolerant behavior; it suggests the limitless possibilities of life in a pluralistic universe, a life to which everyone has a contribution to make. In the conclusion to *Varieties of Religious Experience* James returns to this point, confirming that the pluralistic view is not only a necessity but a cause for celebration:

> I do not see how it is possible that creatures in such different positions and with such different powers as human individuals are, should have exactly the same functions and the same duties. No two of us have identical difficulties, nor should we be expected to work out identical solutions. Each, from his peculiar angle of observation, takes in a certain sphere of fact and trouble, which each must deal with in a unique manner. . . . Each attitude being a syllable in human nature's total message, it takes the whole of us to spell the meaning out completely. (*Writings,* 436–37)

As in the address on Emerson James uses this image of each individual's distinct angle of observation on reality to set up his claim that the various responses to these observations, the different types of work people do, and the way they live their lives, all share in an essential dignity. And while each of these is sufficient in itself, no angle alone can account for the entirety of reality, which is no less than the multitude of perceptions that these observations yield. For James, as for Emerson, to read the meaning of the universe requires an appreciative attention to every syllable of its utterances.

James concludes "On a Certain Blindness" with a summary of the claims that pluralism makes on our behavior:

> It absolutely forbids us to be forward in pronouncing on the meaninglessness of forms of existence other than our own; and it commands us to tolerate, respect, and indulge those whom we see harmlessly interested and happy in their own ways, however unintelligible these may be to us. Hands off: neither the whole of truth nor the whole of good is revealed to any single observer, although each observer gains a partial superiority of insight from the peculiar position in which he stands. (169)

In *Varieties of Religious Experience* he puts it more bluntly: "The first thing to bear in mind . . . is that nothing can be more stupid than to bar out phenomena from our notice, merely because we are incapable of taking any part in them ourselves" (105).

In each of these instances, as throughout his work, James is addressing a mixed audience. On the one hand, he was employed by Harvard University as a professional philosopher and actively participated in the formal discourse of his field. He responded to such contemporaries as Henri Bergson and Bertrand Russell as well as to the standard figures in Western philosophy from Plato to Kant. The frequent invitations he received to deliver distinguished lecture series suggest the seriousness with which his work was received in professional circles. At the same time many of James's lectures and essays appealed to a more popular audience for which interest in the technical debates of philosophy was never more than casual. He spoke to high school teachers, student groups, and fraternal organizations, and published reviews and essays in such magazines as *Atlantic Monthly, The Nation,* and *Popular Science Monthly.* While some of his work was tailored specifically for one or the other of these audiences— *Talks to Teachers* contained some quite informal "talks" while *The Meaning of Truth* collected essays published in professional journals—most of what James wrote enjoyed an overlapping appeal. Indeed, he cultivated this overlap. James insisted that philosophy accord itself with the ordinary details of human experience and he was sure that everyday life could be served by the achievements of philosophical inquiry. His concern with the human susceptibility to blindness and stupidity thus extended from the formal realm of philosophical discourse to the everyday world of human interaction, and his articulation of the demands of a pluralistic universe was directed at professional philosophers and the untrained public alike.

In developing his idea of radical empiricism as a response to these demands, James intended it to serve as both a tool for philosophical practice and a way of navigating through daily life. Radical empiricism originated with James as a theory of knowledge that sought to resist the narrowness of human blindness and accommodate the claims of pluralism; it ultimately influenced every aspect of his thought. He first defined this "philosophic attitude" in the essays collected in *The Will to Believe,* but his most direct statement of it appears in "A World of Pure Experience" published in 1904:

> I give the name "radical empiricism" to my *Weltanschauung.* Empiricism is known as the opposite of rationalism. Rationalism tends to emphasize universals and to make wholes prior to parts in the order of logic as well as in that of being. Empiricism, on the contrary, lays the explanatory stress upon

the part, the element, the individual, and treats the whole as a collection and the universal as an abstraction. My description of things, accordingly, starts with the parts and makes of the whole a being of the second order. It is essentially a mosaic philosophy, a philosophy of plural facts. . . . To be radical, an empiricism must neither admit into its constructions any element that is not directly experienced, nor exclude from them any element that is directly experienced. (*Writings*, 1160)

Consistent with his faith in the essential dignity and necessity of each individual, James seeks a description of the whole of life that gives priority to this plurality of facts and details. In philosophy this view would challenge the assumptions of determinism and rationalism, theories that posit a necessarily partial view of reality and validate only those individual experiences that conform to it while dismissing as unreal those that do not. In terms of everyday human interaction, radical empiricism is a systematic argument for tolerance and respect, a formal acknowledgment of the pluralistic nature of reality and a warning that universals are by their nature incomplete and temporary constructions.

James's argument for radical empiricism is often passionate.[24] Throughout *The Will to Believe* he makes clear his mistrust of the rationalists, determinists, and monists who, whatever their differences, each maintain that reality can be fully and finally known. For James there is simply too much at stake in the world for it to be reduced to a condition of perfect stasis: to see reality as fixed is to see it for much less than what it truly is. He writes:

After all that reason can do has been done, there still remains the opacity of the finite facts as merely given, with most of their peculiarities mutually unmediated and unexplained. To the very last, there are the various "points of view" which the philosopher must distinguish in discussing the world; and what is inwardly clear from one point remains a bare externality and datum to the other. The negative, the alogical, is never wholly banished. Something . . . is still wrong and other and outside and unincluded, from *your* point of view, even though you be the greatest of philosophers. (*Will to Believe*, viii)

In building on these observations in the title essay, James seeks to unsettle traditional assumptions about logic, reason, and the scientific basis for truth. Since we disbelieve "as a rule . . . all facts and theories for which we have no use," systems of logic that aim to prescribe the natural progression of thought or action should enjoy no special claims to authority: The "very law that the logicians would impose upon us . . . is based on nothing but their own natural wish to exclude all elements for which they, in their professional quality of logicians, can find no use" (10–11). This is the inherent human blindness transformed into a systematic rule and cloaked in intellectual authority: while a logician may claim that his is a universally applicable system, what he offers as logical may be little more than his own particular view concealed behind the mask of objectivity.

As in "On a Certain Blindness," James here sees the narrow perspective of the logicians as natural, something to which we are all inclined because of our need to apprehend others in the same terms by which we understand ourselves. Rather than urging us to reject systems of logic outright, he is primarily interested in exposing their subjective nature and warning us not to be seduced by their claims to absolute objectivity. James goes on to make a similar point about our quest for truth: "We may talk of the *empiricist* way and the *absolutist* way of believing in truth. The absolutists in this matter say that we not only can attain to knowing truth, but we can *know when* we have attained to knowing it; while the empiricists think that although we may attain it, we cannot infallibly know when" (12). Truth is no more than a temporary label assigned to a particular set of hypotheses; it assists us in pursuing our day-to-day activities but is never absolutely determined.

James does not doubt that such ideas as truth and logic are useful, but he deplores the persistent and irresponsible denial of their essential indeterminacy:

> Objective evidence and certitude are doubtless very fine ideals to play with, but where on this moonlit and dream-visited planet are they found? I am, therefore, myself a complete empiricist so far as my theory of human knowledge goes. I live, to be sure, by the practical faith that we must go on experiencing and thinking over our experience, for only thus can our opinions grow more true; but to hold to any one of them—I absolutely do not care which—as if it never could be reinterpretable or corrigible, I believe to be a tremendously mistaken attitude. (14)

Again, as in his discussion of logic, James is careful to point out that he wants only to reveal the subjective origins of truth, not do away with it as a viable concept. The possibility of attaining to truth remains for James the necessary object of our efforts and it is in no way diminished simply because it has been stripped of its aura of absolutism: "when as empiricists we give up the doctrine of objective certitude, we do not thereby give up the quest or hope of truth itself. We still pin our faith on its existence, and still believe that we gain an ever better position towards it by systematically continuing to roll up experiences and think" (17). In *The Vari-*

eties of Religious Experience he offered a similar observation: "I reject this dogmatic ideal not out of a perverse delight in intellectual instability. I am no lover of doubt and disorder as such. Rather do I fear to lose truth by this pretension to possess it already wholly" (305). James demands that we live rationally and that we continue to strive after truth, but he also requires that we shed all pretenses of absolutism and be willing to live in a world that is always uncertain.

In 1903 James wrote in one of his manuscript notebooks that he favored philosophic constructions that worked "with concrete elements, with change, with indeterminism" because they are "more objective and cling closer to the temperament of nature itself." Other constructions, he observed, were little more than "subjective caprices":

> All neat schematisms with permanent and absolute distinctions, classifications with absolute pretensions, systems with pigeon-holes, etc. . . . seem to me to violate the character with which life concretely comes and the expression which it bears of being, or at least of involving, a muddle and a struggle, with an "ever not quite" to all our formulas, and novelty and possibility forever leaking in.[25]

This foregrounding of uncertainty and change is a key element of radical empiricism. The perceived construction of the world at any given moment is subject to revision; no view of the whole of it can account for all of its peculiarities, and the way must be left open for successive "facts" and experiences to be brought into the frame. James sees impermanence as the only absolute condition, a given from which any healthy and practical worldview must proceed. What we know of reality, of our physical and emotional worlds, is a process rather than a state, and our beliefs and actions, so far as they are based upon our knowledge, are similarly indeterminate and always evolving. He summarizes this point most effectively in *Varieties of Religious Experience:*

> [T]he safe thing is surely to recognize that all the insights of creatures of a day like ourselves must be provisional. The wisest of critics is an altering being, subject to the better insight of the morrow, and right at any moment, only "up to date" and "on the whole." When larger ranges of truth open, it is surely best to be able to open ourselves to their reception, unfettered by our previous pretensions. (304)

Both the individual world that we immediately inhabit and the larger world that we must try to understand are continuously in flux, and James urges that we accept this condition and find meaning within it.

James was aware that, like his idea of pluralism, radical empiricism challenged many of the assumptions on which people rely in their daily lives. To acknowledge that the world is always changing, that nothing is or ever can be fixed, is a bold enough step; to feel comfortable in such a world is quite another thing. In "On a Certain Blindness" he portrayed pluralism not simply as a fact that we are constrained to accept but as a cause for celebration, the source of a richer and more rewarding life for each individual. He makes a similar case for the rewards offered by the flux and uncertainty that characterize radical empiricism. In the aptly titled "Is Life Worth Living?" James asserts that:

> So far as man stands for anything, and is productive or originative at all, his entire vital function may be said to have to deal with maybes. Not a victory is gained, not a deed of faithfulness or courage is done, except upon a maybe; not a service, not a sally of generosity, not a scientific exploration or experiment or textbook, that may not be a mistake. (*Will to Believe*, 59)

James assumes the tone of a preacher as he proclaims that this uncertainty must be embraced, that a life founded on possibility and chance is the only one worth living. We ultimately live on faith, he observes in "The Sentiment of Rationality," the "belief in something concerning which doubt is still theoretically possible," and in "The Dilemma of Determinism" he argues that chance and indeterminism are the only adequate means of representing a pluralistic world (*Will to Believe*, 90, 175). As radical empiricism admits the experiences of each individual into its understanding of the world the complexion of that world must inevitably change. In turn, it is this very process of continuous change that keeps our lives fresh and endows them with meaning.

The impermanence and lack of certitude that accompany this world of ever-unfolding experience forms the connection between radical empiricism and the other important development in James's thought, pragmatism. If pluralism serves as a description of the universe and radical empiricism as a way of comprehending that universe with all its lack of certainty, then pragmatism represents James's program for action, for making one's way in the world as it evolves over time. Pragmatism is foremost a theory of truth that examines what it means to call something true, how we choose to act upon that truth, and what we perceive to be the desired results of our actions. As such, it pertains to both our private lives and our social relations. To be sure, James initially disclaimed any connection between radical empiricism and pragmatism. In the introduction to his seminal *Pragmatism,* he sought to "avoid one misunderstanding at least" by asserting that "there is no logical connexion between pragmatism, as I understand it, and a doctrine which I have recently set forth as 'radical empiricism.'" However, two years later in *The Meaning of Truth* James would declare that "the establishment of the pragmatist theory of truth is a step of first-rate importance in making radical empiricism prevail."[26] In fact, James's notions of radical empiricism and pragmatism are intimately related, and each doctrine relies on the other for its ultimate importance.

James intended pragmatism to serve as a systematic means of accommodating the world of ever-unfolding experience posited by radical empiricism with what he always acknowledged was a human need for truth. If the experience of each individual must be admitted into the construction of the world then truth, an element of that world on which we base our beliefs and actions, must be conceived of as indeterminate and open to revision. In *The Will to Believe* James had suggested that, as a consequence of radical empiricism, we can say that we have attained to truth and knowledge only for so long as we continue to look for them; once we pretend to have achieved them we are lost. He makes a similar observation in elaborating on pragmatism: "we have to live to-day by what truth we can get to-day, and be ready to-morrow to call it falsehood." Truth thus conceived is an "expedient in the way of our thinking":

> I have already insisted on the fact that truth is made largely out of previous truths. Men's beliefs at any time are so much experience *funded.* But the beliefs are themselves part of the sum total of the world's experience, and become matter, therefore, for the next day's funding operations. So far as reality means experienceable reality, both it and the truths men gain about it are everlastingly in process of mutation. (*Pragmatism,* 583–84)

The cornerstone of this pragmatic theory of truth is the "pragmatic method," an effort "to interpret each notion by tracing its respective practical consequences" and asking the question: "What difference would it practically make to any one if this notion rather than that notion were true?" (506). This test would apply not only to the "metaphysical disputes" occasioned by such questions as "Is the world one or many?—fated or free?—material or spiritual?" but to any idea we encounter in our "stream of experience." For pragmatism, "*theories thus become instruments, not answers to enigmas, in which we can rest.* We don't lie back upon them, we move forward. . . . Pragmatism unstiffens all our theories, limbers them up and sets each one to work" (509–10, emphasis in original). As James had first implied in *The Will to Believe,* such concepts as logic, truth, and reason mean little in themselves; they are mere "attitude[s] of orientation" through which we confront the world, subjective in origin and only as substantial as the practical value they contain.

It is important here to recall that while James extolled the virtues of utility he felt that there were many ways in which something could be deemed useful: bread, poetry, and steam engines each responded to a human need, and ought to be valued accordingly.[27] This is a crucial point: "Pragmatism is willing to take anything, to follow either logic or the senses and to count the humblest and most personal experiences. . . . Her only test of probable truth is what works best in the way of leading us, what fits every part of life best and combines with the collectivity of experience's demands, nothing being omitted" (522). James was particularly eager to demonstrate the way in which pragmatism validated the largely abstract dimensions of religious experience. In "A World of Pure Experience" he posited that radical empiricism may acknowledge only those elements that have been "directly experienced," and with the pragmatic theory of truth he points the way to admitting religious beliefs and experiences into the empirical world. James devoted the concluding chapter of *Pragmatism* to arguing for the probable truth of religious attitudes. Since "on pragmatic principles we can not reject any hypothesis if consequences useful to life flow from it," and since the history of religion is in many respects the history of the human needs that religion has met, then, James concludes, we must accept the reality of religious experiences even if we have never shared in them ourselves (606, 617). He thus returns to the point he had made in "On a Certain Blindness": we have no grounds to judge the ideals or beliefs of others because, due to our own limited experience, we are blind to the purposes they might serve.

In this manner *Pragmatism* brings together the key elements of James's philosophy: The world is pluralistic; it is composed of "an indefinitely numerous lot of *eaches*" who participate in the construction of reality and whose independent experiences radical empiricism compels us to respect (602). The result is a world defined by its impermanence, one that always resists our efforts to pin it down as fixed and absolute. In turn, the pragmatic theory of truth maintains that it is precisely within this mutable reality that individual effort most clearly manifests itself: "In our cognitive as well as in our active life we are creative. We *add,* both to the subject and to the predicate part of reality. The world stands really malleable, waiting to receive its final touches at our hands. . . . Man *engenders* truth upon it" (599). For James, pluralism, radical empiricism, and pragmatism work together to emphasize the supreme importance of each individual to the world in which we live, a world that is essentially of our own making.

Just as James had incorporated Emerson in his early writings on pluralism he found him to be a ready source of support for his subsequent explorations. Indeed, the Emerson James describes in the centenary address comes very near to being an intellectual self-portrait. While he declares the driving force of Emerson's work to be the same pluralistic vision that motivated his own writings, he also claims Emerson as an advocate of ideas that were central to radical empiricism and pragmatism. In the address James quoted a selection of passages to illustrate Emerson's belief in the sanctity of a life lived "at first hand"; he then summarized the message of those passages in terms that spoke directly to his own work: "The world is still new and untried. In seeing freshly, and not in hearing of what others saw, shall a man find what truth is" (*Writings*, 1121). A few pages later James paraphrased Emerson again: "All God's life opens into the individual particular, and here and now, or nowhere, is reality" (1124). By highlighting such ideas as keynotes of Emerson's work James is also appropriating Emerson as a source of validation for his own.

Dana Brand has suggested that the Centenary Address served as something of a watershed in James's intellectual development. In the process of rereading Emerson as he prepared for this address in early 1903, Brand contends, James "discovered" him as a radical empiricist and worked him into a series of essays on the subject that he began later that year.[28] Though Brand is right to point to a connection between James's radical empiricism and similar ideas expressed by Emerson, it is misleading to date this connection from 1903. James had read widely in Emerson before being invited to deliver this address and had referred to him with familiarity throughout his earlier work. Furthermore, he had begun working on radical empiricism well before 1903—as early as *The Principles of Psychology* in 1890—and the parallels with Emerson's work go back just as far.[29] To be sure, the centenary address was an important event in James's intellectual life, but not because of any new discovery he made about Emerson's incipient empiricism or pragmatism. Rather, the address recorded James's recognition of the remarkable convergence between Emerson's essays and the direction his own work had taken.

James did not have to look far in Emerson's writings to find support for his theories of radical empiricism and pragmatism. The idea that reality is mutable and that truth is always evolving and never fixed forms as strong a current in Emerson's work as in James's, and the delight James took in this lack of certainty, like the delight he took in the exhilarating fact of pluralism, shares much with Emerson's own celebration of a world that was always changing. In "Experience" Emerson sets forth his objections to the kind of absolutist attitudes that James would so fervently reject in *The Will to Believe*. Commenting upon the "contracting influences of so-called science" that promise full and final knowledge of the nature of the world and of human character, Emerson declares that "the grossest ignorance does not disgust like this impudent knowingness" (475). The claim that we can know reality in any final way, or that there is a single reality by which individual manifestations may be measured, strikes Emerson as not only demonstrably false but foolish, for it can only hinder individuals from achieving their full human potential: "life is a series of surprises, and would not be worth taking or keeping, if it were not. . . . The results of life are uncalculated and uncalculateable" (483).

As with James, this rejection of absolutism leads Emerson to champion the virtues of change and variety: if people cannot attain to a single and final understanding of the world in which they live, then meaning must be located in the always-evolving collection of details. In "Self-Reliance" he identifies this state of impermanence as the necessary condition for a truly self-reliant life: "Life only avails, not the having lived. Power ceases in the instant of repose; it resides in the moment of transition from a past to a new state, in the shooting of the gulf, in the darting to an aim" (271). This opposition between power and repose, and the argument that life is fully realized only as an ongoing series of transitions, occurs throughout Emerson's work. In "Intellect" he anticipates James in asserting that truth itself is a process rather than a fixed quantity:

> God offers to every mind its choice between truth and repose. Take which you please,—you can never have both. Between these, as a pendulum, man oscillates. He in whom the love of repose predominates will accept the first creed, the first philosophy, the first political party he meets. . . . He in whom the love of truth predominates will keep himself aloof from all moorings, and afloat. He will abstain from dogmatism. . . . He submits to the inconvenience of suspense and imperfect opinion, but he is a candidate for truth. (426)

Emerson acknowledged that truth was a necessary object of human endeavor, but he also believed that by its very nature it must always remain indeterminate. This "inconvenience of suspense" was thus a measure of our proximity to truth rather than an obstacle in our way to achieving it.

As James wrote in *The Varieties of Religious Experience,* "to admit one's liability to correction is one thing, and to embark on a sea of wanton doubt is another. Of willfully playing into the hands of skepticism we cannot be accused. He who acknowledges the imperfectness of his instrument, and makes allowance for it in discussing his observations, is in a much better position for gaining truth than if he claimed his instrument to be infallible" (304).

Emerson developed his version of this theme more fully in his essay "Circles." The uncertainty of the world leaves everything in that world subject to revision: "There is not a piece of science but its flank may be turned to-morrow; there is not any literary reputation, not the so-called eternal names of fame, that may not be revised and condemned. The very hopes of man, the thoughts of his heart, the religion of nations, the manners and morals of mankind, are all at the mercy of a new generalization." Aware of how unsettling this condition must be, Emerson goes on to urge men to cultivate the "valor" that "consists in the power of self-recovery": only by "preferring truth to his past apprehension of truth" and frankly accepting "the intrepid conviction that his laws, his relations to society, his Christianity, his world, may at any time be superseded and decease" will a man be adequately prepared to lead a life that is radically unpredictable (407). Toward the end of the essay Emerson summarizes what it means to live in such a world, providing a statement of what that life offers and the terms on which it can best be lived:

> There is no sleep, no pause, no preservation, but all things renew, germinate, and spring. . . . In nature every moment is new; the past is always swallowed and forgotten; the coming only is sacred. Nothing is secure but life, transition, the energizing spirit. . . . No truth so sublime but it may be trivial to-morrow in the light of new thoughts. People wish to be settled; only as far as they are unsettled is there any hope for them. (412–13)

In *Pragmatism* James offered a similar description of how he himself intended to confront an uncertain world: "I find myself willing to take the universe to be really dangerous and adventurous, without therefore backing out and crying 'no play.' . . . I am willing that there should be real losses and real losers, and no total preservation of all that is." This attitude, which James defines as "pragmatistic theism," recognizes that the world is radically unpredictable but rejects the "crude naturalism" that would see human life on a course of aimless drift. Rather, like Emerson before him, James urges individuals to embrace this lack of certainty and the risks that go along with it. A universe that is both pluralistic and indeterminate offers one clear path to an active and significant life: a man must be "willing to live on a scheme of uncertified possibilities which he trusts [and] willing to pay with his own person, if need be, for the realization of the ideals which he frames" (617–18). For both Emerson and James, the daunting implications of an indeterminate world are a challenge to be met rather than a handicap to be overcome, an opportunity for individual human beings to endow their own lives with dignity by boldly accepting conditions that are in any event unavoidable.

James's notion of "pragmatistic theism" suggests a further point of comparison between his work and Emerson's. He introduced the idea in a chapter on "Pragmatism and Religion" in which he argues for a reconsideration of religious experience on pragmatic grounds. As I noted above, this was one of his primary aims in working out the theory of pragmatism, for he felt that it was crucial to rescue religion from both the negations of scientific absolutism and the numbing repressions of dogmatic theology. In "Is Life Worth Living?" James wrote that "Our faculties of belief were not primarily given us to make orthodoxies and heresies withal; they were given us to live by. And to trust our religious demands means first of all to live in the light of them and to act as if the invisible world which they suggest were real" (*Will to Believe,* 56). James stresses that outward religious forms are subordinate to the individual experience, the immediate perception of a divine presence from which religious faith originates, and in this way he approaches religion on essentially the same terms as did Emerson.

In the opening paragraph of *Nature* Emerson expressed regret that while "the foregoing generations beheld God and nature face to face" people of his own generation were content with secondhand knowledge. Convinced that each individual is open to a direct apprehension of the divine spirit and that the meaning of religion inheres in this fact, Emerson devoted much of his subsequent work to affirming the significance of personal religious experience. His most concise statement of these views is "The Divinity School Address," delivered at Harvard in 1838 and sufficiently controversial that he was not asked to return to his alma mater for nearly thirty years. Instead of elaborating on the role of the ministry or explicating the fine points of theological doctrine, topics that would surely have pleased school officials, Emerson hailed the supremacy of the "religious sentiment" that is revealed to each individual soul:

> The sentiment is divine and deifying. It is the beatitude of man. It makes him illimitable. Through it, the soul first knows itself. It corrects the capital mistake of the infant man, who seeks to be great by following the great, and

hopes to derive advantages *from another,*—by showing the fountain of all good to be in himself, and that he, equally with every man, is an inlet into the deeps of Reason. (78)

Emerson here introduces a theme variations of which comprise his entire body of work: the religious sentiment begins with an individual perception, an experience of the immanent divinity in all things. Every individual is capable of such a perception on his own terms because each individual is an instrument of God. From this it follows that religion, whatever outward form it takes, must acknowledge this private feeling as its necessary origin:

> [W]hilst the doors of the temple stand open, night and day, before every man, and the oracles of this truth cease never, it is guarded by one stern condition; this, namely; it is an intuition. It cannot be received at second hand. Truly speaking, it is not instruction, but provocation, that I can receive from another soul. What he announces, I must find true in me, or wholly reject; and on his word, or as his second, be he who he may, I can accept nothing. On the contrary, the absence of primary faith is the presence of degradation. (79)

As Emerson proceeds it is clear that he finds this "absence of primary faith" to be characteristic of the religion of his day, and the consequent degradation widespread: "From the views I have already expressed, you will infer the sad conviction, which I share, I believe, with numbers, of the universal decay and now almost death of faith in society. The soul is not preached. The Church seems to totter to its fall, almost all life extinct" (83). Concerned more with its institutional forms, rituals, and points of dogma, the "Church" has ignored the very element upon which it is built: the individual experience of the religious sentiment. For Emerson, this failure is most immediately evident in the field of preaching, a vocation to which his audience was soon to be graduated and from which he would soon resign. In its ideal form, "preaching is the expression of the moral sentiment in application to the duties of life." It must come from the soul and demonstrate that the religious sentiment is a living and vibrant fact. In this country, however, preaching is too often characterized by tradition: "it comes out of the memory, and not out of the soul; it aims at what is usual, and not at what is necessary and eternal." Thus, "historical Christianity destroys the power of preaching, by withdrawing it from the exploration of the moral nature of man, where the sublime is, where are the resources of astonishment and power" (84–86). In failing to heed this primary call, the church has cut itself off from its true source of vitality and legitimacy.

James collected his own observations on religion in *The Varieties of Religious Experience,* published five years before *Pragmatism* and a year before he delivered his address at the Emerson centenary.[30] In the opening lecture he echoes Emerson's "Divinity School Address" as he outlines his project:

> I speak not now of your ordinary religious believer, who follows the conventional observances of his country. . . . His religion has been made for him by others, communicated to him by tradition, determined to fixed forms by imitation, and retained by habit. It would profit us little to study this second-hand religious life. We must make search rather for the original experiences which were the pattern-setters to all this mass of suggested feeling and imitated conduct. These experiences we can only find in individuals for whom religion exists not as a dull habit, but as an acute fever. (*Writings,* 15)

James recognized that his choice to focus on personal religious experiences rather than on the institutional forms and doctrinal issues that surround those experiences was an unusual approach to the study of religion. Many members of his audience had dedicated their lives to examining the organized structures through which religion was transmitted between generations and between cultures, and to simply ignore such topics as promising little profit no doubt struck them as brash. Nonetheless, James defended his approach as providing the truest insight into the nature of religion: "In one sense at least the personal religion will prove itself more fundamental than either theology or ecclesiasticism. Churches, when once established, live at second-hand upon tradition; but the *founders* of every church owed their power originally to the fact of their direct personal communion with the divine. . . . [S]o personal religion should still seem the primordial thing, even to those who continue to esteem it incomplete" (35).

James would return to this point throughout the book, emphasizing in a manner parallel to Emerson that the essential nature of religion is its origin in personal experience. He thus brings to his study of religion the same criteria that informed his understanding of pluralism and radical empiricism: "What keeps religion going is something else than abstract definitions and systems of concatenated adjectives, and something different from faculties of theology and their professors. All these things are after-effects, secondary accretions upon those phenomena of vital conversation with the unseen divine, of which I have shown you so many instances, renewing themselves *in saecula saeculorum* in the lives of humble and private men" (401). This is religion as an element of a pluralistic world, a truth that emanates from the "humble and private man" rather than being imposed from outside by subjective and incomplete theories of theology.

Ultimately, James concludes that "the uses of religion, its uses to the individual who has it, and the uses of the individual himself to the world, are the best arguments that truth is in it. We return to the empirical philosophy: the true is what works well" (411). The whole weight of his explorations in *Varieties* attests to the fact that religion, as an intense and undeniable form of personal experience, has positive, practical effects; it "works well" and, by the standards of pragmatism, is true. James thus joins with Emerson in maintaining that personal religion, the manifestation of each individual's communion with the divine, be accorded the philosophical and intellectual respect that has for too long been enjoyed only by "second-hand" religious forms.

In the final chapter of *Pragmatism* James brings together his various observations on pluralism, radical empiricism, and pragmatism in a characteristically expansive summary of what it means to live in the kind of world he has described. Above all, it is a world that affords each individual an angle of observation on and participation in its making:

> Our acts, our turning-places, where we seem to ourselves to make ourselves grow, are the parts of the world to which we are closest, the parts of which our knowledge is most intimate and complete. Why should we not take them at their face-value? Why may they not be the actual turning-places and growing-places which they seem to be, of the world—why not the workshop of being, where we catch fact in the making, so that nowhere may the world grow in any other kind of way than this? (613)

While James once again affirms that our understanding of the world begins with our own personal experience of it, he hastens to add that "in our world, the wishes of the individual are only one condition. Other individuals are there with other wishes and they must be propitiated first." In this way the world would grow "piecemeal by the contributions of its several parts." James admits that this view is only an hypothesis, a mere supposition as to how the world might actually develop, but he urges that we take this hypothesis seriously as one that carries significant implications:

> Suppose that the world's author put the case to you before creation, saying: "I am going to make a world not certain to be saved, a world the perfection of which shall be conditional merely, the condition being that each several

agent does its own 'level best.' I offer you the chance of taking part in such a world. Its safety, you see, is unwarranted. It is a real adventure, with real danger, yet it may win through. It is a social scheme of co-operative work genuinely to be done. Will you join the procession? Will you trust yourself and trust the other agents enough to face the risk?" (614)

This passage echoes the selection from Emerson's "Spiritual Laws" that James quoted in his centenary address: "The fact that I am here certainly shows me that the Soul has need of an organ here, and shall I not assume the post?" Yet within this echo are certain discordant notes that result from Emerson and James emphasizing different terms for accepting the challenge to live in this world. Emerson dedicated himself to liberating the private individual from the encumbrances of society, a liberation he saw as prerequisite to living a full life. Though on the whole he balanced his rhetoric of radical individualism with an equally intense vision of duty, responsibility, and self-surrender, Emerson's paeans to the infinitude of the private man make up his most recognizable legacy. Indeed, it was this angle of his thought that led critics like Van Wyck Brooks and Waldo Frank to condemn his "corrosive individualism" and to doubt his relevance for twentieth-century literature. "Nothing is at last sacred but the integrity of your own mind" he wrote in "Self-Reliance," just after observing that "society everywhere is in conspiracy against the manhood of every one of its members" (*Essays*, 261). In such passages as these, which abound in his work, Emerson disavows any interest in the day-to-day relationships among individuals as all such entanglements prevent a man from heeding the simple injunction to follow his own genius.

While James shared Emerson's faith in the sufficiency of each individual to his own task, he was far more explicit in acknowledging the demands that a world full of such individuals must inevitably impose. As he reminds his readers in *Pragmatism,* "the wishes of the individual are only one condition. Other individuals are there with other wishes." James is committed to seeing his vision of the dignity of each individual result in a greater awareness of shared purpose: life is "a social scheme of co-operative work" that is dependent to some degree on each member of society conscientiously attending to his own duty. Indeed, James advances his idea of pluralism primarily as a means of calling our attention to the worth of other individuals rather than simply promoting our need to liberate ourselves. Pluralism stresses a plurality of independent selves working interdependently as opposed to the single solitary self that often emerges from Emerson's work.

For James, the "workshop of being" is always a cooperative affair; for Emerson, most important work is done in solitude.

This difference is most readily apparent in James's description of how society absorbs the always evolving experiences of its constituent individuals. At various points he sought to ensure that his notions of pluralism and radical empiricism did not dissolve into mere relativistic confusion. In the preface to *Talks to Teachers* he was careful to define the practical point of pluralism as the "outward tolerance of whatever is itself not intolerant," and he would go on, in "What Makes a Life Significant," to search for a principle by which "our tolerance may be less chaotic" (*Talks*, 19, 172). James was keenly aware that his pluralistic world implied limitations as well as opportunities, and that these limitations imposed real choices. In "The Moral Philosopher and the Moral Life" he describes the "tragic situation" that confronts a world of competing individual needs and desires:

> [The] question here is most tragically practical. The actually possible in this world is vastly narrower than all that is demanded; and there is always a *pinch* between the ideal and the actual which can only be got through by leaving part of the ideal behind. There is hardly a good which we can imagine except as competing for some space and time with some other imagined good. Every end of desire that presents itself appears exclusive of some other end of desire. . . . Some part of the ideal must be butchered. (*Will to Believe*, 202–3)

To decide which desires and "goods" must be given up and which ones accommodated in furthering the "social scheme" of life is for James the most important and the most sensitive task we face.

Emerson, too, acknowledged the limitations faced by the individual in a world full of other individuals but, unlike James, he did not see this as an issue demanding explicit attention. Indeed, he seemed singularly indifferent to the question that James considered crucial: How does society mediate between the conflicting demands of those whose equal participation is vital to the world's growth? This indifference is occasioned in part by Emerson's greater focus on the individual self and his consequent minimizing of the role of social relationships in the lives of individual men. In Emerson's scheme society is what the self-reliant individual ought to shun; it is in any event not something to be promoted. What arbitrating force Emerson's world does require comes through the influence of the over-soul. Even in such essays as "Fate" and "Compensation" where he details the injustices and frustrations that befall the most conscientious adherents to the doctrine of self-reliance, Emerson still maintains that a divine breath "blows eternally through the universe of souls in the direction of the Right and Necessary" ("Fate," 956). This faith would seem to obviate any sustained attention to such questions as which ideals ought to be butchered. Where James sees individuals actively mediating between conflicting ideals in the course of their social relations, Emerson sees the over-soul performing the same function in a far more subtle and impersonal manner.

Though his moral sensibility was no less acute, Emerson did not share James's conviction that the good of society was something to be pursued through deliberate, practical effort. He would declare in various ways his belief that "independence, and cheerful relation . . . are the essentials,— these, and the wish to serve,—to add somewhat to the well-being of men," yet he also delighted in flaunting his indifference to whether the world he described turned out well or poorly.[31] In a manner that would endear him to Nietzsche, he often denied any responsibility to uphold goodness and vowed to "live then from the Devil" if that was whence his impulses originated ("Self-Reliance," 262). This paradox is evident in a frequently cited passage from "Circles":

> I own I am gladdened . . . by beholding in morals that unrestrained innundation of the principle of good into every chink and hole that selfishness has left open, yea, into selfishness and sin itself; so that no evil is pure. . . . But . . . let me remind the reader that I am only an experimenter. . . . I unsettle all things. No facts are to me sacred; none are profane; I simply experiment, an endless seeker, with no Past at my back. (411–12)

Here, advancement of the principle of good is not a goal in itself but only the fortuitous side effect of radical experimentation. Emerson argued a similar point in "Self-Reliance" where he wrote that "he who would gather immortal palms must not be hindered by the name of goodness, but must explore if it be goodness" (261). While James, too, would maintain that no facts are sacred and would agree with the assertion that we must never accept goodness as an absolute term, he insisted that the goal of our experiments be some realization of the general social good, however contingent and impermanent that good might be. Emerson, whose faith in the benevolent guidance of the over-soul assured him that his impulses did not, after all, come from the devil, evidently considered such insistence superfluous.

The boast that Emerson makes about having no past at his back points to another issue on which he and James place differing emphasis, and again Emerson's writing on this point is paradoxical. In such seminal essays as "The American Scholar" and "History" Emerson urged his audience not to be guided by its understanding of the past but to live only in the present tense where the forces of innovation and originality triumph over the oppressive weight of tradition. At the same time he articulated a vision of growth that was gradual, suggesting that the present is continuously built upon the accumulated foundation of the past.[32] While both of these readings find ample support in his work, Emerson's call to cast off the shackles of the past is the one that most impressed his early audiences, and his critics and admirers would come to consider this stance his trademark.

For his part James left little doubt that he was aware of the past at his back and that he understood its necessary function. From pluralism to *Pragmatism* his work points to the fact that change is piecemeal, a gradual process of grafting the new onto the old. For the individual encountering a constant flow of new experiences, each suggesting new truths and new facts, this careful accommodation of the new was a necessity. As James noted, "we can hardly take in an impression at all, in the absence of a preconception of what impressions there may possibly be" (595). It was in this way that the pragmatic theory of truth made sense of the often chaotic world of radical empiricism:

> A new opinion counts as "true" just in proportion as it gratifies the individual's desire to assimilate the novel in his experience to his beliefs in stock. It must both lean on old truth and grasp new fact. . . . That new idea is truest which performs most felicitously its function of satisfying our double urgency. It makes itself true, gets itself classed as true, by the way it works; grafting itself then upon the ancient body of truth, which thus grows much as a tree grows by the activity of a new layer of cambrium. (514)

For James, this measured process of social evolution offers the fairest and most reliable means of mediating between conflicting forces in a pluralistic world. The existing stock of truths provides a foundation, both for the individual, whose own sense of the past guides his response to new experiences, and for the society of individuals, which relies on the filtering of innovation through tradition in order to avoid anomie. And of course, this foundation itself remains unfixed and open to revision:

> We patch and tinker more than we renew. The novelty soaks in; it stains the ancient mass; but it is also tinged by what absorbs it. Our past apperceives and co-operates; and in the new equilibrium in which each step forward in the process of learning terminates, it happens relatively seldom that the new fact is added *raw*. . . . New truths thus are resultants of new experiences and of old truths combined and mutually modifying one another. (559–60)

In this way James smoothes the radical edges of Emersonian individualism and grounds it in a context of social interaction and hopeful meliorism, which is not to say that Emerson's vision was socially detached but that James was more inclined to recognize the need for and the positive potential of social interaction. Emerson saw society as existing in opposition to the interests of the individual, while James saw it as composed precisely of those interests. For James, individuals frame their own place within the world and, in the process, contribute to the construction of the broader world in which they live. And though this world is still indeterminate and remains open to the always unfolding stream of experience, each new experience must "become humanized in the sense of being squared, assimilated, or in some way adapted to the humanized mass already there" (595). Thus, when Frank Lentricchia writes that modernism "in its William Jamesian phase" seeks "to wipe out tradition and history, to experience life as if for the first time, without mediation," he has misconstrued the impetus of James's thought.[33] Instead of unsettling all things through his endless experimentation, he seeks a cautious assimilation, a new equilibrium between past and present, old and new, society and the individual. To live life "as if for the first time" is, for James, to live with an awareness of what has gone before and a determination to join in shaping what will come. Starting with Emerson's unqualified faith in the sufficiency of the individual and his rejection of all forms of absolutism and determinism, James goes on to envision a community that is built around the various needs, gifts, and ideals of the individuals who comprise it rather than imposed on those individuals as a predetermined structure. His modern individual is one who willingly participates in a society both of his own choosing and of his own making, someone who acknowledges the claims of others to be as worthy as his own.

I here diverge from Cornel West's account of the connection between Emerson and James. West asserts that "James moves the focus of Emersonian theodicy away from the community and back to the individual person," and he finds James's persistent attempts to mediate between opposing forces to be pale and timid: "For James, as for Emerson, abundant life is always found on the highway. Yet for him, such life can be sustained only in the middle lane. Openness, flexibility, and improvisation characterize his intellectual attitude and personal temperament, but he always ends by residing in the golden mean, between extremes." Clearly West finds this approach inadequate and sees it as indicative of both Emerson and James's limitations: "Emerson and James simply fail to entertain the possibility that overcoming a limitation or reconciling extremes may result in an outcome that is worse than its antecedent conditions; they cannot imagine wholesale regression owing to human will and action." This failure, in turn, would eviscerate any claim Jamesian pragmatism might make to being a progressive social philosophy for, like Emerson, James "is prohibited by his individualism from taking seriously fundamental social change; instead, he opts for gradualism supported by moral critique."[34]

While West's argument is compelling, it rests on what I believe is a hasty characterization of James's thought. First, if James moved the "focus of Emersonian theodicy" anywhere it was in the direction of the community and not toward the individual. He exhibited a greater sensitivity to the interaction between the individual and the community and believed that an individual's experience is always mediated through and interdependent with social relations. Indeed, James rejected the very premise of West's contention by refusing to consider the individual and society as contending forces. West's misstatement here is complicated by his linking James's emphasis on mediation and gradualism with his supposed commitment to individualism. As I have argued, James's gradualism grew out of his effort to contribute to a keener appreciation of the interdependence of social relations and personal experience; it was not, as West implies, a screen for sacrificing the needs of the community to the desires of the individual.

More persuasive is James Kloppenberg's argument that James in fact offered an intellectual basis for the emerging theories of progressivism and social democracy. Kloppenberg admits that there is a "certain amount of truth to [the] familiar argument" that James was oriented more toward the individual, but he asserts that this is so only in a superficial way: "James, like Dewey, recognized that social relations lay at the heart of lived experience. Characteristically, he never speculated whether man is social or egoistic by nature, both because he constantly opposed dualism and because the search for an 'essence of man' was alien to his style of thinking." Kloppenberg goes on to conclude that James, again like Dewey, "considered experience itself to be fundamentally social." While James "demanded that all truth must ultimately be confirmed in personal experience," he also believed that "social relations are part of personal experience" and that "the contradiction between individual and social tests of truth can be exaggerated."[35] For Kloppenberg, the "philosophers of the *via media*," including James and Dewey, approached politics as they did any other aspect of human knowledge: it was something that was provisional, was never absolute, and resisted all determinist efforts to reduce it to one or two causal principles. As a result, they promoted a healthy gradualism as the best way to avoid the chaos that might otherwise accompany an indefinitely mutable political scene: "we can skirt despair if we use the compass of accumulated cultural experience" to maneuver our way through a changing world (45).

Kloppenberg's linking of James with John Dewey suggests the way in which Dewey, too, appropriated Emerson in his work. Like James, Dewey scattered references to Emerson throughout his writings and the wide selection of essays from which he quotes suggests that he was familiar with most of what Emerson wrote. In *Democracy and Education* (1916) Dewey defended his theory of education against charges that it abandoned peda-gogical authority and instructional content in favor of indulging the whim of the student. To clarify his own position he turns to Emerson:

> The true principle of respect for immaturity cannot be better put than in the words of Emerson: "Respect the child. Be not too much his parent. Trespass not on his solitude. But I hear the outcry which replies to this suggestion: Would you verily throw up the reins of public and private discipline; would you leave the young child to the mad career of his own passions and whim-sies, and call this anarchy a respect for the child's nature? I answer,—Respect the child, respect him to the end, but also respect yourself. . . . keep his nature *and arm it with knowledge in the very direction in which it points.*"[36]

This passage not only links Emerson with an important part of Dewey's philosophy but is representative of Dewey's overall assessment of Emerson's significance. More explicitly than James, Dewey invokes Emerson as a voice of mediation, someone who boldly proclaimed the dignity and suffi-ciency of individual endeavor but at the same time recognized that such endeavor could not prosper in isolation.[37]

On the same day that James delivered his address at the Emerson Cen-tennial in Concord, Dewey read his own tribute at the University of Chi-cago. And, much like James, Dewey found in Emerson confirmation of some of his own most fundamental principles. He first sets out to defend Emerson against the "condescending patronage" of philosophers and liter-ary critics who would point to his lack of cohesiveness as justification for their own inattention to his thought. In fact, Dewey asserts, Emerson had a logic and a system of his own, complex and internal but still "compact and unified" and concentrated in "form and effect." Failure to comprehend this resulted less from the elusiveness of Emerson's thought than from the shortcomings of critics who need "every reason carefully pointed out and labelled, and are incapable of taking anything for granted." To more per-ceptive and original thinkers, Emerson's writings cohere in a clear and powerful statement of the priority of individual experience in a world where philosophical, political, and economic systems leave little room for anomalous details.[38]

Dewey firmly believed that philosophy should be submitted to the test of everyday experience. It is thus not surprising that he identifies as the most characteristic trait of Emerson's work the fact that he "takes the distinctions and classifications which to most philosophers are true in and of and because of their systems, and makes them true of life, of the common experience, of the everyday man." It is this tactic that gives both shape and significance to Emerson's thought: "I fancy he reads the so-called eclecticism of Emerson wrongly who does not see that it is a reduction of all the philosophers of the race, even the prophets like Plato and Proclus whom Emerson holds most dear, to the test of trial by the service rendered the present and immediate experience" (27–28). Echoing William James, Dewey here finds in Emerson an incipient pragmatism and radical empiricism, a pronounced tendency to reassert the primacy of individual experience over impersonal intellectual systems that would transcend the details of real life.

Dewey suspects that the major reason professional philosophers have resisted claiming Emerson as one of their own is his rejection of this distinction between the real and the ideal. All of Emerson's efforts tended toward affirming the simple truth that every individual enjoys an equal claim on the insights afforded by philosophical inquiry, a truth that was, to say the least, not widely shared:

> [T]he idealist has too frequently conspired with the sensualist to deprive the pressing and so the passing Now of value which is spiritual. Through the joint work of such malign conspiracy, the common man is not, or at least does not know himself for, an idealist. It is such disinherited of the earth that Emerson summons to their own. "If man is sick, is unable, is mean-spirited and odious, it is because there is so much of his nature which is unlawfully withholden from him."

For Dewey, this is Emerson's most important contribution: "Against creed and system, convention and institution, Emerson stands for restoring to the common man that which in the name of religion, of philosophy, of art and of morality, has been embezzled from the common store" (29).

Dewey's reading of Emerson parallels that of James in many ways. Both stressed the importance of ensuring that ideas—whether philosophical, political, social, or otherwise—remain congruent with individual experience, and each identified this as a prominent feature of Emerson's thought as well. As Dewey wrote, Emerson "finds truth in the highway, in the untaught endeavor, the unexpected idea," and his ideas "are not fixed upon any Reality that is beyond or behind or in any way apart" from immediate lived experience, an observation similar to one James had made. And, just as James had located the wellspring of Emerson's work in his assertion that each individual is open to the mystery of the universe and participates in its ongoing revelation, Dewey saw as fundamental Emerson's belief that "every individual is at once the focus and the channel of mankind's long and wide endeavor." Dewey goes on to declare that, in Emerson, such sentiments "cease to be statements of a separated philosophy and become natural transcripts of the course of events and of the rights of man" (29). On the evidence of these transcripts Dewey proclaims Emerson the "Philosopher of Democracy" and concludes that "one may without presumption believe that even if Emerson has no system, none the less he is the prophet and herald of any system which democracy may henceforth construct and hold by, and that when democracy has articulated itself, it will have no difficulty in finding itself already proposed in Emerson" (30).

In claiming Emerson as the "Philosopher of Democracy" and praising his defense of individualism, Dewey intended precise definitions for his terms. He saw democracy not as a fixed condition of government to which any group might finally attain, but as a process of constant striving, an ever-evolving political culture. In *Freedom and Culture* he argued that democracy was not simply a matter of maintaining democratic forms of government, but required for its sustenance a thorough infusion of democratic principles into every corner of human experience. More than a set of institutions, democracy was an experimental method dedicated to "maintaining an ever-increasing release of the powers of human nature, in service of a freedom which is co-operative and a cooperation which is voluntary."[39] Dewey makes a similar point with Emerson in an essay on the Belgian writer Maurice Maeterlinck: "Emerson, Walt Whitman, and Maeterlinck are thus far, perhaps, the only men who have been habitually, and, as it were, instinctively aware that democracy is neither a form of government nor a social expediency, but a metaphysic of the relation of man and his experience to nature."[40] As man's experience continues to unfold, so, too, must democracy remain open-ended and evolve in the direction of a culture that supports a broad understanding of personal freedom.

In addition to his efforts to refine the public discussion of democracy, Dewey promoted a revisionist view of the concept of individualism, an idea that was the cornerstone of American social and political discourse. In his most important works on social philosophy— *The Public and Its Problems* (1927), *Individualism Old and New* (1929), *Liberalism and Social Action*

(1935), and *Freedom and Culture* (1939)—Dewey unfolds his argument that the traditional view of the individual and the social as antithetical inter- ests has become a dangerous anachronism. Rooted in seventeenth- and eighteenth-century political philosophy and a staple of nineteenth-century American thought, the idea that the individual can prosper only when free of social entanglements has, Dewey believes, been responsible for the pov- erty of recent social and political thought and the growing chasm between American ideals and American reality. Indeed, the very premise of this "old individualism" is obsolete, for the reality of twentieth-century America with its widespread economic organization and centralization has rendered the rugged individual essentially powerless. Still, the ideals of the old individualism have retained their grip on the American imagination and continue to obstruct necessary economic and political reforms.

For Dewey, the persistence of the old individualism has placed the modern individual in something of a double bind. On one side, the identi- fication of liberal individualism with laissez-faire economic and political ideas leaves it open to charges of wanton exploitation and casts suspicion on any theory claiming to promote the interests of individuals. This clearly poses a threat to the foundation of a democracy that revolves around the idea of individual rights. On the other side, the "monstrosity of the doc- trine that assumes that under all conditions governmental action and indi- vidual liberty are found in separate and independent spheres" ensures that collective social action, however necessary, remains almost unthinkable.[41] The result is an individualism that has been discredited and at the same time rejects its only opportunity for revitalization. Dewey states the issue succinctly in *Individualism Old and New*:

> It is difficult for us to conceive of individualism except in terms of stereotypes derived from former centuries. Individualism has been identified with ideas of initiative and invention that are bound up with private and exclusive economic gain. As long as this conception possesses our minds, the ideal of harmonizing our thought and desires with the realities of present social conditions will be interpreted to mean accommodation and surrender. It will even be understood to signify rationalization of the evils existing in society. A stable recovery of individuality waits upon an elimination of the older economic and political individualism, an elimination which will liberate imagination and endeavor for the task of making corporate society con- tribute to the free culture of its members. Only by economic revision can the sound element in the older individualism—equality of opportunity—be made a reality.[42]

As the means of restoring personal autonomy, dignity, and equality of opportunity to the modern individual, Dewey advocates a thorough rejection of the outworn economic individualism of old and a greater awareness of the corporate nature of modern life and the social context in which all individuals move. The "new" individual will emerge from the democratic commitment to "experimental procedure" which "carries with it the idea of continuous reconstruction of the ideas of individuality and of liberty, in their intimate connection with changes in social relations."[43]

Given his interest in reconstructing the idea of individuality it was inevitable that Dewey would have offered a revised understanding of Emerson's role as the great champion of American individualism. We have already seen that V. F. Calverton, Van Wyck Brooks, and Waldo Frank, among others, believed that Emerson underwrote the acquisitive individualism that Dewey sought to replace; Dewey's interpretation of Emerson serves as an indirect response to these critics. In *Individualism Old and New* Dewey endeavored to reconcile the conflicting observations Emerson had made in "Self-Reliance" about the nature of society, and in the process he claimed him for the new individualism:

> The same Emerson who said that "society is everywhere in conspiracy against its members" also said, and in the same essay, "accept the place the divine providence has found for you, the society of your contemporaries, the connection of events." Now, when events are taken in disconnection and considered apart from the interactions due to the selecting individual, they conspire against individuality. So does society when it is accepted as something already fixed in institutions. But "the connection of events," and "the society of your contemporaries" as formed of moving and multiple associations, are the only means by which the possibilities of individuality can be realized. (122)

In Dewey's telling, the society that Emerson rejects as conspiring against its members is the kind of society imagined by the old individualism. It is a system of fixed institutions that refuses to accommodate the unfolding revelations of individual experience and thus clearly runs counter to everything that Emerson and Dewey cherish. Yet Emerson was also aware that society could be understood in a different way, as the medium through which individuals confront their world and a set of institutions that they constantly revise. This is the vision of society that Emerson urges us to accept, the one that Dewey sees as crucial to the development of a new individualism: "Our garden is our world, in the angle at which it touches our own manner of being. By accepting the corporate and industrial world in which we live, and by thus fulfilling the pre-condition for interaction with it, we, who are also parts of the moving present, create ourselves as we create an unknown future" (123). Though Emerson had little to say about the corporate and industrial world, Dewey found in him the key perception that "individualism" and "society" were not absolutes but ideas the meaning of which must vary with the moving present.

In his essay of 1903 Dewey defined Emerson's project as an effort to restore to the common man that which had been "embezzled" from him. A significant part of this task involved identifying those ideas, insights, and forms of knowledge that had been appropriated as private property by the few and returning them to the "common store." Emerson thus stands not only for the invigoration of the individual but for the revitalization of the community: in both word and deed he declared that what appears to be private insight is in fact a product of accumulated social experience and can attain its full value only as it is shared with the public. Dewey addresses this larger theme in *The Public and Its Problems,* an extended examination of the nature and function of the democratic state. In the course of summarizing his argument about the dependence of "personal intellectual endowment" on the "flow of social intelligence" that proceeds from personal participation in a democratic community, Dewey turns to Emerson in what are the final two sentences of the book:

> Ideas which are not communicated, shared, and reborn in expression are but soliloquy, and soliloquy is but broken and imperfect thought. It, like the acquisition of material wealth, marks a diversion of the wealth created by associated endeavor and exchange to private ends. It is more genteel, and it is called more noble. But there is no difference in kind. . . . We lie, as Emerson said, in the lap of an immense intelligence. But that intelligence is dormant and its communications are broken, inarticulate and faint until it possesses the local community as its medium.[44]

All of Emerson's insights about the nature of the universe, or the dynamics of human interaction with that universe, remained unfulfilled until they were communicated, a task which Emerson himself undertook through his public lectures and collections of essays and which Dewey sought to complete. For Dewey, Emerson both represents and champions the intelligent individual freely and actively participating in a growing democratic community, the kind of individual on which the very future of such a community would depend.

Both James and Dewey embraced Emerson as a figure of enduring importance and drew on his work in pursuing their own speculations. In very specific ways each man saw him as authorizing his own particular understanding of democracy and social experience and, in their tributes at the centennial of his birth, each proceeded to cast Emerson in his own image. This stands in marked contrast to the neglect and rejection Emerson endured at the hands of the vast majority of critics writing between 1880 and 1940, the years in which James and Dewey produced their most important work. Indeed, James and Dewey deserve a significant share of the credit for rescuing Emerson from this oblivion and for carrying forward some of his ideas. Emerson, James, and Dewey shared a deeply felt belief about what it meant to live in a world that was at the same time individualistic, pluralistic, and democratic. Dewey's conclusion to *Freedom and Culture* may serve as an apt accounting of each man's final word:

> We must know that the dependence of ends upon means is such that the only *ultimate* result is the result that is attained today, tomorrow, the next day, and day after day, in the succession of years and generations. Only thus can we be sure that we face our problems in detail one by one as they arise, with all the resources provided by collective intelligence operating in cooperative action. At the end as at the beginning the democratic method is as fundamentally simple and as immensely difficult as is the energetic, unflagging, unceasing creation of an ever-present new road upon which we can walk together. (134)

CHAPTER FOUR

W.E.B. Du Bois and the Implications of Pragmatism

Born in 1868 and productive until his death at the age of ninety-five, W.E.B. Du Bois wore many hats during his long and prolific career. At various times he filled the roles of educator, journalist, civil rights leader, cultural critic, and political agitator. His published works include efforts in history, sociology, poetry, fiction, and theatrical pageants. Even in his more formal treatments of the political and economic condition of black Americans, Du Bois displayed an appreciation of, and a sensitivity to, the spiritual and aesthetic dimensions of human experience. As fully as anyone of his generation, Du Bois deserved the label "man of letters": he never tired in his pursuit of learning and refused to be limited by the artificial barriers between disciplines. The range of his interests and the sheer diversity of his writings alone should have ensured him prominent status in any accounting of American intellectual life, yet few scholars have endeavored to locate his work in that broader context. Instead, most Du Bois scholarship focuses on his debate with Booker T. Washington, his work as a founding member of the NAACP, his theory of races, or his advocacy of "Pan-Africanism."

Though Du Bois certainly merits attention for his efforts in these fields, the effect of this attention has been to pigeonhole his work as race-specific, of importance primarily to those interested in issues of African American history. Not only has this obscured Du Bois's contributions to American intellectual and cultural history, but it has effectively declared that the subjects he explored—the manifestations of "the problem of the color-line" in all areas of American life—have little bearing on the way that history is understood. Both of these conditions are regrettable, particularly since Du Bois was uniquely situated to bring the concerns of black Americans to bear on the "main streams" of intellectual and cultural discourse. His reflections on the interests, achievements, and frustrations of black Americans parallel, in both form and content, the work of many of his contemporaries, including the pragmatism of William James and John Dewey, the educational philosophy of Dewey, the radical pacifism of Randolph Bourne, and the progressivism of Walter Lippmann. At the same time, Du Bois worked to broaden these discussions through his unflagging attention to the consequences of racism. To consider Du Bois in this context is to begin to consider the ways in which the experiences of black Americans both challenge and illuminate these prominent modes of American thought.

It was a desire to meet just this challenge that motivated Arnold Rampersad's valuable study of Du Bois's "art and imagination." Puzzled by the ongoing neglect of Du Bois's contributions to American intellectual history, Rampersad set out to fill that "void of commentary" with an account of his "extraordinary and virtually indefinable power as a thinker and an artist." Noting his commitment to "the necessity of liberal learning, the value of culture, the importance of a leading class, (and) the spirituality of life," Rampersad goes on to observe that Du Bois brought to the issue of race relations in America a "peculiar synthesis" of liberal ideas that had its roots in "various elements of the teachings of Calvin, Carlyle, Emerson, and Matthew Arnold." Moreover, Du Bois wrestled with the same paradox that had driven American thought since the time of John Winthrop, a paradox represented at various moments in American history by the seemingly contrary pairing of puritanic restraint with democratic assertiveness, humility with egocentric individualism, and a code of self-sufficiency with "the democratic need for social liberalism and generosity."[1] By viewing Du Bois's career as a struggle to reconcile this paradox in its many manifestations, Rampersad points the way to further study of his contributions to American intellectual history.

Building on Rampersad's essentially ground-breaking effort, Cornel West cast Du Bois as a key player in his "Genealogy of Pragmatism," a lineup that begins with Emerson, William James, and John Dewey, and spreads out to include Reinhold Niebuhr, Sidney Hook, Lionel Trilling, and Richard Rorty. West portrays pragmatism as the most vital and influential tradition in American thought, a tradition—defined by its commitment to the ideals of democracy and individual freedom—that has ranged broadly across the fields of literary and cultural criticism, political theory, religious studies, and philosophy.[2] At the same time, West points to a "crisis" in the pragmatic tradition, a persistent blindness to the ways in which racism, sexism, and imperialism have denied many people the chance to share in the ideals that America has promised. Highlighting its "unashamedly moral emphasis and its unequivocally ameliorative impulse," West aims to re-imagine American pragmatism in a way that responds to this blindness and that serves as a more responsive agent of social, political, and cultural change.

Within this scheme West turns to Du Bois as providing both an illustration of this crisis and a model of response to it (138). Though working very much in the tradition of Emerson and James, Du Bois also had a keen awareness of the blindness that restricted their vision. From the vantage of what might ironically be termed this "privileged insight," Du Bois "provides American pragmatism with what it sorely lacks: an individual perspective on the impetus and impediments to individuality and radical democracy" that has grown out of his experience as a black American (147). Indeed, West concludes that, for Du Bois, "an Emersonian culture of creative democracy had become a mere chimera" once he recognized that "a racist, sexist, and multinational capitalist America had no potential whatsoever to realize the pragmatist ideals of individuality and radical democracy" (149). Du Bois's task, then, and the task of other "mid-century pragmatic intellectuals" who faced this dilemma, was to restore this potential by creating a pragmatism that would openly confront this crisis. In West's telling, Du Bois provides a reality check for the American intellectual tradition, a reminder that rhetoric and ideals must remain in touch with actual experience.[3]

West's argument is provocative, and the eclectic nature of his genealogy suggests important new ways of thinking about the tradition of pragmatism in American thought.[4] In particular, his placing Du Bois within that tradition is an important step in the process of reassessing his place in American intellectual history. However, West paints only a partial portrait. While claiming that Du Bois both subverted and revised the pragmatism of Emerson, James, and Dewey, West has little to say about how and where Du Bois actually engaged their ideas in his work. To be sure, Du Bois left few signposts pointing to such moments, but his work is nonetheless replete with passages that bear a striking similarity to the work of his liberal pragmatist predecessors. In the second of his three autobiographies he describes his general vocation in terms that recall both Emerson and James: "It had always been my ambition to write; to seek through the written word the expression of my relation to the world and of the world to me."[5] His exploration of the many questions raised by the American commitment to "democracy" and "individualism," and his understanding of the roles that education and politics should play in American life, locate him squarely within the broadly defined tradition of pragmatism articulated by Emerson and refined by James and Dewey.[6] Du Bois demonstrated not only the relevance of pragmatism to black Americans but the important lessons black America could teach pragmatism.[7]

The influence of William James is only one of the many aspects of Du Bois's career that have been inadequately addressed by scholars. As a student at Harvard from 1888 to 1892, Du Bois studied philosophy with James, wrote a thesis on ethics under his direction, and cultivated an acquaintance that lasted until James's death in 1910. James provided Du Bois with a letter of introduction to his brother Henry, then living in England, and, after reading *Souls of Black Folk* upon its publication in 1903, sent a copy to Henry praising it as a "decidedly moving book." Du Bois also recruited James to serve on an advisory board he had set up for a proposed *Encyclopedia Africana,* although, for financial reasons, the project lay dormant until 1961. The clearest evidence of Du Bois's indebtedness to James, however, can be found in his letters and autobiographical writings, where his references to his Harvard mentor convey a strong sense of both gratitude and admiration. Remembering James as "my friend and guide to clear thinking," Du Bois identified three aspects of James's influence that were of lasting significance to his own career: James's role in guiding his vocational path, his developing theory of pragmatism, and his commitment to an inclusive and progressive vision of democracy. Each of these combined to help form the foundation of the entire corpus of Du Bois's work.[8]

As an undergraduate at Fisk University Du Bois had devoted special attention to the study of philosophy, and he sought admission to Harvard in part because he hoped to make a career as a professional philosopher. Reflecting on his early interest in philosophy, Du Bois recalled: "It opened vistas. It made me determined to go further in this probing for truth. Eventually it landed me squarely in the arms of William James at Harvard, for which God be praised." Du Bois was grateful to James, however, not for pointing the way to the philosopher's guild but for redirecting his energies. James recognized that his student's interest in probing for the truth lacked a specific focus, a context without which that search would be little more than an academic exercise. After tactfully suggesting that it would be difficult for Du Bois actually to make a living as a philosopher, James encouraged him to turn his attention to "United States history and social problems."[9] Clearly, James saw that Du Bois was divided between his passion for the ideals and achievements of Western philosophy and his awareness of the obstacles barring his own full participation in the culture which that philosophy aimed to describe. As Du Bois recalled in 1939, concluding with words that echo both James and Emerson, "I was extremely emotional on the race problem while I was at Harvard and my emotion was curbed by the philosophy of William James and the historical research under [Albert Bushnell] Hart. They did not quench; they directed it. . . . I did not want to be a historian. I wanted to be an unhampered intelligence, but history pointed a path."[10] Heeding James's advice and encouragement, Du Bois merged his emotion on "the race problem" with his quest for philosophical truth and evolved a probing analysis of the conditions that separated the ideals of Western culture from the actual experience of those who lived within it.

While James directed Du Bois toward the study of social problems in part because he did not see him making a good philosopher, this turn represented for both men less an abandonment of philosophy itself than a change of focus. At the time that Du Bois enrolled in Harvard, the discipline of philosophy in America was undergoing something of a revolution. Men such as James, Josiah Royce, and Charles Peirce questioned many of the premises of nineteenth-century philosophy—especially its commitment to absolutism, determinism, and epistemology—and challenged the very understanding of philosophy that Du Bois had brought with him from Fisk.[11] James, in particular, was devoted to reconnecting philosophy with lived experience and ensuring that philosophical systems respected individual circumstances rather than being imposed upon them as absolute structures. In this context, James might have imagined Du Bois's study of social problems as more an extension of philosophy than an alternative to it.

For his part, Du Bois found much in James's philosophy that would help shape his own work, and in turning his focus toward social problems he did not turn away from the ideas of his teacher. In a third autobiography, Du Bois recalls the good fortune that allowed him to become "a devoted follower of James at the time he was developing his pragmatic philosophy," and refers to James as "my salvation" because he "guided me out of the sterilities of scholastic philosophy to realist pragmatism."[12] Though James would not begin formal work on *Pragmatism* until 1905—during Du Bois's time at Harvard he was busy completing his *Principles of Psychology*—he had already begun fleshing out the ideas that would animate the later work. And, indeed, by "realist pragmatism" Du Bois has in mind the whole intricate mixture of pluralism, radical empiricism, and pragmatism that had characterized James's thought since the 1880s, when he began the essays that would make up *The Will to Believe*. Du Bois's Philosophy IV notebook offers a portrait of James at work, introducing ideas that he would later develop in *Pragmatism* while also discussing those central to pluralism and radical empiricism. Mixed in with these notes are Du Bois's own, appreciative reflections on James's ideas, and it is clear that he followed these lectures quite carefully.[13] Throughout his work Du Bois can be seen applying the lessons he learned from James, demanding that America accept its pluralistic nature and admit the experiences and contributions of its black citizens into its understanding of itself.

Part of the attraction of James's philosophy for Du Bois was the generous democratic faith that accompanied it, indeed, that seemed to grow out of it. In "Harvard and Democracy," an unpublished essay of 1925, Du Bois lamented that, with the passing of James, "who belonged to the world," Harvard no longer enjoyed "that clear, fine vision of democracy" which had so distinguished its finer moments.[14] Outspoken in his opposition to imperialism, his support of women's suffrage, and his condemnation of lynch law in the South—positions that seemed to belie his elite social standing— James represented the very combination of intellectual achievement and political commitment for which Du Bois yearned. As Arnold Rampersad suggests, James's appeal to Du Bois was rooted in a seductive mixture of sentiment, intellect, ideals, and personal flamboyance; James "validated the integrity of ideas and traditions that might otherwise have been discredited by men who, with the best of intentions, could not convincingly apply them to the realities dominating the thought of a young black man like Du Bois."[15] On more than one occasion Du Bois would remark that his own "attention from the first was focused on democracy and democratic development and upon the problem of the admission of my people into the freedom of democracy."[16] Through his work and example, James not only provided Du Bois with some of the tools necessary to examine this problem, but also stood as proof that, in the process, the political, intellectual, and emotional need not be relegated to separate spheres.

To be sure, Du Bois did not always work within the orbit prescribed by James's ideas. Summarizing his career in the second autobiography he wrote—at the age of seventy-two—Du Bois recalled that, after World War I, he had revised his Jamesian pragmatism through his study of Freud and Marx. Abandoning, at least in part, his attempts to win recognition for American blacks based upon their intellectual and cultural achievements, he adopted an increasingly international perspective, one which emphasized the responsibility of capitalism and imperialism for the suffering of the "darker races" around the world.[17] While not an outright rejection of the culture that James represented, Du Bois's turn did suggest that he found that culture to be irrelevant as long as it remained inaccessible to black Americans. Still, he always returned to James as the first and most important influence on the work he chose to pursue, and from his Harvard commencement address on "Jefferson Davis as a Representative of Civilization" in 1890 through his commentary on the release from prison of Earl Browder, general secretary of the American Communist party, in 1942, that influence is richly evident.

If the lines connecting Du Bois and James are fairly clear, those connecting Du Bois with Emerson are much more elusive. Du Bois owned a number of anthologies of American literature, each containing a generous sampling of Emerson's writings, and he used selections from Emerson—as well as from Carlyle, Thoreau, Tennyson, and others—as epigraphs for many of his *Crisis* essays. For the most part, however, Du Bois appeared to lump Emerson in with the other literary figures who served as generic representatives of the "commonwealth of culture" to which he himself aspired. In none of his published work does he directly address Emerson or any of his writings, and the exhaustive microfilm collection of his unpublished papers is also silent on this point. Still, given his New England upbringing, his Harvard education (which included studying with Barrett Wendell), and his passion for the ideals that Emerson did so much to define, it is likely that Du Bois read Emerson, and read him with some care. In addition, Du Bois certainly got a good deal of his Emerson at second hand. As I have argued above, James found in Emerson support for the most important elements of his own thought, and it was these, in turn, that struck such a chord with Du Bois. In his reflections on the way in which the particular experience of black Americans illuminated such cherished American values as "individualism" and "democracy," Du Bois put himself directly in the line that passed from Emerson through William James. In the process he demonstrated that that tradition was more than the collection of detached musings and high-sounding nonsense that many critics were making it out to be.

Du Bois's long and productive life presents a special challenge to those looking for continuity in his career. He was committed to the full integration of blacks into American society, yet made perhaps his most lasting contribution by articulating a vision of black nationalism; he was a fierce defender of folk culture with a professed passion for the high culture of England and France; and he was an advocate of the downtrodden while investing many of his hopes and aspirations with the "talented tenth." No single one of the ideological labels that he adopted throughout his life—progressive, Marxist, socialist, Pan-Africanist—describes more than isolated fragments of his thought. As his longtime friend and literary executor Herbert Aptheker observed, above all else "Du Bois was a Du Boisite." Yet, though his "political affiliations or affinities varied as times changed, as programs altered, and as he changed," the defining mark of his thought remained constant: "All his life Du Bois was a radical democrat."[18]

Beginning with Aptheker's assessment, Manning Marable has looked at Du Bois's career and concluded that the "central thesis" connecting all of his work was a commitment to "cultural pluralism" (36). While Marable is correct to identify this as the cornerstone of Du Bois's work—and to point to James as one of its sources—it is important to see the way in which Du Bois's understanding of both pluralism and culture gradually evolved. As reflected in the descriptions of his early interest in philosophy, Du Bois for a time subscribed to the idea that Truth and Beauty were absolute values which existed somewhere "out there," and that "culture" was the path one followed in order fully to enjoy those values. His earliest aspirations were to find the entrance to this path and join in the pursuit of all that was beautiful and true. Even after enrolling in Harvard and coming under the tutelage of James, Du Bois continued to see culture as something to which one sought admission and through which one came to a finer appreciation of certain fixed ideals. In an address to the National Colored League of Boston in 1891, he urged his audience to join in the pursuit of culture because "Truth, Beauty and Virtue are ends worth attaining."[19] While sincere in offering these worthy ideals to the general population, Du Bois was principally motivated at the time by his own burning desire to gain admission to "the kingdom of culture," a kingdom that promised him intellectual equality, spiritual sustenance, and full participation in the grand human experiment.

It was in this context that Du Bois was first introduced to James's pluralism. At the beginning of his Philosophy IV notebook, Du Bois transcribed James's admonition that we have "no *a priori* right to exclude any sentient being" from our conception of the universe, a principle that James identified as the driving force of his own work.[20] James offered pluralism as an alternative to absolutism, arguing that any adequate philosophical system must begin with a broad appreciation of the varieties of individual experience rather than a fixed understanding of the nature of reality against which those individual experiences were measured. As James observed in his address at the Emerson centenary, pluralism enjoyed its fullest affirmation in Emerson's abiding faith in the inherent dignity of the individual and the value of each "individual angle of observation on the universe." It was this faith that Du Bois inherited from James and molded into the guiding principle of his own life's work.

Du Bois initially understood pluralism to be a variation on individualism, a promise that any individual sufficiently inclined and adequately prepared could enter the kingdom of culture and share in the ideals it offered. As he became increasingly aware that he was in fact seeking admission to a restricted club, Du Bois was forced to acknowledge that, rather than being welcomed into a pluralistic universe, he was to be one of those sentient beings whose "conditions and ideals" were always judged beyond the pale. His desire—and the frustrations he began to meet in pursuing it— is best captured in this well-known passage from *The Souls of Black Folk:*

> I sit with Shakespeare and he winces not. Across the color line I move arm and arm with Balzac and Dumas, where smiling men and welcoming women glide in gilded halls. From out the caves of evening that swing between the strong-limbed earth and the tracery of stars, I summon Aristotle and Aurelius and what soul I will, and they come all graciously with no scorn nor condescension.[21]

Du Bois embraced the achievements of Western culture that his education had taught him to value, but he saw that his full participation in that culture was blocked by its refusal to validate the gifts and abilities of a member of the Negro race. Stunned by the incongruity that he could sit with Shakespeare but not at the front of the bus, Du Bois turned his enormous critical energies from the quest for Truth and Beauty to an analysis of the "Negro Problem."[22]

By his own account, Du Bois's awareness of the pervasive nature of American racism was rather slow in developing. He observed in *Dusk of Dawn* that, as a child growing up in Great Barrington, Massachusetts, he was only vaguely aware that his being black was an issue of significance. Similarly, his recollections of life at Fisk and Harvard suggest that his race caused him little more than the occasional inconvenience. Only after returning from Europe in 1894, where he had spent two years studying at Friedrich Wilhelm University in Berlin, did he begin to confront the full extent of racial prejudice in America, and even then he apprehended it primarily as an obstacle to his own individual aspirations: "What the white world was doing, its goals and ideals, I had not doubted were quite right. What was wrong was that I and people like me and thousands of others who might have my ability and aspiration, were refused permission to be a part of this world" (573–74). Not yet ready to demand that the terms of cultural discourse be changed, Du Bois sought only to gain admission to the discussion.

Du Bois's initial efforts at analyzing the Negro Problem in American society thus focused on the conditions that precluded blacks like himself from sharing in the opportunities and achievements of that society: How did it come to pass that a Harvard Ph.D., who had studied in Europe, is deemed both legally and socially subordinate to an illiterate white cracker from Georgia? In "Of the Sons of Master and Man," first published in 1901 and revised for *The Souls of Black Folk,* Du Bois lamented the lack of contract between the "best" of both races:

> [T]here is almost no community of intellectual life or point of transference where the thoughts and feelings of one race can come into direct contact and sympathy with the thoughts and feelings of the other. . . . Between [the best element of the black race] and the best element of the whites, there is little or no intellectual commerce. . . . Here is a land where, in the higher walks of life, in all the higher striving for the good and noble and true, the color-line comes to separate natural friends and co-workers; while at the bottom of the social group, in the saloon, the gambling-hall, and the brothel, that same line wavers and disappears. (488–90)

As a degree-bearing member of the intellectual elite, Du Bois clearly thought himself to be among the best that the black race had to offer, and he was frustrated that white society persisted in judging him as if he were no different than those at the bottom of the social ladder. While he quickly moved beyond the narrow elitism of this perception, it nonetheless represents the beginning of his interest in civil rights and was the fundamental motivation for his earliest efforts toward improving the lot of black Americans.[23]

If Du Bois learned a hard lesson about the obstacles that separated him from the company of Emerson and James, his response to that situation demonstrated the remarkable resilience of his faith in their principles. James had held forth on the virtues of pluralism not only because it captured the democratic spirit of fairness and equity but because it was essential to the happiness, well-being, and completeness of the entire society; it was in equal parts a responsibility, a necessity, and a cause for celebration. Suspecting that direct appeals to America's moral duty to its black citizens would meet with little success, Du Bois concentrated instead on popularizing the cultural achievements of black Americans and the vital contributions they could make to the health of American society. Whereas James had argued that any view of human experience was impoverished to the degree that it failed to account for individual perspectives on that experience, that is, that it failed to be pluralistic, Du Bois focused on correcting one crippling example of such a failure. In the process he aimed to demonstrate not only that American society was the poorer for its exclusion of blacks, but that the experiences and achievements of black folk contained the seeds of American redemption.[24] He outlined this claim in "Of Our Spiritual Strivings," the initial chapter of *Souls:* "there are to-day no truer exponents of the pure human spirit of the Declaration of Independence than the American Negroes. . . . all in all we black men seem the sole oasis of simple faith and reverence in a dusty desert of dollars and smartness" (370).

In pursuing his goal of cultural pluralism in this manner, Du Bois confronted a sticky dilemma. If he focused his energies on promoting black pride and the achievements of the black race as a whole, he fell into just the trap he was trying to avoid: an argument built on race-specific qualities rather than pure individual potential. However, his own experience had taught him that the color line was etched so deeply in the American landscape that it was futile to expect individual blacks to transcend racial barriers and be judged on their own merits. Unfazed, Du Bois followed a two-tiered approach, highlighting the general characteristics of the race as a context for individual achievement, and pointing to individual achievement as a way of raising the dignity of the race. On the one hand, he argued that blacks possessed special qualities *as a race* that were vital to the future well-being of American society, and that individual blacks should thus be welcomed into full membership in that society. On the other hand, he offered the achievement of individual blacks as proof that the race as a whole deserved equal recognition and respect. In *The Souls of Black Folk* Du Bois offered a rough sketch of what the practice of pluralism might accomplish for blacks and for the white world beyond: "the rich and bitter depth of [black people's] experience, the unknown treasures of their inner life, the strange rendings of nature they have seen, may give the world new points of view and make their loving, living, and doing precious to all human hearts" (438).

Du Bois first explored the "new point of view" that blacks might bring to American society in "Jefferson Davis as a Representative of Civilization," his 1890 Harvard commencement address. Taking pains to portray Davis himself as a noble figure, Du Bois was primarily interested in "the type of civilization which his life represented," a civilization based on "the idea of the strong man" toward whose development modern history had long been

striking. As "a typical Teutonic hero," Davis stood for a society founded on
the idea of "individualism coupled with the rule of might," a society that
made virtues out of murdering Indians, waging a disgraceful war with
Mexico, and defending slavery. While providing "a field for stalwart manhood and heroic character," such a civilization also fostered a climate of
"moral obtuseness and refined brutality." In short, Davis stood for a civilization that promoted "the advance of a part of the world at the expence of
the whole." Though "the world has needed and will need its Jefferson
Davises," such a type is "incomplete and never can serve its best purpose
until checked by its complementary ideas."[25]

These "complementary ideas," Du Bois went on, were best developed in
the experience of the Negro, who stood in a unique position to correct
civilization's too-narrow devotion to the Teutonic Strong Man:

> The Teutonic met civilization and crushed it—the Negro met civilization
> and was crushed by it. The one was the hero the world has ever worshipped,
> who gained unthought of triumphs and made unthought of mistakes; the
> other was the personification of dogged patience bending to the inevitable,
> and waiting. In the history of this people, we seek in vain the elements of
> Teutonic deification of Self, and Roman brute force, but we do find an idea
> of submission apart from cowardice, laziness or stupidity, such as the world
> never saw before. This is the race which by its very presence must play a part
> in the world of tomorrow; and this is the race whose rise, I contend, has
> practically illustrated an idea which is at once the check and complement of
> the Teutonic Strong Man. It is the doctrine of the Submissive Man—given to
> the world by strange coincidence, by the race of whose rights, Jefferson Davis
> had not heard. (812–13)

It was William James who had suggested to Du Bois that a system that
focused its energies on pursuing a single ideal effectively forfeited any claim
to completeness or wholeness and tended to the grotesque. In the case of
Jefferson Davis and the Teutonic Strong Man, Du Bois takes James's analysis to the level of Western, and in particular American civilization. Poisoned by its singular devotion to this blend of individualism and brute
force, America risks "abnormal development" and can regain its balance
only by embracing the qualities of submission that have supposedly been
the province of its black citizens. Du Bois's summary of how this might
work reveals just how deeply he was influenced by James's idea of pluralism:

> What then is the change made in the conception of civilization, by adding to
> the idea of the Strong Man, that of the Submissive Man? It is this: the
> submission of the strength of the strong to the advance of all—not in mere

aimless sacrifice, but recognizing the fact that, "To no one type of mind is it given to discern the totality of Truth," that civilization cannot afford to lose the contribution of the very least of nations for its full development.

Du Bois is clearly paraphrasing James here, and his words bear a striking resemblance to the passage in "On a Certain Blindness in Human Beings" where James writes: "neither the whole of truth nor the whole of good is revealed to any single observer, although each observer gains a partial superiority of insight from the peculiar position in which he stands." However, James did not write this piece until 1896, six years after Du Bois delivered his address, and it is likely that Du Bois was drawing instead on James's lectures for Philosophy IV where, as we have seen, James had devoted considerable time to defining his vision of pluralism. Sharing James's belief that "the facts and worths of life need many cognizers to take them in," Du Bois committed himself to the task of explaining why the perspective of a previously excluded group of cognizers was essential to the full development of American civilization.[26]

While Du Bois's address shows the guiding influence of James, it also echoes certain passages in Emerson. In chapter 3 I noted the connection between Emerson's understanding of individualism and James's concept of pluralism; it is thus not surprising that Du Bois's working definition of pluralism recalls, as well, Emerson's assertion that "no sentence will hold the whole truth."[27] For Emerson, as for James and Du Bois, each individual perspective on reality contributed to the overall understanding of human experience, and the development of any human society depended on the variety of perspectives granted admission. Emerson, too, recognized the tendency of society to elevate a particular set of ideas and values to the exclusion of others, and to concentrate these in certain representative individuals. In *Representative Men* he offers portraits of six individuals who typified particular ideals or movements, highlighting not only what was gained but what was lost through their narrow concentration of a single force. Throughout, Emerson stresses the need for a variety of perspectives representing a full range of ideas: "The centripetence augments the centrifugence. We balance one man with his opposite, and the health of the state depends on the see-saw" (628).

The parallels between Du Bois's assessment of Davis and Emerson's understanding of representative men are most evident when we turn to the latter's essay, "Napoleon; or, the Man of the World." Emerson frankly admired Napoleon's ability to overcome obstacles and follow the dictates of his will, the effective way in which he combined "animal force and insight . . . the natural and the intellectual power" (730). At the same time, he felt that Napoleon was "singularly destitute of generous sentiments" and served as a warning about "the power of intellect without conscience" (743–44). Like Jefferson Davis, who demonstrated the excesses as well as the successes of the doctrine of the Strong Man, Napoleon excelled in both the virtues and the vices of the ideal he represented. Both men embodied an aggressive selfishness that subordinated the aspirations of the many to the achievement of the few, and each stood as proof that a healthy society must not limit itself to developing a single ideal or point of view. In appending his own chapter to Emerson's *Representative Men,* Du Bois offered the unique perspective of black Americans as the first step toward realizing the pluralistic vision of William James.

Du Bois would return to this point many times in his career, each time refining his sense of what was unique in the black experience and how it might help restore American society to health. In *The Gift of Black Folk,* a volume he contributed to a Knights of Columbus series that promoted awareness of ethnic diversity, he surveyed the history of black life in America and highlighted the achievements in such areas as politics, education, music, literature, science, and military service.[28] It is in the chapter on "The Gift of the Spirit," however, that Du Bois states unequivocally what he takes to be the most important gift that blacks have to offer America, a gift that has yet to be either appreciated or accepted. After a brief sketch of black religious life in which he betrays his discomfort with the influence of some forms of religion in the black community, Du Bois concludes on an affirmative note:

> [B]ehind the half childish theology of formal religion there has run in the heart of black folk the greatest of human achievements, love and sympathy, even for their enemies, for those who despised them and hurt them and did them nameless ill. . . . they have been good and true and pitiful to the bad and false and pitiless and in this lies the real grandeur of their simple religion, the mightiest gift of black to white America. (337)

As he had in the address on Jefferson Davis and in *The Souls of Black Folk,* Du Bois here suggests that the essence of the black experience in America, the experience of slavery and oppression and systematic persecution, has nurtured the very qualities that America needs to embrace if it is to move beyond its legacy of enslavement and oppression. He continues:

> [T]he black man has brought to America a sense of meekness and humility which America never has recognized and perhaps never will. . . . it has become almost characteristic of America to look upon position, self-

assertion, determination to go forward at all odds, as typifying the American spirit. . . . it is in many of its aspects a dangerous and awful thing. It hardens and hurts our souls, it contradicts our philanthropy and religion; and here it is that the honesty of the black race, its hesitancy and heart searching, its submission to authority and its deep sympathy with the wishes of the other man comes forward as a tremendous, even though despised corrective. (339)

Pointing to the unique insight of the race rather than that of individual blacks, Du Bois is urging America to recognize itself as a pluralism of cultures, to embrace a variety of ideals and points of view in an effort to correct its narrow commitment to aggressive individualism and self-assertion. Not only should this mighty gift of black folk, developed over centuries of suffering and mistreatment, be seen as a way to bring American society into balance, it should be recognized as the only hope America has of saving its soul and achieving its full promise.

For Du Bois, black folk would contribute to the spiritual renewal of America on a number of levels. In religion they would stand as "the last and terrible test of the ethics of Jesus Christ," a constant reminder to American Christians that they must be ever vigilant in their response to the gospel; in politics as well, black folk would provide a "peculiar test of white profession," ensuring that the vital ideals of democracy did not wither away through unfulfilled promises. And in "Criteria of Negro Art" Du Bois moves into a third area, arguing that a black aesthetic is called on to counter the increasingly materialistic trend in American culture.[29] He begins by recounting his visit to the land of Scott's "Lady of the Lake" and the romantic idyll he enjoyed wandering in the peaceful forest. All too soon, however, the mood was broken by a "rush of excursionists," mostly "loud and strident" Americans, whose behavior captures for Du Bois the essential perversity of American attitudes toward culture and toward life:

> They all tried to get everywhere first. They pushed other people out of the way. They made all sorts of incoherent noises and gestures so that the quiet home folk and the visitors from other lands silently and half-wonderingly gave way before them. They struck a note not evil but wrong. They carried, perhaps, a sense of strength and accomplishment, but their hearts had no conception of the beauty which pervaded this holy place.

Du Bois then goes on to ask whether the things that such a people value— fast cars, elaborate estates, expensive clothes, and other forms of conspicuous consumption—are true measures of happiness and success. Answering for an audience composed of members of the Chicago area NAACP, he concludes:

Even as you visualize such ideals you know in your hearts that these are not the things you really want. You realize this sooner than the average white American because, pushed aside as we have been in America, there has come to us not only a certain distaste for the tawdry and flamboyant but a vision of what the world could be if it were really a beautiful world; if we had the true spirit; if we had the Seeing Eye, the Cunning Hand, the Feeling Heart; if we . . . lived in a world where men know, where men create, where they realize themselves and where they enjoy life. It is that sort of a world we want to create for ourselves and for all America. (994–95)

In the latter part of the essay Du Bois stresses the responsibility of black artists to remain loyal to their own aesthetic principles, to produce literature, music, paintings, and architecture that reflected their own special insight into what was beautiful and what gave life value. Here, he is concerned less with the renewal of American values than with correcting the skewed portrait of blacks perpetuated in the work of white artists. At the same time he still sincerely believes that the nature of black experience, once recognized and accepted on its own merit, will not stand alone but rather add to the overall picture of American culture, enhancing it and correcting its failures. In making this point Du Bois urges that we recognize a wider range of expression as being the stuff of art. Just as James had sought to expand the field of philosophical truth by calling attention to the varieties of experience, so does Du Bois hope to broaden the field of beauty: "I remember tonight four beautiful things: The Cathedral at Cologne . . . a village of the Veys in West Africa . . . the Venus de Milo; a single phrase of music in the American South." For Du Bois, the essence of beauty is in its variety, and it is precisely variety that black Americans will bring to American culture:

> The world is full of [beauty]; and yet today the mass of human beings are choked away from it, and their lives distorted and made ugly. . . . Who shall right this well-nigh universal failing? Who shall let this world be beautiful? We black folk may help for we have within us as a race new stirrings; stirrings of the beginning of a new appreciation of joy, of a new desire to create, of a new will to be . . . [bearing with us] a new determination for all mankind. (995)

Throughout his career Du Bois was guided by his belief that, in following its own special insight, the black race would not only elevate itself but would redeem the values and ideals of the wider culture, whether of Harvard, of America, or of the world. At the age of seventy he restated the principle that he had first explored at twenty-two, a principle that had its roots in the work of his most important teacher: "The colored world must be seen as existing not simply for itself but as a group whose insistent cry may yet become the warning which awakens the world to its truer self and its wider destiny" (*Dusk of Dawn*, 680). Appropriating James's pluralism as a pluralism of cultures, Du Bois explained the problem of the color line as an obstacle to white and black aspirations alike. In presenting his solution to that problem, he appealed not only to the wider world's sense of justice but to its enlightened self-interest as well.

While detailing the unique insight provided by the experience of black Americans and the contributions they could make, as a race, to American civilization, Du Bois never lost sight of Emerson's faith that the root of all achievement, all activity, and all significant experience lay in the individual. In "The American Scholar" Emerson had asked: "Is it not the chief disgrace in the world, not to be an unit;—not to be reckoned one character;—not to yield that peculiar fruit which each man was created to bear, but to be reckoned in the gross, in the hundred, or the thousand, of the party, the section, to which we belong; and our opinion predicted geographically, as the north, or the south?" (71). As one whose individual character had always been subsumed under the larger category of his race, Du Bois eagerly joined Emerson in agreeing that this was, indeed, a disgrace. It was a condition, however, that he could not transcend simply by declaring it disgraceful. His own experience had taught him over and again that, whatever his desires, abilities, or achievements, he was before all else a black man. In "The Conservation of Races" he somewhat ruefully observed: "the history of the world is the history, not of individuals, but of groups, not of nations, but of races," a statement that was less an argument for the inherent significance of race than an observation of a practical truth.[30] Desperately wanting his own history to be that of an individual, Du Bois knew that he must first provide a history for his race out of which such an individual might emerge.

While Du Bois's efforts aimed to make the ideals of Emersonian individualism accessible to all Americans, he undertook at the same time a revision of the very idea of individualism, a revision that paralleled similar efforts by James and, especially, John Dewey. As an American black Du Bois realized not only that the culture of individualism held for him an empty promise, but that concepts such as individual rights and freedom had in fact long been used to support the legal practice of oppression and discrimination. As early as the address on Jefferson Davis he was suggesting that the popular understanding of individualism as unhampered self-assertion and freedom from restraint needed to be replaced. In explaining what civilization would gain by "adding to the idea of the Strong Man, that of the Submissive Man," Du Bois cited the fact that "not only the assertion of the I, but also the submission to the Thou is the highest Individualism." This was a submission that served to bind individuals to the community, providing a context that would nurture and give meaning to their strivings. In turn, the spoils of narrow self-assertion, such as social status, power, and wealth, would no longer be recognized as the true measure of an individual's achievement—a possibility left open by Emerson—but would be displaced by the degree to which those efforts promoted the well-being of the group.

Of course, Emerson himself had made much of the virtue of submission and was usually careful to distinguish his understanding of individualism from any aggressive assertion of the I. In such essays as "Self-Reliance," "The Over-Soul," and "Fate," he exclaims with equal emphasis that we must both live from within and heed the voice of the "immense intelligence" in whose lap we lie; throughout his work images of surrender and obedience to a higher force enclose his advocacy of self-reliant individualism. In the opening chapter of *Representative Men* he explicitly recognizes the need for some agency to guard individuals against each other's incursions: while every individual strives to "impose the law of its being on every other creature, Nature steadily aims to protect each against every other" (628). While Emerson had faith that the method of nature, the over-soul, or the breath of the divine will would provide structure and purpose to individual strivings and look after the health of the group, Du Bois required something more severe. Far more explicitly than Emerson, he demanded that this higher individualism, this blend of submission and assertion, be directed toward the interest of the general good, and he leaves Emerson behind when he suggests that the state should serve as the agent of enforcement.

Du Bois's most direct statement of this comes in his biography of John Brown. Though he derives almost all of the biographical material from previously published work, he appends an original and provocative chapter that considers Brown's legacy for the twentieth century. Unlike Jefferson Davis, whose bold individualism served the interests of a privileged few, Brown's act was one of sacrifice, a selfless effort to redeem the American people from the sins of slavery. From Brown's martyrdom and the national cataclysm of civil war that ultimately realized his goal, Du Bois draws this fundamental lesson: "the cost of liberty is far less than the price of repression." Yet in making his case for liberty, Du Bois takes care to point out that this is not the same empty promise inscribed in the Declaration of Independence. Rather, out of Brown's example there "will arise a new interpretation of the word freedom. There must be left a wide individualism and yet no individual must be allowed to infringe upon another's freedom. . . . the future will not be free in the sense that anyone can do what he pleases, but freedom in the larger sense of having his acts work for the best interests of the peoples of the world."[31] Brown thus emerges as Du Bois's answer to Davis, a strong, heroic individual who nonetheless submits his efforts to advancing the good of all: the definitive manifestation of the higher individualism for which Du Bois had called.[32]

This would be a fairly common theme in Du Bois's work of the thirties and forties. Like so many other American intellectuals who were seeking an alternative to the decaying capitalist order, Du Bois was attracted to socialism. He had visited the Soviet Union in 1926 and, like Lincoln Steffens, was convinced that the future worked. Of course, Du Bois was particularly interested in applying the theories of Marx to the problem of the color line, and in addition to exploring this in a variety of articles, he taught a seminar, "Marx and the Negro," at Atlanta University in 1933. In Marx, Du Bois found a map to the relationship he had long posited between economics, politics, imperialism, and racism, and he quickly developed a political stance we might loosely define as democratic socialism. In the revealingly titled "Individualism, Democracy, and Social Control," a speech he delivered in 1944 at Prairie View State College, he again made his case for a reimagined individualism, casting the issue in terms fully consistent with James's pragmatism: "It is always a good thing to reconsider a general idea in times of distress and difficulty because words continually lead us astray." This time, however, Du Bois makes the broader political dimensions of his vision explicit: "You have got to have fullness of individualism. You have got to have individual development carried on by all men. . . . The object of all this is full freedom. Compatible with this is social control. You only get this by sacrifices you will have to make for the advantage of the whole group."[33]

This basic formula serves as the most succinct statement of Du Bois's mature political thought. In a 1938 address at Fisk University he asserted: "Democracy does not and cannot mean freedom. On the contrary it means coercion. It means submission of the individual will to the general will and it is justified in this compulsion only if the will is general and not the will of special privilege." Twelve years later, at the age of eighty-two, he presented his case for socialized medicine before the College of Medicine at the

University of Illinois: "One man can be free; two men cannot. Just as soon as society grows in numbers and intricacy of organization just so soon individual freedom of action must be curtailed. The curtailment . . . can and will lead to many compulsions. But in the end it can and must mean that individual effort will be curbed and conditioned for the common good. The individual must bow to the interests of society."[34]

While in each of these cases Du Bois assumes a rather authoritarian tone, his sense of how individual effort was to be curtailed is far from draconian. Indeed, Du Bois was too much the maverick himself to subscribe to any rigid system of social control, and his emphasis was ever on directing, rather than prohibiting, individual effort. In this, again, he differed only modestly from Emerson, who always preferred the carefully directed flow of initiative to individualism run amok. In fact, Du Bois's sense of the proper balance between the individual and society was fully consistent with that of both William James and John Dewey who, as we have seen, incorporated Emerson's deep faith in the priority of the individual within their own attention to social relations. While James was concerned with how society was to absorb the often competing claims of its constituent individuals, and Dewey offered a "new individualism" that would respond to the need for collective social action, Du Bois, too, envisioned individuals working within and for a larger social unit, enjoying true "freedom of thought" without the misleading distractions of "freedom for private profit-making."[35]

Du Bois's political thought, then, though it assumed different outward forms at different points in his career, remained firmly rooted in this eclectic blend of pluralism, pragmatism, and progressivism.[36] When Dewey asserts that, for Emerson, "democracy is neither a form of government nor a social expediency, but a metaphysic of the relation of man and his experience to nature," he is not only describing his own definition of democracy but that of Du Bois—and James—as well: more than a set of public institutions, democracy must penetrate to the depths of culture, promoting in all areas of human experience "a freedom which is co-operative and a cooperation which is voluntary."[37] The full scope of Du Bois's political and social thought, and its deep resonance with Emerson, James, and Dewey, is suggested by two lengthy meditations on the nature of democratic government, one written in 1917 and the other in 1942. In "Of the Ruling of Men," a moving and richly detailed argument for the full extension of the franchise to women, blacks, and the poor, Du Bois sets forth the "real argument for democracy":

[I]n the people we have the source of that endless life and unbounded wisdom which the rulers of men must have. A given people today may not be intelligent, but through a democratic government that recognizes, not only the worth of the individual himself, but the worth of his feelings and experiences to all, they can educate, not only the individual unit, but generation after generation, until they accumulate vast stores of wisdom. Democracy alone is the method of showing the whole experience of the race for the benefit of the future. . . .

The addition of the new wisdom, the new points of view, and the new interests must, of course, be from time to time bewildering and confusing. . . . The appearance of new interests and complaints means disarrangement and confusion to the older equilibrium. It is, of course, the inevitable preliminary step to that larger equilibrium in which the interests of no human soul will be neglected. These interests will not, surely, be all fully realized, but they will be recognized and given as full weight as the conflicting interests will allow. The problem of government thereafter would be to reduce the necessary conflict of human interests to the minimum.[38]

The next passage is found in Du Bois's comment on the release of Earl Browder from federal prison in 1942. Browder, general secretary of the American Communist party, had received the unusually stiff sentence of four years for a passport violation in 1941 but was released one year later amidst the wartime climate of cooperation between the United States and the Soviet Union. Browder's release spurred Du Bois to these reflections:

Democracy is not simply the right of electing our own rulers; it is not simply the right of working people to have a voice in the conduct of industry. It is a vaster and more inclusive ideal: the right to accumulate and use a great reservoir of human thought and experience out of which people may choose the best policies of government and conduct, and have their choices mean more because the sum of all human knowledge is open to their understanding. It is in thought and concept that real freedom lies: not just a matter of physical movement or the election of officials, either of which could be easily frustrated and meaningless; not even simply economic freedom. Rather, freedom of thought and planning by which the world, with a broad basis of fact and knowledge of experience, can slowly and laboriously work out a way of life for the mass of men.[39]

With Emerson, Du Bois believed that government can only and must only be a collective expression of the entire population it represents; with both Emerson and James he understood that society was fluid and ever-changing, and that a government must be responsive to those changes and the disruptions that accompany them. Du Bois shared James's vision of a plurality of individuals participating in a "social scheme of co-operative work," contributing their own individual experiences to the ongoing experiment of human life. Finally, Du Bois believed with Dewey that democracy must move beyond its commitment to political and economic individualism and focus instead on directing the "collective intelligence" of the people, drawn from their accumulated experience, in a program of "cooperative action."[40] Though keenly aware that the broadly conceived culture of democracy articulated by Emerson, James, and Dewey offered little of immediate value to black Americans—or, in fact, to many white Americans—Du Bois nonetheless cast himself directly in their line of thinking, determined that their vision and his might yet meet.

While Du Bois's understanding of democracy and of the complex relationship between the individual and the society places him clearly within the tradition that I have been tracing, his writings on the function and purpose of education, particularly the education of black Americans, suggests an even deeper connection. Once again, the resonance with James is striking, but Du Bois also echoes Emerson in developing his vision of self-culture and in waging his famous campaign against Booker T. Washington and the Tuskegee philosophy. Indeed, the debate between Du Bois and Washington may be framed, in part, as a clash between two conflicting appropriations of Emerson's thought. Washington articulated a narrow vision of self-reliance that promoted economic individualism and an up-by-your-own-bootstraps approach to improving the condition of black Americans; this was clearly reflected in his emphasis on technical and agricultural training as the primary goal of Negro education. Du Bois, as we have seen, rejected economic individualism and the ethic of self-sufficiency as running counter to the best interests of society, and he saw education as playing a vital role in creating a broad-based democratic culture that would bind individuals of all races to the larger group.

The earliest statement of Du Bois's educational philosophy is the 1891 address "Does Education Pay?" delivered before the National Colored League of Boston. Though clearly a product of Du Bois's youth—it reads in many places like a classroom exercise in late Victorian rhetoric, complete with lofty invocations of Truth, Beauty, and Virtue—this work introduces some of the themes of Du Bois's mature thought on education. The principle argument of the piece is that education—in its ideal form—is the very process of civilization, the "organized continuous effort" through which human beings may come "to realize all that life means." One generation inherits from the previous one "a fund of experience" to which it may add in turn, thereby making the heritage of future generations greater: "life is built on life, truth joined to truth, experience given to experience." And, as the means by which this fund was both improved and distributed, education represents no less than the value of life itself: "it is not only of the greatest use in fulfilling your present life, but it will furnish you a larger, broader life to live."[41]

In this buoyant passage Du Bois is almost certainly drawing on his studies with James, for his words echo James's description of how new experiences and new truths are grafted onto the body of accumulated tradition: "Men's beliefs at any time are so much experience *funded.* But the beliefs are themselves part of the sum total of the world's experience, and become matter, therefore, for the next day's funding operations."[42] For Du Bois, a liberal education is the surest means of access to this fund, a way of sharing in what it offers and participating in its ongoing formation. In making this point, he goes beyond the allusion to James and explicitly invokes Emerson:

> [W]e have, by tradition, by Art, and by Literature, the great heritage of the age, the great conglomerate which we call knowledge; the accumulated experience of millions of human beings like you is yours: men who have had the same thoughts, have striven under the same difficulties—laughed in your joy, and sorrowed in your sorrow. All this the living bequest of a million millions human souls is the property of you, the children of the Nineteenth Century, if you choose to take it. There is none so humble but can say with Emerson:
>
> > "I am the owner of the sphere
> > Of the seven stars and solar year;
> > Of Caesar's hand, and Plato's brain,
> > Of Lord Christ's Heart and Shakespeare's strain."
>
> (3–4)

Like Dewey, Du Bois recognized part of Emerson's project to be the task of "restoring to the common man that which . . . has been embezzled from the common store," namely, the ability of each individual to share in the accumulated wisdom of experience and to participate in its making. Emerson had written that the true mark of genius comes when we recognize images of our own thoughts in those of the past, and that a tradition means nothing unless we actively make it our own. In stressing the importance of liberal education to his audience of young black Americans, Du Bois not only urges them to stake their own claim to this tradition, but challenges them to accept their responsibility for shaping and transmitting this fund of experience to future generations.

Du Bois was aware that many in his audience looked upon liberal education as a frivolous luxury, favoring instead the more "useful" schools of technical and vocational training. Indeed, the task Du Bois set himself of convincing them otherwise served as something of a warm-up for his debate with Washington some years later. By answering an enthusiastic "Yes!" to the question posed in the title, Du Bois hoped to persuade his audience that higher education would provide a valuable return on their investment: "you only realize the possibilities of the world in which you live in just such a degree as you have liberally educated yourselves either in the high school or college, or in the long, careful, and diligent self-culture" (6). Targeting the short-sightedness of those who would focus exclusively on technical training, Du Bois cautions: "Never make the mistake of thinking that the object of being a man is to make a carpenter—the object of being a carpenter is to be a man."[43] These words, which Du Bois would repeat more than a dozen times over the course of his career, call to mind Emerson's admonition that our efforts should aim not to train farmers, but to produce men-who-farm. Eager to recognize the virtues of the hoe and the spade, Emerson nonetheless maintained that the too narrow devotion to a particular task runs counter to "the main enterprise of the world" which is "the upbuilding of a man."[44] Du Bois found Emerson's message to be of special interest in his exploration of the subject of black education, for it affirmed his belief that a system built upon technical training would deny individual blacks full participation in the ongoing creation and accumulation of wisdom.

Du Bois's primary goal, then, was to persuade his audience that the "organized continuous effort" of liberal education was vital not only for their own individual improvement but for the well-being of the race as a whole. After outlining his plan for a system of self-culture, including suggestions for properly chaperoned amusements and a reference to one's "moral duty to see Edwin Booth play 'Hamlet,'" Du Bois concludes his talk with a call to arms: "So tonight the great warm bursting heart of the mother of God is calling us to be men in the race that needs us, in the world that awaits us. Will you do it? Can you do it?

> 'So near is grandeur to our dust,
> So near is God to man;
> When duty whispers low thou must,
> The youth replies—I can.'"

(18)

Du Bois here gives Emerson the final word, quoting the stanza from "Voluntaries" that James would identify as the purest distillation of Emerson's thought. But whereas James focused on the first couplet and its affirmation of man's essential divinity, Du Bois is more interested in the youth's eager acceptance of duty. Nine years later, in a similar context, Du Bois quoted the same passage. Addressing a meeting of black school teachers in Athens, Georgia, he outlined the importance of "cultivating and developing that careful intellectual culture the elements of which you received in school." He then goes on to restate his case for a life-long commitment to liberal learning:

> [T]he truly educated man is he who has learned in school how to study and in life what to study. . . . And this he can do—in spite of sordid surroundings in the absence of all incitements to self-culture, in spite of the demands of home and school and work, he can—you can leave time for self-cultivation and self-development—for the realization of some of the high ideals of your youth—you can do it because others have done it and above all because you *must:* "So near is grandeur to our dust. . . ."[45]

In stressing the importance of the Emersonian ideal of self-culture, Du Bois turns to Emerson himself for the words of encouragement and affirmation necessary to its pursuit. He offers this final image to his audience in the hope that they might accept the challenge of liberal education and go on to serve the needs of the race.

Though Du Bois's educational philosophy shifted in emphasis as he grew older, it remained firmly rooted in the principles he introduced in these early pieces, principles that, in turn, drew on the thought of Emerson and James: liberal education is a responsibility as well as a privilege and demands continuous effort; its ultimate purpose is to produce well-rounded individuals whose experience will contribute to the ongoing accumulation of wisdom; it holds the key to lifting the black race into full participation in the pluralism of cultures; and the exclusive focus on technical training serves to perpetuate a system that views blacks as second-class citizens. Within these parameters Du Bois came to focus more on what blacks would contribute to the commonwealth of culture and less on the opportunities it would bestow upon them. In part, this reflected his gradual acceptance of de facto segregation as a condition within which he had to work. If blacks were going to be excluded from the institutions of American civilization simply because they were black, then Du Bois recognized that he must begin to fight the effects of that isolation from within the excluded race. Even then, however, he advocated no crude racial separatism but sought to portray the black experience as both different from and essential to the dominant white culture.[46]

In "The Talented Tenth" (1903), his most direct appeal to the responsibility of blacks to their own race, Du Bois restates his argument for liberal education within an essentially segregated context:

> If we make money the object of man training we shall develop money makers but not necessarily men; if we make technical skill the object of education, we may possess artisans but not, in nature, men. Men we shall have only as we make manhood the object of the work of the schools—intelligence, broad sympathy, knowledge of the world that was and is, and the relation of men to it—this is the curriculum of that Higher Education which must underlie true life. On this we may build bread winning, skill of hand and quickness of brain, with never a fear lest the child and man mistake the means of living for the object of life.[47]

For Du Bois, the ability of his race to claim its place in the wider world, a place that had long been denied it through a combination of economic, political, and cultural forces, rests on its ability to produce individuals of intelligence and broad sympathy. Such individuals, while segregated, would accumulate their own store of wisdom and experience, accepting, if only temporarily, the condition of American blacks as "a group within a group"; then, as the force of their achievements begin to crack the color line, they would bring the special gifts and insights of their race to bear on the experience of the wider world, achieving in the process a fuller realization of cultural pluralism and an effective undermining of the notion of racial separateness itself.

Du Bois's approach to education thus represents a creative synthesis of Emerson and James, promoting the diligent practice of self-culture as the path to individual improvement and, in turn, putting that individual improvement to work in the task of uplift. In *The Souls of Black Folk* he demonstrated most clearly his allegiance to Emerson's belief that the purpose of education, and indeed of all our strivings, is to draw individuals out of the "calamity" of the masses: "The function of the Negro college, then, is clear: . . . beyond all this it must develop men. Above our modern socialism, and out of the worship of the mass, must persist and evolve that higher individualism which the centres of culture protect; there must come a loftier respect for the sovereign human soul that seeks a freedom for expansion and self-development" (437). And, in *Dusk of Dawn,* he observed that it was through this higher individualism that real equality might be achieved: "when we compare the gift of one human soul with that of another, are we not seeking to measure incommensurable things; trying to lump things like sunlight and music and love? And if a certain shadowy Over-soul can really compare the incomparable with some transcendental yardstick, may we not here emerge into a super-equality of man? At least this I can quite believe" (661). Central to Emerson's work, from *Nature* through the late essays, was a belief that equality among individuals begins with the observation that each may serve as a channel for the divine will animating the universe; Du Bois's path to racial equality through liberal education shares the same point of origination: "it would not do to concenter all effort on economic well-being and forget freedom and manhood and equality. Rather Negroes must live and eat and strive, and still hold unfaltering commerce with the stars" (557).

In James's ideas of pluralism, radical empiricism, and pragmatism, Du Bois found the materials with which to build on this Emersonian foundation. In "The Negro College" (1933) he expands on his earlier observations about the vital contributions blacks can make to politics, religion, and literature, challenging black institutions to produce "the only college which stands for the progress of all": "No system of learning—no university—can be universal before it is German, French, Negro. Grounded in inexorable fact and condition . . . it may seek the universal and haply it may find it—and finding it, bring it down to earth and us."[48] Here, Du Bois recalls James's description of his method as beginning with particulars and treating the universal as "a being of the second order."[49] For James, this was the intersection of pluralism and radical empiricism: any system, whether philosophical, political, or social, must first accommodate individual experience before it can claim to speak for any wider, universal interest. Du Bois, in the context of his commitment to cultural pluralism, argues that the modern system of learning must find its universality first in the particular experience of individual cultures and races. Focusing on the actual experience of life—its facts and conditions—as the only material from which a proper system of education might be built, Du Bois adds another layer to his vision of cultural pluralism, an educational pluralism which strives to keep the universal and the particular working cooperatively for the progress of all.

For Du Bois, education rightly conceived is the most important of all social institutions, and its influence extends well beyond any mere system of schooling. More than an institute for the acquisition of skills or a vehicle for imparting information, even more than a place where one might indulge in the commonwealth of culture, the chief "function of the university" is to be "the organ of that fine adjustment between real life and the growing knowledge of life, an adjustment which forms the secret of civilization." Above all else, human education is a continuous effort to make "that ever necessary combination of the permanent and the contingent—of the ideal and the practical in workable equilibrium."[50] This idea of life as a continuous process of adjusting to new knowledge, of grafting new truths onto the accumulated body of tradition, forms the very core of James's philosophy and is a significant aspect of Emerson's as well. By incorporating it into his vision of education, Du Bois reveals the extent to which their ideas undergirded his own.

Looming in the background of all of Du Bois's writing on education is the history of his disagreement with Booker T. Washington. This disagreement centered not only on the question of which type of education would best serve the needs of black Americans but involved two distinctly different visions of the future of American society.[51] Du Bois favored liberal education because it nurtured individuals of "intelligence and broad sympathy," individuals who were essential to realizing his commitment to cultural pluralism and democratic socialism. In his scheme, the opening up of America, and indeed of the entire Western world, to a fuller realization of black experience would fundamentally alter the values and goals that guided that world. Washington, on the other hand, was a devoted disciple of the captains of industry and a sometimes fierce defender of Western-style industrial capitalism; he looked to technical training to ensure that American blacks would gain access to the kingdom of the invisible hand. Unlike Du Bois, Washington was an outspoken opponent of labor organization, writing contemptuously of the "professional labour agitators" who were committed to destroying the prosperity of happy, hard-working coal-miners. And, while Du Bois's experience abroad endowed him with a deeper appreciation of the cultural, economic, and political lives of the world's peoples, Washington saw the significance of his own international experience somewhat differently: "It was worth the trip to Holland, too, just to get a sight of three or four hundred fine Holstein cows grazing in one of those intensely green fields." Indeed, the thing that most impressed Washington on his travels was the "deference" shown by servants to their masters in England and the degree to which the English class of servants accepted the role for which they had been prepared.[52] With an intense singleness of purpose, Washington called on blacks to cultivate the only intelligence of any lasting value, the intelligence to recognize and secure their place in the capitalist order.

If Du Bois came to Emerson through the expansive air of William James and turn-of-the-century Harvard, Washington evidently encountered the pocket-sized collection of aphorisms favored by Andrew Carnegie and Henry Ford. He refers to Emerson occasionally in his letters and speeches, always in a context that highlights Emerson's commitment to self-reliance. As president of Tuskegee Institute, Washington organized an Emerson Club which met every Tuesday for the purpose of searching "that learned gentleman's sentences" for lessons in self-improvement and self-mastery.[53] Representative of Washington's understanding of Emerson is his 1891 Tuskegee commencement address:

> It is said of Ralph Waldo Emerson, the great philosopher, that at one time one of his friends noticed him standing near a window seemingly intently gazing at something in the distance. When the question was asked, "What are you looking for, Mr. Emerson?" the answer came, "I am trying to find Ralph Waldo Emerson." Ladies and gentlemen . . . I would remind you to remember Emerson's reply. Find yourselves as often as possible.[54]

While this injunction suggests the possibility of a broad field for self-discovery, consistent with Du Bois's open-ended vision of liberal education, Washington quickly narrows the scope, indicating that his idea of self-discovery is closer to the controlled "mastery of self." Rather than a commitment to the life-long experiment of cooperative learning, exploration, and growth, Washington urges his audience to remember that "you must be your own checks, your own spurs, your own props, your own guides."

Washington, of course, encountered a variety of dissenters from his plan. In addition to such malcontents as Du Bois and William Monroe Trotter, he faced opposition from more respectable sources, most notably Harvard president Charles William Eliot. Though he greatly admired Washington's efforts and shared his social conservatism (recall Eliot's "discovery" of Emerson's incipient opposition to organized labor), Eliot pleaded with Washington to devote more attention to the academic branches of learning. Fearful of alienating potential benefactors like Eliot, Washington nonetheless held his ground, offering vague assurances that he would consider his suggestions.[55] Interestingly, Washington's expressed attitude toward such criticism calls to mind Emerson's assertion in "The American Scholar" that if "the single man plant himself indomitably on his instincts, and there abide, the huge world will come round to him" (70). For Washington, "the thing to do, when one feels that he has said or done the right thing, and is condemned, is to stand still and keep quiet. If he is right, time will show it" (232). Of course, as Louis Harlan and others have noted, Washington's way of keeping quiet included often extraordinary efforts to stifle his critics through behind-the-scenes machinations. Still his fierce, indeed righteous determination suggests the variety of ways in which Emerson's call for self-trust could be interpreted.

Central to Washington's vision, then, is a rather narrow interpretation of Emersonian self-reliance. Indeed, his entire argument for the priority of industrial education for black Americans, as presented in *Up from Slavery,* is consistent with a carefully drawn selection of Emerson's observations on the value and meaning of work and the function of education. In summing up the experience of slavery, Washington not only finds room to appreciate its introduction of Western agricultural techniques to otherwise backward Africans, but suggests that its most regrettable legacy was that it "took the spirit of self-reliance and self-help out of the white people" (17). With the misguided era of reconstruction having sapped blacks of this self-reliance as well, Washington sees his mission—and the mission of black education generally—to be one of restoration. That same spirit of self-help which had seen blacks through slavery was now called on to ensure that they would enjoy economic security within the capitalist order. The surest path to this was education along the Hampton-Tuskegee model.

In almost every way, Washington's plan for education was the antithesis to Du Bois's. Where Du Bois saw the brick-mason as raw material for the well-rounded individual, Washington valued the brick-mason as an end in himself. In "The Talented Tenth" Du Bois made his case for educating the black race from the top down; in *Up from Slavery* Washington argued just the opposite: "No race can prosper till it learns that there is as much dignity in tilling a field as in writing a poem. It is at the bottom of life that we must begin, not at the top" (220). While Du Bois found Emerson to support his broad vision of liberal education, Washington's narrowness of purpose focused on Emerson's eloquent testaments to the value of life on the farm and the dignity of manual labor, to the thinness of an education that is gotten from books, and to the wastefulness of extensive training in dead languages, all observations which he himself made with great zest.[56]

Washington did not care much for books, preferring instead lessons that were drawn out of real life experience: "The older I grow, the more I am convinced that there is no education which one can get from books and costly apparatus that is equal to that which can be gotten from contact with great men and women. Instead of studying books so constantly, how I wish that our schools and colleges might learn to study men and things!" (55). In addition to teaching his students how to bathe, how to brush their teeth, and how to care for their rooms properly, Washington hoped "to give them such practical knowledge of some one industry, together with the spirit of industry, thrift, and economy, that they would be sure of knowing how to make a living after they had left us. We wanted to teach them to study actual things instead of mere books alone" (126). Unlike Emerson, who always qualified such statements as these, and in direct contrast with Du Bois, Washington emphasized the attainment of practical skills and the ability to make a living as an absolute and nearly exclusive end in itself. He had little room in his scheme for such "frivolous" sentiments as those stressed by Du Bois in *Souls:* "the true college will ever have one goal,—not to earn meat, but to know the end and aim of that life which meat nourishes" (420).

Washington's aversion to liberal education carried particular force when he came to the subject of foreign languages. Emerson had once remarked on the absurdity of students devoting "four, or six, or ten years" to the "parsing of Greek and Latin," and Washington seized on this condition as representative of all that was wrong with liberal education. Second only to the apparently ridiculous desire to hold public office, the "craze for Greek and Latin learning" among blacks during the 1870s was a measure of the failure of Reconstruction (80). Washington is relentless in his attacks on what he considers a pathetic symbol of wastefulness: "In fact, one of the saddest things I saw during the month of travel which I have described was a young man, who had attended some high school, sitting down in a one-room cabin, with grease on his clothing all around him, and weeds in the yard and garden, engaged in studying a French grammar" (122). Nowhere are the limits of Washington's imagination more evident than in his failure to see anything hopeful, anything encouraging, in this scene, a scene which Du Bois, James, or Emerson would have found full of promise and dogged determination.

Ultimately, the disagreement between Washington and Du Bois comes down to the question of whether a commitment to individual achievement, economic self-sufficiency, and the pursuit of practical knowledge was the right program for black Americans. For Washington, the way for blacks to overcome prejudice and discrimination was simple, and in charting this path he offers yet another dig at the ridiculousness of liberal education: "The individual who can do something that the world wants done will, in the end, make his way regardless of his race. One man may go into a community prepared to supply the people there with an analysis of Greek sentences. The community . . . may feel its need of bricks and houses and wagons" (155). To build a better mousetrap, then, is the challenge Washington urges on black Americans, for he believes that once members of his race prove their usefulness, the destructive forces of white racism will crumble before the rational pursuit of economic self-interest. This simple but deep faith defined all of Washington's efforts: "The great human law that in the end recognizes and rewards merit is everlasting and universal" (318).

It was precisely this simple faith that Du Bois rejected, for in his experience this "great human law" was in fact temporal and particular. To rely, as did Washington, on economic self-sufficiency as the sole means of defeating racism was an irresponsible delusion. While the rational pursuit of self-interest might motivate some of the people some of the time, Du Bois found human behavior to be far more complex. His study of economics had taught him that modern capitalism was actually sustained by the exploitation of race and class differences, and was as likely to appropriate as reward meritorious achievement. For Du Bois, the fact that blacks might prove their usefulness as farmers and laborers would guarantee nothing more than their continued confinement to the field and the factory while the rest of the world held commerce with the stars. This was why he emphasized the need to work across a broad front, striving for achievement in the fields of culture and politics as well as economic production. In this lengthy passage from *The Souls of Black Folk,* Du Bois articulates his alternative to Washington's model of industrial education and, in the process, gives full expression to the ideal of cultural pluralism that he adapted from Emerson and James:

To be really true, all these ideals must be melted and welded into one. The training of the schools we need to-day more than ever,—the training of deft hands, quick eyes and ears, and above all the broader, deeper, higher culture of gifted minds and pure hearts. The power of the ballot we need in sheer self-defence,—else what shall save us from a second slavery? Freedom, too, the long-sought, we still seek,—the freedom of life and limb, the freedom to work and think, the freedom to love and aspire. Work, culture, liberty,—all these we need, not singly but together, not successively but together, each growing and aiding each, and all striving toward that vaster ideal that swims before the Negro people, the ideal of human brotherhood, gained through the unfying ideal of Race; the ideal of fostering and developing the traits and talents of the Negro, not in opposition to or contempt for other races, but rather in large conformity to the greater ideals of the American Republic, in order that some day on American soil two world-races may give each to each those characteristics both so sadly lack. (370)

In *Nature,* Emerson challenged Americans to "build, therefore, your own world," a challenge that Du Bois and Washington each took up on behalf of black Americans. Washington's world reflected a narrow interpretation of Emersonian self-reliance, while Du Bois envisioned a pluralism of cultures committed to the ongoing accumulation of knowledge and wisdom. Du Bois was not blind to the obstacles that blacks continued to face in their effort to join such a world. In "Of the Coming of John" he tells the story of a young black man who goes off to college, acquires an appreciation for music, art, and literature, and tries to live according to the principles that his education had taught him to value. However, his achievements fail to protect him from the cruelties of prejudice and he grows increasingly uncomfortable with the taunts and slurs designed to keep him in his place. Upon returning home to rural Georgia, his restlessness and frustration lead to a series of events that culminate in his being lynched.[57] While Washington would have offered this story to illustrate his critique of liberal education—not only is it a waste of time, like studying French and reading novels, but in creating false expectations it can be dangerous as well—Du Bois leaves no doubt that, though tragic, the story of John carries a lesson in perseverance. The only way to break the suppression of black aspirations is to continue struggling against it on all fronts; the risk incurred points to the richness of what is to be gained.

In the opening chapter of *The Souls of Black Folk,* Du Bois declared that his goal was "not to Africanize America, for America has too much to teach the world and Africa"; nor was it to "bleach [the] Negro soul in a flood of white Americanism" because the Negro, too, "has a message for the world." Rather, he "simply wishes to make it possible for a man to be both a Negro and an American . . . a co-worker in the kingdom of culture" (364–65). This vision of cultural pluralism drives all of Du Bois's work; his exploration of its implications for the color line stands as his most important contribution to American thought. Drawing on the ideals of Emerson and James, Du Bois demonstrated that the world they imagined and the world in which he lived need not, indeed must not, remain separate spheres: "I insist that the question of the future is how best to keep these millions from brooding over the wrongs of the past and the difficulties of the present, so that all their energies may be bent toward a cheerful striving and co-operation with their white neighbors toward a larger, juster, and fuller future" (436–37). That Du Bois came, in the last years of his long life, to see this goal as at best a cause deferred does not diminish its urgency. He continued to maintain that the future of America, of Western civilization, and indeed of the world, depended upon its ultimate attainment. In a now somewhat famous journal entry reflecting on the death of his young son Waldo, Emerson wrote: "I am *Defeated* all the time; yet to Victory I am born."[58] Du Bois could well appreciate the spirit of this sentiment—realistic yet hopeful—as it reflected on his lifelong effort to resolve the problem of the color line.

CHAPTER FIVE

Inclusiveness without Redundancy:
William Carlos Williams in the Emersonian Grain

Though recognized by a substantial and diverse body of scholarship, William Carlos Williams has only recently come to receive the kind of critical attention devoted to his modernist contemporaries. Among a generation of poets who came of age with "The Waste Land" and who carried on their work in the shadow of what Hugh Kenner calls "the Pound Era," Williams played the role of yeoman laborer: the poet-doctor from New Jersey who quaintly insisted on leading a "real life" while scribbling his poems on prescription blanks between house calls. In large part, his awkward standing among critics has resulted from the variety of genres in which he worked. The definitive edition of his collected poetry fills three weighty volumes; he also published four novels, numerous plays and short stories, critical essays, philosophical meditations, an autobiography, and an impressionistic history of American culture. However, while critics have paid ample attention to Williams's individual efforts, few have attempted to make sense of his oeuvre as a whole.[1] Apparently taking his cryptic warnings against looking for ideas in his work at face value—"no ideas but in things"—most critics have presented him as a predominantly nonintellectual, if not anti-intellectual figure, whose achievements are best examined piecemeal.

While apparently disavowing any intellectual pretensions, Williams also strove to present himself as a poet who worked, in Emerson's words, with no past at his back. His was an irascibly independent voice, and he eagerly cultivated the image of someone operating beyond any recognizable tradition. With the exception of a few tepid tributes to Whitman, he avoided associating his work with any figure from the past, evidently anxious lest his own work be diminished through the comparison. Williams dedicated himself to throwing off the mindless allegiance to tradition that he saw as crippling the development of American art, and was openly contemptuous of the "intellectuals" who forced individual forms of expression into "schools" for the sake of an imaginary continuity.

Within the last ten years, as scholars have come to examine the broader political, cultural, and intellectual dimensions of literary modernism, Williams has gained—in spite of himself—a modest status as a writer of ideas, a poet with something to say. In his essays on the function of the artist, the priority of the local, and the immediacy of knowledge and experience; in his stories that detail the lives of the poor and working-class patients he served in Rutherford and New York City; in his ambitious and esoteric project of rewriting American history; and, of course, in his poetry, Williams emerges as a serious and articulate intellectual who explored the important issues of his day through a variety of forms.[2] In addition, critics have begun the task of locating Williams's work in a wider literary and intellectual context. Carl Rapp has argued persuasively that, despite his frequent and vehement denunciations of romanticism, Williams's work nonetheless represents an extension of the romantic idealism of Wordsworth, Coleridge, and Emerson. Rapp goes on to claim Emerson as the precursor of Williams's ideas on the form and function of poetry, and suggests other instances in which Williams relies on "Emersonian habits of interpretation." More ambitiously, Stephen Tapscott has located Williams within a tradition that is rooted in Walt Whitman and branches out to include Emerson and John Dewey, a tradition that accommodated both a strenuous artistic freedom and a firm grounding in "the local."[3]

While Tapscott and Rapp have opened the door to a significant reconsideration of Williams's place in American cultural history, few other critics have endeavored to cross that threshold. Some of the most compelling scholarship on American modernism has highlighted the way in which Emerson and William James served as precursors for such figures as Robert Frost, Gertrude Stein, and Wallace Stevens, but no attempt has been made to link Williams with this larger cast.[4] Most notable has been the work of Frank Lentricchia and Richard Poirier, who offer provocative and important suggestions about the sources and the significance of American modernism. In various but complementary ways, Poirier and Lentricchia each construct a tradition that begins with Emerson, passes through James, and reaches fruition in the work of Frost, Stein, Kenneth Burke, and Stevens. For Lentricchia, the key link in this chain is the "pluralism and antinomianism" that James adapted from Emerson and transmitted to the younger generation of poets and intellectuals. Drawing on this source, Stevens and Burke articulated a vigorous and liberating aesthetic that stood in sharp contrast to the restrictive and authoritarian modernism of Eliot and Pound.[5] Like Lentricchia, Poirier sees James as "the point of transmission" linking Emerson to Frost, Stein, and Stevens, each of whom was a student at Harvard during James's tenure. Poirier presents his cast of characters, too, as embodying a vital alternative to Eliot. While the pragmatists saw language as "the instrument of a saving uncertainty and vagueness," Eliot's "potential Emersonianism gave way to the urgency of his personal need for semblances of order and, ultimately, for the God of Anglo-Catholicism."[6]

Given his own opposition to Eliot, whose influence on American letters he considered to be a "great catastrophe," Williams is an obvious choice for inclusion in the lineup that Poirier and Lentricchia have assembled. Many aspects of his work correspond precisely to the themes that they trace, and his absence from their accounts is conspicuous. In *The Renewal of Literature* Poirier dismissed Williams as "not difficult enough" to be taken seriously as a member of the "Emersonian contingent," while in the later *Poetry and Pragmatism* he took a more charitable approach, suggesting that the account of Williams's place in "the tribe of Waldo" should be left to someone more appreciative of his work.[7] With considerably less equivocation, Lentricchia concludes his account of the link between pragmatism and modernism by suggesting that Williams was superfluous to the wider work of liberation implicit in modern poetry: "very little, maybe nothing at all, depends upon a red wheelbarrow."[8]

It is my argument that Williams's work places him squarely within this "tribe of Waldo." His attitude toward history and tradition, his contempt for imposed structures of order, his vision of a pluralism of literary voices, and his sense of experience and knowledge as always-evolving fields reflect ideas that were articulated by Emerson and revised and transformed by James, Dewey, and Du Bois. Indeed, Williams's Emersonian modernism stands in stark contrast to the modernism of Eliot who, we should recall, had dismissed Emerson as "already an encumbrance" in 1919. Implicit in my argument, of course, is the contention that Williams does have contributions to make to the traditions articulated by Poirier and Lentricchia, though ultimately my terms and theirs differ significantly. More than a devotee of linguistic skepticism or a post-Marxist voice of aesthetic liberation, Williams stands in a line of writers who struggled with the conflicting forces of individualism and community, tradition and innovation, stability and an ever-unfolding newness. By locating his work in this context, we can better appreciate the contributions he made not only to modern poetry but to American intellectual and cultural discourse.

Given his abiding concern with the poet's responsibility for rejuvenating a present rendered sterile by the impositions of the past, it is remarkable that Williams had so little to say about Emerson, whose attitudes toward history and the role of the poet so closely mirrored his own. While Williams recognized Emerson's efforts to encourage an indigenous and original American culture, he concluded that the "Sage of Concord" was a "poet lost in the making," one whose genius was "too often circumscribed by a slightly hackneyed gentility."[9] Williams expressed his discomfort with Emerson more vividly in *The Great American Novel,* where he damns him as the "complacent Concordite," while later, in *The Autobiography,* he recalls that on a visit to Concord his wife Floss became "sick on somebody's grave" (GAN, 211; A, 130). In part, Williams's aversion to Emerson is consistent with his refusal of influence, his desire to keep his work independent of any association with writers out of the American past. It was these writers, after all, who represented the very body of writing that Williams sought to leave behind. At the same time, his attitude toward Emerson suggests the influence of Van Wyck Brooks's *America's Coming-of-Age,* which Williams read sometime prior to beginning his research for *In the American Grain.*[10] Brooks's conclusion that Emerson was disconnected from the forces that governed real life may well have confirmed for Williams what he already suspected: that Emerson's "spiritual assertions" lacked authenticity and did not fulfill the "underlying necessity" of relating creativity to immediate experience (SE, 155).

The extent to which Williams was familiar with Emerson is difficult to assess. In none of the literature, including Paul Mariani's massive biography, is there any indication that Williams actually read Emerson, and those who are sure that he did—Rapp, Tapscott, and Bryce Conrad—rely entirely on inference. Still, Williams's work so closely parallels the ideas Emerson developed in "The American Scholar," "History," and "The Poet" that such an inference seems fully justified. Williams and Emerson shared similar attitudes toward history; they both called on American artists to reject tradition and the "courtly muses of Europe" in the quest for a truly native form; each stressed the value of discarding the old and starting anew; and each called on the poet, who worked with language in its most primitive and uncorrupted state, to ensure that all aspects of American culture remained fresh and open to new experience. In "The American Scholar," his epoch-marking call for America's cultural independence from Europe, Emerson writes of the "helpful giant" who comes along seeking to "destroy the old or to build the new."[11] Though he may not have emerged from the "unhandselled savage nature" out of which Emerson's giant arose, Williams took that giant's task as his own and devoted his career to fulfilling it.

Throughout his prose and poetry, Williams writes of the need to clear away the old, inherited traditions and standards in order to pave the way for the creation of newer and more vibrant ones. In *In the American Grain* this serves as the basis for his appreciation of Edgar Allan Poe, who, by attempting to sweep aside "all colonial imitation," paved the way for Whitman and his descendants to begin writing a distinctly American poetry (IAG, 219). Williams was not exactly calling for a revival of Poe's poetry, which he felt failed as an expression of anything truly American. Rather, as E. P. Bollier has argued, Williams was drawn to Poe because he recognized the prior necessity of Poe's "sinking to the ground."[12] As such, Williams focused on Poe's criticism, presenting his "crusade against plagiarism" as an effective contribution to the important task of ground-clearing. Like Emerson before him, Williams was aware that a new American language, or poetry, or culture, could not simply be added on as an ornament of the old. As he wrote in his chapter on Sam Houston, "we have no other choice: we must all go back to the beginning; it must all be done over; everything that is must be destroyed" (IAG, 215).

Williams's most compelling treatment of this theme is his account of the burning of the library in book 3 of *Paterson,* where he identifies books—and reading—with the persistence of the old traditions that must be destroyed. The library, which adjoins the tumultuous Paterson Falls, offers a "sanctuary to our fears," the comforting presence of books that

> give rest sometimes against
> the uproar of water falling
> and righting itself to refall filling
> the mind with its reverberation
>   shaking stone. (97)

While the Passaic River thunders by outside the window, people immerse themselves in "dead men's dreams" and the oppressive "roar of books," protected from the onrushing force of life and content to relive the thoughts and deeds of those who have come before (100). Instead of nourishing creativity and imagination, then, the library "sweats of staleness and of rot," giving off a smell of "stagnation and death" (101–3). The source of this "library stench," of course, is the books, repositories of those dead dreams that "enfeeble the mind's intent" (102). To the active, creative life, books can only be "antagonistic" because they

> cannot penetrate and cannot waken, to be again
> active but remain—books. (116)

The fire that destroys the library and its contents is thus a "beautiful thing," the beginning of a process of rebirth that "breaks through the skull of custom" and clears the ground for fresh acts of creation:

> Papers
> (consumed) scattered to the winds. Black.
> The ink burned white, metal white. So be it. (117)

With the old words gone and the pages blank, the security of reading must give way to the risky but far more essential work of composition.

Williams uses this opposition between writing and reading throughout his work as a metaphor of the conflict between creativity and security. In *The Embodiment of Knowledge,* he makes his case explicit:

> Why not avoid writing and read? For the wisdom of the age is inaccessible. Mountains of dead words, cemeteries of words befog the mind. Now another book. It cannot be helped. The conviction that fills the whole body of a man is nearer to him than all the books that have ever been written. And these other books, the great philosophies, the endless treatises of science, the books of religions and the lives of other men—the biographies, the histories—what are they? They are part of the very oppressive, stupid, aimless, ignorant world which has driven him to shelter, to prison within himself, to defeat from which he must escape. (105)

As in *Paterson,* books here are oppressive, stifling the creative impulses that Williams has committed himself to liberating. While reading may provide respite from the intensity of the present, it ultimately leads to a deeper, more confining prison, a dungeon of dead words from which we can escape only when we (re)turn to writing.

It was the act of writing that Williams sought to encourage, the constant creation and re-creation of the self, rooted in the experience of the present and not in the dusty records of the past. Foremost among the reasons why "one should want to write and not merely read" is that "there is an antagonism between the ages. Each age wishes to enslave the others. Each wishes to succeed." To limit one's efforts to reading is to allow an earlier age to dominate the present. Immersed in the world of books "we are somehow convinced that we are not quite alive, that we are less than they—who lived before us. . . . To read, while we are imbibing the wisdom of the ages, we are at the same time imbibing the death and the imbecility, the enslaving rudeness of the ages." It is this enslavement, this death, that the act of writing strives to overcome, for through it we assert not only our own individual vitality but that of our "age" as well: "WE are the center of the writing, each man for himself but at the same time each man for his own age first." We write, then, with the simple but awesome goal of making our own existence comprehensible to ourselves and to our contemporaries (106–7).

While Williams sees the reading of books as posing a threat to the dynamics of life, his point is not that books are inherently oppressive and sterile but that the way in which people use them makes them so. The fire in *Paterson* was necessary because the act of reading had become a distraction from the work of creativity rather than a search for fresh inspiration. Emerson had declared that the purpose of books was to inspire, to liberate our own creative energies through the whispers of genius that they contain; Williams recognized the same potential:

> For there is a wind or ghost of a wind
> in all books echoing the life
> there, a high wind that fills the tubes
> of the ear until we think we hear a wind,
> actual   .   (P, 96)

The problem arises when readers focus on the original source of this echo instead of exploring its reverberations in their own thoughts. Williams does not ask us to ignore the record of the past, only to use it properly: "The fatal illusion of learning is that the works of antiquity, the philosophies, art pieces, political schemes, have endured; whereas they exist for us merely as symbols—of that which has lived and might live again. . . . What we see is the track of something which has passed" (EK, 93). The past can only live actively, as it is remade in the present and in the lives of each individual: "All one needs learn from the past is that it existed. It must be put down each for himself, read each for himself" (EK, 106). To "endure," after all, is merely to linger.

In all of these reflections on creativity and reading Williams is echoing Emerson, whose own attitude toward books strikes a remarkably similar tone. Emerson begins "The American Scholar" by observing that books are, in fact, "the best type of the influence of the past." The "theory of books is noble," for, in writing his book, the scholar has taken the world he sees and given it "the new arrangement of his own mind," transforming "dead fact" into "quick thought." The best books are those which communicate these thoughts to future generations: "There is some awe mixed with the joy of our surprise, when this poet, who lived in some past world, two or three hundred years ago, says that which lies close to my own soul, that which I also had wellnigh thought and said." However, the point of recognizing this shared thought is not to worship the record of the past but to use it as inspiration for creating a record of the present: no one can write a book that "shall be as efficient, in all respects, to a remote posterity, as to contemporaries," because each generation, in order to see rightly, must see anew. Thus, "each age . . . must write its own books" (56–58). Some years later, Williams would make a similar point: "the same truth in art must be restated continually in each age in the materials of that age to be true" (EK, 87–88).

For Emerson, as for Williams, the "great mischief" of books arises when "the sacredness which attaches to the act of creation,—the act of thought,— is transferred to the record." It is in such cases of misuse that "the book becomes noxious," its influence destructive. Books do not comprise bodies of "accepted dogma" to which our own efforts must conform, but should serve merely to inspire those efforts: "Books are the best of things, well used; abused, among the worst. . . . I had better never see a book, than to be warped by its attraction clean out of my own orbit, and made a satellite instead of a system." Both Emerson and Williams stress that people must remain true to their individual creative orbits, committed to rendering their own immediate experience into comprehensible form unimpeded by the influence of older systems. To ensure this, Emerson insists, reading must be "sternly subordinated" so that "Man thinking" is not "subdued by his instruments. Books are for the scholar's idle times. When he can read God directly, the hour is too precious to be wasted in other men's transcripts of their readings" (58).

The price of misusing books, of esteeming too highly the text and ignoring the life it reveals, is high. Williams offers an unforgiving picture of the cultural and spiritual decay that results from worshipping the transcripts of the past, while Emerson, too, fears that the failure to practice "creative reading" invites stagnation: "The book, the college, the school of art, the institution of any kind, stop with some past utterance of genius. This is good, say they,—let us hold by this. They pin me down. They look backward and not forward." Instead of "Man Thinking," which Emerson identified as the highest goal of human education, the narrow worship of books produces "the bookworm," one who would retreat to the security of Paterson Library rather than accept the risk of direct communion with life. For Williams, the task of restoring life to a culture suffocating under this "library stench" may well require stern measures. As he wrote in "Against the Weather" (1939): "To stop the flames that destroy the old nest prevents the rebirth of the bird itself. All things rot and stink, nothing stinks more than an old nest, if not recreated" (SE, 208).

For Williams, this intimate cycle of destruction and rebirth was fundamental to the creative process. To live creatively, actively, and in the present, that is, to live at all, we must first discard the restrictive detritus of the past. Anything that outlasts its usefulness—or its timeliness—not only grows stale but inhibits new growth. In "Burning the Christmas Greens," Williams details this process of destruction and rebirth and suggests what is at stake if we refuse our individual responsibility to stoke the flames. The scene is a simple one in which the family members set about disassembling the Christmas decorations:

> Their time past, pulled down
> cracked and flung into the fire
> [the greens] go up in a roar

Immediately, however, the image turns from one of destruction to one of re-creation:

> All recognition lost, burnt clean
> clean in the flame, the green
> dispersed, a living red,
> flame red, red as blood wakes
> on the ash—

The greens are not simply burned, they are transformed, and what emerges, what "wakes" on the ashes of the old, is a new life, "a living red . . . red as blood." After this initial image of destruction and rebirth, Williams recounts the original gathering of the greens when

> At the thick of the dark
> the moment of the cold's
> darkest plunge

the family carried branches of the "living green" indoors, to brighten and enliven the house. Quickly, however, he returns to the burning:

> Their time past,
> relief! The room bare. We
>
> stuffed the dead grate
> with them upon the half burnt out

> log's smoldering eye, opening
> red and closing under them
>
> and we stood there looking down.

The greens, which had been a

> solace
> a promise of peace, a fort
> against the cold

now bring the "dead grate" and the "half burnt-out log" to life. At the same time, and at the very moment that they are consumed by the flames, they become part of a new life themselves:

> Violence leaped and appeared.
> Recreant! Roared to life
> as the flame rose through and
> our eyes recoiled from it.
> . . . .
> and quick in the contracting
> tunnel of the grate
> appeared a world! Black
> mountains, black and red

Though our eyes recoil from the fire as the greens are destroyed, we quickly become aware of a new world, one "as yet uncolored—and ash white" that offers us "an infant landscape." Born in the destruction of the old world, this new one now stands ready, awaiting our efforts to color it and to make it our own. This is the central metaphor of Williams's work, the continuous process of rebirth out of the destruction of the old. To be sure, this process carries an element of discomfort and risk, but it is also marked by an exhilarating sense of possibility:

> and we, in
> that instant, lost,
>
> breathless to be witnesses,
> as if we stood
> ourselves refreshed among
> the shining fauna of that fire.[13]

James Guimond has suggested that the key to understanding this poem is the fact that Williams—or the narrator—himself takes an active part in "the destructive-recreative process," implying that "men can help the 'catastrophic birth' of the new if they are willing to destroy the old."[14] In fact, considered in context with the rest of Williams's work, this poem argues that new birth is possible *only if* individuals are willing to undertake the work of ground-clearing. Burning and destruction thus serve as both midwife and mother to the new form. Twenty years before "Burning the Christmas Greens," in *Kora in Hell*, Williams observed: "It's no use trying to deceive me, leaves fall more by the buds that push them off than by lack of greenness" (KH, 80).

For Williams, this image served as the clearest representation of the development of human culture, and it was the poet who was to assume primary leaf-pushing responsibility. Emerson, too, had recognized the poet as the figure best suited to this process of rejuvenation. He observes in "The Poet" that "the experience of each new age requires a new confession," and for this "the world seems always waiting for its poet" (450). The poet is "representative," standing "among partial men for the complete man"; he "apprises us not of his wealth, but of the commonwealth" (448).[15] This service is particularly wanted in America, where people have relied for too long on the confessions of some earlier age: "We do not, with sufficient plainness, or sufficient profoundness, address ourselves to life, not dare we chaunt our own times and social circumstance" (465). The poet, as "the Namer, or Language-maker" whose genius it is to "repair the decays of things," is the one who can best articulate the newness of the world and recall us to life (456–57). Like Williams, who invoked Thomas Jefferson in calling for a revolution in language every generation, Emerson asked the poet to clear the ground of dead usages: "all language is vehicular and transitive, and is good, as ferries and horses are, for conveyance, nor as farms and houses are, for homestead" (463). It is the poet's task to continuously reinvent new means of transport, for if we settle too long in any one mode it will no longer take us where we need to go.

Emerson called on the poet not simply to revitalize old forms of expression but to create new expressions that have an immediate vitality of their own, to give words "a power which makes their old use forgotten" (456). Emerson's poet is "a liberating God" who gives to the present its own voice, enabling the work of creation to begin across the culture (462). Williams, too, had an abiding faith in the regenerative potential of the poem and portrays his poet as bearing the light of liberation into the dark corners of tradition-bound culture. In "Caviar and Bread Again: A Warning to the New Writer," written in 1930, Williams declares: "on the poet devolves the most vital function of society: to recreate it—the collective world—in time of stress, in a new mode, fresh in every part," in order to once again "set the world working or dancing" (SE, 103). Williams's perception that the world, particularly the American world, had ceased to work or dance helps to explain the sense of urgency with which his metaphors of destruction and rebirth are imbued. As he would imply in *Paterson,* the accumulated detritus of tradition had reached a critical level and demanded quick action:

> Poet, poet! sing your song, quickly! or
> not insects but pulpy weeds will blot out
> your kind. (83)

If Emerson waited with benign impatience for the emergence of his American poet, Williams was issuing a call to arms, summoning poets to the pressing task of rejuvenating an American culture struggling through a wasteland of rotting nests, stench-filled libraries, and dead leaves.

Williams diagnosed America's social and cultural malaise as resulting from a lingering devotion to European modes of language, criticism, and form. Not only was the so-called "American tradition" hopelessly corrupted by the influence of eighteenth and nineteenth-century European sources, but contemporary American artists—poets, painters, novelists—rather than searching for their inspiration at home, declared themselves lost and set sail for England and France. Williams is relentless in skewering those who—like Eliot and Pound—gave up on America and chose to live abroad, for he feels that in doing so they abandoned their responsibility, and surrendered their opportunity, to cultivate a truly indigenous art. Instead, he praises Kenneth Burke as "one of the rarest things in America," an artist who "lives here: has a family, a house" (SE, 133). Some four generations after Emerson had first called for America's cultural independence from Europe, Williams not only has to contend with what he sees as the same old rotten traditions, but is confronted with a generation of cultural expatriates as well.

Williams's efforts to liberate the American arts from a critical tradition rooted in Europe did not lead him to dismiss European culture as corrupting in itself. Rather, he granted the appropriateness of European culture for the Europeans (French culture for the French, English for the English) while at the same time demanding that America shed its adolescent dependence on inherited forms of cultural authority. He makes this point most succinctly in *In the American Grain* when he writes: "if we will not pay heed to our own affairs, we [will be] nothing but an unconscious porkyard and oilhole for those, more able, who will fasten themselves on us" (IAG, 109). It is at this lack of attention to America's indigenous material that Williams—like Emerson before him—directs most of his energy, for it is both cause and symptom of the pervading stagnation: "Europe is nothing to us.

Simply nothing. Their music is death to us. . . . God, I would like to see some man, some one of the singers step out in the midst of some one of Aida's songs and scream like a puma" (GAN, 174). Only the irruption of such an unabashedly American voice can break the hold of European culture and demonstrate to Americans that they have a cultural voice of their own. Once again, this highlights the critical role of the poet as creator of the first order, for before people can recognize a culture as their own it needs to be created.

Williams asserted the need for a distinctively American voice throughout his work, but he presented his case most directly in "The American Background." In a prologue to this essay he relates a story of the first settlers to the New World who, upon encountering "birds with rusty breasts," called them robins after a similarly colored English bird. Thus, from the very beginning, an "America of which they could have no inkling drove the first settlers upon their past." Confronted with the unknown, they "retreated for warmth and reassurance to something previously familiar," and in the process committed the first in a series of mistakes: "For what they saw were not robins. They were thrushes only vaguely resembling the rosy, daintier English bird." The American bird was "larger, stronger, and in the evening of a wilder, lovelier song," yet this was all lost in the blur and confusion of the unknown and the new (SE, 134).

For Williams, the difference between the American thrush and the English robin is crucial, and the failure of the settlers to recognize this is representative of the failure of American culture to break free of European forms. While he admits that this "example is slight," it is nonetheless "enough properly to incline the understanding." The new continent "induced a torsion in the spirits of the first settlers, tearing them between the old and new." At the very beginning, "a split occurred in that impetus which should have carried them forward as one into the dangerous realities of the future." America demanded of these settlers "great powers of adaptability, a complete reconstruction of their most intimate cultural make-up, to accord with the new conditions. The most hesitated and turned back in their hearts at the first glance." The cost of retreating to the past when confronted with the new and unknown was, Williams believed, high. To be sure, it offered security and safety, but in trying to avoid the "dangerous realities" the settlers, and many who came after them, also surrendered any hope of developing an indigenous and vital American culture. Instead of the wild and lovely song of the thrush, they failed to hear anything but the dainty chirping of the robin.

Williams recognized that for the early settlers, adrift in a "strange and difficult" new world, this tendency to fall back on the security of their old traditions, while "retrograde," was nevertheless "necessitous." America had borrowed its culture in moments of "poverty and danger," when it seemed to have no other choice; as those moments faded into the past, the borrowing should have been displaced by making. Even into the present day, however, this "acquisition of borrowed European culture was [not] in itself a bad thing." It was only when European culture was "taken to be virtue itself" that its influence became destructive. Instead of complementing an indigenous American culture, these borrowed forms drown it out or, worse, mutate it into forms more like themselves (SE, 144). The result is an America that is prevented from speaking its own language because it has been lulled into thinking that another's language is more suitable. Williams observed in the chapter on Poe in *In the American Grain:* "Americans have never recognized themselves. How can they? It is impossible until someone invent the ORIGINAL terms. As long as we are content to be called by somebody else's terms, we are incapable of being anything but our own dupes" (IAG, 226). And since, as he writes in *Spring and All,* life exists only when we name it, the price America pays for its cultural dependence is dear: lacking the terms to name life for itself, America in effect stops living (SA, 115).

Given his commitment to clearing the ground of dead traditions and breaking free of the gravitational pull of the past, it was inevitable that Williams would turn his attention to the field of American history, that vast accumulation of dead traditions through which the past perpetuated its hold on the present. Yet, while he was quick to point to history as the most immediate source of America's cultural crisis, he left behind the slash-and-burn rhetoric that characterized so much of his other writing. Williams acknowledged that history should not, and in fact could not simply be burned away. When properly conceived, an awareness of the past could provide a useful frame of reference for those searching to give expression to the new. History should be "a left hand to us, as of a violinist," he observed, but instead we "bind [it] up with prejudice, warping it to suit our fears" (IAG, 189). His aim was thus to rewrite history, not write it off. Paul Jay has suggested that Williams's *In the American Grain* is the Ur-text of American modernism's paradoxical attitude toward history, presenting the past as "both the source of America's present degradation *and* of its renewal."[16] In his effort to reconstruct American history Williams tackled both halves of that paradox: "I wish only to disentangle the obscurities that oppress me, to track them to the root and uproot them. . . . I seek the support of history, but I wish to understand it aright, to make it show itself" (IAG, 116).

Like many critics of his generation, Williams wanted to construct a usable past, to create from the events and characters of that past a tradition that would, in effect, lead up to and validate his own work. He was interested in men and women who had made contact with America, whose "most intimate cultural make-up" had emerged from the actual conditions of the New World; he was interested in those who were willing to embrace what was strange and unfamiliar as the defining characteristics of that world; and he was interested in artists who left the safe conventions of Europe and England behind and allowed America to shape its own cultural forms. What Williams found, however, was that everything in which he was interested, all that represented the "true character" of the American experience, had been lost in a "chaos of borrowed titles" (v). The accepted "schoolbook" version of American history was little more than a chronicle of figures who, like the earliest settlers, fell back upon the past because they feared what was new and unknown. What Williams took to be the very cause of America's social and cultural stagnation, the history books translated into a story of virtue and heroism. Given the condition of their recorded history, then, it was not surprising that "Americans have lost the sense . . . that what we are has its origin in what the nation in the past has been; that there is a source in AMERICA for everything we think or do" (109). It was this source that Williams set out to recover.

Everywhere he looked Williams was overwhelmed by "the niggardliness of our history, our stupidity, sluggishness of spirit, the falseness of our historical notes, the complete missing of the point." He was particularly disturbed by "the tenacity" with which the fear of the new continued to mold America's laws and customs, so that now "almost nothing remains of the great American New World but a memory of the Indian" (157). The organized suppression in the past of what was original in the American experience led to a history that obscured even those acts of suppression: "History, history! We fools, what do we know or care? History begins for us with murder and enslavement, not with discovery" (39). Instead of celebrating newness and variety, then, American history constructed a legacy of "thrift, timidity and security" around which it twisted the rest of the story. Beyond the simple fact that this was an inaccurate and misleading picture of the past, it also bound up the creative energies waiting to break free in the present. Williams concluded that such a history could only have been

written by those who, "never content in the malice with which they surround each living moment" must therefore "extend their ill will backward,
jealous even of a freedom in the past" (189).

Williams follows a rather simple pattern in *In the American Grain,*
unmasking the forces of suppression that dominate the historical record
while highlighting selected "secondary" figures as more fully representative
of the American character. The limitations of recorded American history
are revealed most clearly in three of its central figures: the Puritans, Ben
Franklin, and Alexander Hamilton. The Puritans, by "their very emptiness" were "the fiercest element in the battle to establish a European life on
the New World," and their legacy has been little more than "an atavism
that thwarts and destroys" (63, 68). Following closely in their stead was
Franklin, the "dike keeper," who kept "out the wilderness with his wits."
Instead of devoting his "omnivorous energy" to exploring the full creative
potential of the New World, Franklin sought only enough information
with which to control that newness. In fact, it was nothing more than
"fear" of the unknown that "drove his curiosity" (155). Finally there was
Hamilton, the archetypal villain who tried to possess the land in an un-
natural way, "to harness the whole, young, aspiring genius to a treadmill"
for his own personal, material gain (195). For Williams, America's understanding of itself was shaped by the enduring influence of these figures: a
refusal of what was original in the American experience, a stubborn insistence on European and English conventions, and such an intense fear of
the new, the unknown, and the untamed that the appearance of such
would provoke violent repression. Such a climate—past or present—was
inimical to the creativity Williams hoped to promote.

Yet if the source of America's cultural degradation lay embedded in this
textbook version of its history, the spring of its rejuvenation could be found
in a history that had, in effect, been covered up. As alternatives to the
sterility and timidness of Franklin, Hamilton, and the Puritans, Williams
offered readings of such figures as Eric the Red, Daniel Boone, Aaron Burr,
and Sam Houston, each of whom manifested the trait that he deemed most
essential: a willingness to allow the immediate reality of America to guide
their experience of it. Representative of these figures was Boone, who had
"run past the difficulties encountered by his fellows in making the New
World their own." Unlike the French, who tried to possess the wilderness
by filling it with Frenchmen, Boone descended to "the ground of his
desire," possessing the wilderness "as the Indian possessed it," that is, on its
own terms (136–37). Houston also sought to accept America on its own
terms, refusing to shrink in fear from the unknown or the unexplored and

willing to descend to the ground (213). And—unlike Hamilton, who saw America developing along narrow, materialistic lines—Burr imagined a future for America that was free and open, always ready to accommodate new experiences and adjust to native realities (197). As someone looking to make space for himself in that future, Williams clearly hoped to rehabilitate a vision of America that embraced rather than destroyed these native sources of inspiration.

In a letter to Horace Gregory, who was preparing to write an introduction for the 1939 edition of *In the American Grain,* Williams describes how he came to write the book:

> Of mixed ancestry, I felt from the earliest childhood that America was the only home I could ever possibly call my own. I felt that it was expressly founded for me, personally, and that it must be my first business in life to possess it; that only by making it my own from the beginning to my own day, in detail, should I ever have a basis for knowing where I stood. I must have a basis for orienting myself formally in the beliefs which activated me from day to day. (SL, 185)

In many ways this represents Williams's response to Emerson's challenge in "History": "The student is to read history actively and not passively; to esteem his own life the text, and books the commentary" (239). All but invoking the man he would dismiss as a "complacent Concordite," Williams rails against a history that subordinates the present to the past, that "is concerned only with the one thing: to say everything is dead" (IAG, 188). Emerson believed that no one could "read history aright, who thinks that what was done in a remote age, by men whose names have resounded far, has any deeper sense than what he is doing to-day." Williams, too, looked to history neither to discredit it nor to change the names of its heroes, but to set it right. He simply wanted to liberate from the bonds of American history those energies and perceptions that would serve to inspire individuals to live creatively in the present, to descend to the ground upon which they themselves stood. In short, Williams asked his readers to cultivate, at the very least, an original relation to America.

While Williams's work is infused with the rhetoric of Americanism, it is far from the provincial patriotism of which he has sometimes been accused. He saw his own greatest achievement as a poet to be his experimenting with different "American forms," and he consistently urged that criticism take into account the American idiom. Yet throughout, Williams's use of "American" is inextricably bound up with his understanding of "the local," an idea he adapted in part from John Dewey.[17] Rather than attempting to replace one overarching theory of "The American Experience" with another, Williams affirms that there is no single American experience. Instead, "America" is comprised of a wide variety of experiences rooted in local conditions. The poet's task was "not to talk in vague categories but to write particularly, as a physician works, upon a patient, upon the thing before him, in the particular to discover the universal" (A, 391). Williams's analogy to his medical practice is telling: to treat an individual patient as if she were a generalization drawn from a textbook was not only a violation of professional ethics but a risk to the patient's well-being.

It was his firm commitment to the idea of the local, rather than any narrow provincialism, that led Williams to focus so much of his creative energy—from *The Doctor Stories* to *Paterson*—on the history of his New Jersey community and the lives of those with whom he came in daily contact. For Paul Mariani, this commitment alone confirms Williams as the single most important poet of the twentieth century. In a 1944 letter to Horace Gregory, Williams expounded on his understanding of the local:

> The interchange from the local toward the general, and the refreshing of the general from the local . . . is what we are after. . . . It is in the wide range of the local only that the general can be tested for its one unique quality, its universality. The flow must originate from the local to the general as a river to the sea and then back to the local from the sea in rain. (SL, 225)

At the time of this letter Williams was already at work on *Paterson,* and the central theme of the poem can be found in the image of the river flowing to the sea and then returning as rain. This passage also connects *Paterson* with *In the American Grain,* where Williams sought to rehabilitate the local conditions that had been obscured by the generalized textbook version of American history. In each work, Williams highlights the interaction of individuals with their local conditions in the formation of local cultures, and argues that any generalized notion of "Americanness" must emerge from these local cultures. In addition, he emphasizes that these interactions are never static and fixed but always evolving: rivers change and are in turn changed by the land formations through which they flow, and what the sea gives back in rain varies widely over time.

Attention to the local, then, was not merely the necessary task of the poet; it was the key to understanding and maintaining American democracy. While he detested the cultural stagnation that resulted from the quest for sameness and generalization, Williams also feared that this quest would produce a narrowly construed understanding of national identity. Such a fixed notion of American identity would, he knew, be rooted in the vision

of the Franklins and the Hamiltons: a suffocating uniformity and conformity, a repression of anything that was new and different. Hamilton's
villainy lay in his pursuit of national goals in ignorance of, and at the
expense of, "local conditions." He sought to impose his old-world vision of
America as a center of manufacturing and finance upon a region that had a
decidedly different sense of itself. For Williams, Hamilton's vision for the
Passaic River Valley should have been guided by what was actually there;
instead, he saw a land ripe for the development of large-scale mill works in
the English style. On one level a sin against culture, this was also reflective
of Hamilton's elitist, centralizing, antidemocratic politics. Williams thus
offered the local as an antidote to both cultural and political decay.

Williams's concern for the local had a final, deeply personal dimension:
it included not only the village of Rutherford but the heritage of his middle
name as well. As the earlier letter to Gregory indicates, Williams identified his mixed ancestry as an essential component of his connection to
America. He was aware from his earliest childhood of what we would today
call his multicultural heritage. His father had been born in Britain under
mysterious circumstances—possibly involving indiscretions within the
Wollstonecraft-Shelley family—and he never gave up his British citizen-
ship. His mother, whom Williams would identify as the most important
influence on his life, was born in Puerto Rico, spoke Spanish, and had
studied art in Paris. She was, in the words of Williams's son, the "product of
a tropical hotbed on a West Indian island, [a] multinational mongrel
gentlewoman transplanted to a north temperate zone suburb of a major
metropolis that was infested with WASP entrepreneurs."[18] That such an
alien figure could make a home for herself in such a place without subsuming her uniqueness was, for Williams, the highest measure of America's
promise.

In *The Autobiography,* Williams recalls his decision to use his middle
name as being based on his sense that it was "most revealing and therefore
better" (108). From the start, then, he affirmed both his cultural uniqueness
and his fundamental Americanness: he himself was part of the "wide range
of the local" that would test the universality of the American general. In
this way, Williams aligned his project with that of Du Bois, whose own
mixed ancestry was further diversified by the element of race. Both Du Bois
and Williams sought to revitalize the interaction of the particular and
the general, in Du Bois's words, "to make it possible for a man to be
both a Negro and an American . . . a co-worker in the kingdom of culture" (*Souls,* 364–65). Each man knew that an America devoted to consistency and universality would be an America that demanded conformity, a

WASPish, Hamiltonian conformity that the black Du Bois could never achieve and that neither man desired. In asserting that the local and the individual were prior to and fundamental components of the general, Williams and Du Bois were pursuing more than the rejuvenation of American culture: they sought nothing less than to ensure themselves a place within the American project.

Williams rejected the old version of American history because it forced individuals and events into narrow "generic patterns," denying the extraordinary variety of forces that had shaped the American experience. Vera Kutzinski has noted that Williams created his own myth of history by striving to "reintroduce contradictions and acknowledge differences," offering *In the American Grain* as an alternative to the old myth of unity and sameness.[19] By breaking through these imposed patterns, he not only hoped to rehabilitate muffled voices from the past but to legitimize a wider variety of cultural voices in the present. He urged painters, poets, and artists of all stripes to discard the safe conventions upon which they had previously relied and revitalize their work by exploring the contradictions and differences at the heart of the American story. In his own poetry he experimented with a variety of forms and subjects, and he looked for and encouraged this experimentation in others. Williams's work thus constitutes not only a rejection of the American literary and historical canon, as Kutzinski suggests, but a radical opening up of the field of "legitimate" literature to reflect the newness and variety that have always defined American experience.

While Williams was primarily concerned with artistic expression, his pursuit of diversity nonetheless had wider implications. As Paul Mariani has noted, "there was a political and social judgment implicit in telling the world that a poem could be made of anything."[20] Williams himself was aware that his work carried a certain political weight, and he accepted the basic premise that culture and politics were intimately related areas of human development. Clearly, a central feature of *In the American Grain* had been Williams's identification of cultural stagnation with a narrow, conservative view of American history; elsewhere, he was quick to see a relationship between the aesthetic failures of Eliot and Pound and their reactionary politics. However, his temperament and his intellectual framework prohibited him from identifying with any particular party or ideology, and he fiercely defended his aesthetic vision from the challenges of both political poles.

Williams was repulsed by a conservative politics that stood for the main-tenance of traditional values and institutions in the face of change. Since these politics tended to exert a constricting and anti-experimental pressure on the arts, Williams was confident that his work must stand in sharp opposition to them. He found his relationship to the politics of the left far more complicated. While he appreciated the support that radical politics often gave to the cultural avant-garde, he was also increasingly aware that the kind of organized political opposition represented by the American left in the 1930s and 1940s threatened his notion of artistic independence. To demand that art promote the workers' revolution was no less a tyranny than to demand that it promote the ideals of thrift, timidity, and security, and Williams thus found himself standing in opposition to those on the left who demanded a faithful adherence to the appropriate codes of realism.

Williams's most explicit treatment of this problem is "The Basis of a Faith in Art," an essay written sometime after 1935 but not published until *The Selected Essays* was issued in 1954. Here, Williams seems to be respond-ing to some of the ideas presented at the American Writer's Congress that he observed in New York in the spring of 1935. Paul Mariani describes how Williams kept a low profile because he was uncomfortable with the leftist dogma of most of the speeches. In fact, as Williams wrote in a letter to Louis Zukofsky, the only speech that really impressed him was Waldo Frank's cautious rejection of "oversimplified propaganda" in favor of as-signing to art the task of "conditioning the proletarian mind [and] making it ready for revolution."[21] While Frank was convinced that "the cause of the socialist society" was above all "a cultural problem," he stressed that the work of art must not be subordinated to the "political-economic aspects of the re-creation of mankind." Rather, it must represent in itself an "*autono-mous kind*" of political action.[22] It was precisely this kind of "political" action that Williams could imagine his own work performing, for he had great faith in the poem as the "revolutionary attribute of a free people" (SE, 243). In so far as he was to participate in the revolution, then, his task would be to prepare as many minds as possible for the radical work of the poem.

Many of the other speeches Williams heard dealt with the "usefulness" of art for the party and the priority of propaganda over questions of "mere aesthetics," and it was at such remarks that "The Basis of a Faith in Art" was directed. Williams suggested that the apparent "uselessness" of art might actually constitute its principal use. Since the work of art is usually an attempt to preserve something of value from the "sordid, scurrilous world" and the "destroying, falsifying, besmutching agencies with which [the artist] is surrounded," it comes to symbolize that which makes the world the revolutionaries seek worth striving for (SE, 179–80). Far from useless, then, the independent work of art fulfills a vital function, and only a "jackass of a party man" would try to twist that art to serve a purpose other than its own (SE, 183). In *In the American Grain* Williams observed that it was through literature alone that "humanity is protected against tyrannous designs" (IAG, 189). In this later essay, he makes it clear that to interfere with that literature in order to make it "useful" to some particular cause may only contribute to the extension of those designs.

Since Williams took poetry as his own "field of action," he was keenly interested in presenting the poem as a weapon in the struggle against tyranny, a tyranny that was both cultural and political. Poetry must constitute itself as a "rival government," always in opposition to those agencies that would oppress or deny the artist's vision (SE, 180). The poet is thus foremost a critic of the government in power, guarding against the "usurpation" of that government by "a class, a group, a set of any sort" that threatened to "subvert the freedom of the individual for some temporary need." In part, Williams portrays poets as canaries in the coal mine, though not the caged and helpless kind. As the artist who represents individual freedom in its purest and most original form, the poet is extremely vulnerable to the forces of oppression and must therefore assume a position on the front lines of battle. By "breaking down" the "imposed tyrannies over his verse forms" and admitting "all classes of subject to his attention," the poet becomes a "social regenerator" (SE, 194). Again, Williams makes explicit the link he sees between the world of art and the world of politics: it takes a free society to produce and nurture a free poet, and a free poet to ensure a free society.

It was in this light that Williams saw his own work. His was a poetry of inclusiveness, a poetry that actively imposed a democracy of form and materials on the poetic field. Not only did this revitalize poetry, it provided a stirring challenge to a political and social order that sought to obliterate differences in pursuit of a narrow vision of the "universal." At the same time, Williams maintained that his art, and any art, could never achieve its goal of social regeneration if it were subordinated to the demands of a particular ideology or cause. The individual act of expression, as the most fundamental and original unit of human experience, must in all cases remain independent and unsullied. Once again, Williams here gives a nod to Emerson, who insisted that whatever wider purpose art might serve, it could do so only on its own terms. In "Against the Weather," Williams summarized his own position nicely:

Who cares anything about propaganda ... unless the best thought is built newly, in a comprehensive form of the day, into the structure of the work? And if such a basis is accepted then, indeed, propaganda can be thoroughly welcomed. Built into the structure of a work, propaganda is always acceptable for by that it has been transmuted into the materials of art. It has no life unless to live or die judged by an artist's standards.

But if, imposing an exposed, a depleted, restrictive and unrealized form, the propagandist thinks he can make what he has to say convincing by merely filling in that wooden structure with some ideas he wants to put over—he turns up not only as no artist but a weak fool. (SE, 218)

At the same Writer's Congress that inspired "The Basis of a Faith in Art," Williams's friend Kenneth Burke was excoriated for his paper, "Revolutionary Symbolism in America." In the paper, Burke pleaded for the symbol of "the people" as "more basic, more of an ideal incentive, than that of 'the worker,'" and went on to say "I am suggesting fundamentally that one cannot extend the doctrine of revolutionary thought among the lower middle class without using middle-class values." Moreover, by "informing his work mainly from the standpoint of this positive symbol," the poet would come to see that he "does not sufficiently glorify his political cause by pictures of suffering and revolt." Rather, the poet makes his most significant contribution by remaining "alive to all the aspects of contemporary effort and thought (in contrast with a certain anti-intellectualist, semi-obscurantist trend among some of the strictly *proletarian* school)."[23] Burke's suggestion was immediately attacked as heresy, for in abandoning the idea of the worker he was abandoning what many of those at the congress felt was the only proper subject for literature. Furthermore, the idea of "the people" that he proffered as an alternative symbol was so fraught with "bourgeois aestheticism" as to be considered ridiculous.[24] Though a committed Marxist, Burke was both ideologically and aesthetically opposed to the oversimplified propaganda of the proletarians, and he shared Williams's belief that though art does have a significant revolutionary potential, it can only approach that potential on its own terms.

Like "Revolutionary Symbolism in America," Burke's *Counter-Statement* contains a critique of the propagandist's position and an alternative vision of art's political usefulness, a vision that is quite similar to Williams's own. Burke states his position at the outset: "Art's very accumulation (its discordant voices arising out of many systems) serves to undermine any one rigid scheme of living."[25] This recalls what Kutzinski described as Williams's work of subversion, his delegitimization of a rigid literary tradition through his commitment to the liberation of "discordant voices." In "The American

Spirit in Art," Williams echoes Burke even more clearly, writing that "the basic idea which underlies our art must be, for better or worse, abundance, that is, permission for all."[26] This notion of abundance was an integral part of Williams's insistence on the suitability of all materials for the work of art, and it serves as a key link between his vision of an active American poetry and Burke's interest in literature as a means of positive social change: to the degree that it is committed to variety and inclusiveness in its own form and subject, art may serve to undermine the broader social tyranny that depends upon illusions of unity and sameness.

In a chapter titled "Program," Burke sets out to explain just how the artist can add his voice to those fighting against economic and social oppression. The artist, as the champion of aesthetic values, is always in confrontation with the practical tendencies of the age, tendencies which correspond to the increasing supremacy of "industrialism" and the reliance on consumption as the supreme palliative (108). The artist's role, then, is to align himself consciously and aggressively on the side of the aesthetic for the purpose of "keeping the practical from becoming too hopelessly itself" (112). That is, the artist must actively promote the ideals of art, such as democracy, experimentalism, curiosity, and risk, as a means of countering the practical (and thus anti-aesthetic) ideals of efficiency, prosperity, and material security. Burke does not expect to eliminate these tendencies entirely, but he does believe that it is important to maintain an alternative vision—what Williams called a rival government—as a means of keeping them in check. For both Burke and Williams, culture plays a prominent role in the formation and development of human society, shaping how individuals see themselves and how they understand their relationship to other individuals. To properly fulfill the role of social regenerator, art—and the artist—must be given free play. These ideas echo not only through the work of Williams and Burke, but through that of Emerson and James as well.[27]

For Williams, the fundamental unit of human experience was the individual act of perception and expression, and throughout his work he insisted that each such act be respected as fresh and independent. Like Emerson, with whom he shared this belief, Williams maintained that creative expression must remain free of any imposed forms, whether those forms originated in the cultural conventions of Europe, the demands of particular social or political causes, or the accumulated force of tradition. Yet while Williams stated more forcefully than Emerson the need to destroy the old forms through which the past exerted its influence over the present, he nonetheless acknowledged more explicitly than Emerson the need for some kind of tradition, some understanding of the past, in which to root these new and emerging voices. For Emerson, it was better that history be ignored than misread, and he felt no pressing need to re-imagine it; for Williams, any history that lends itself to misreading can and must be replaced. Williams considered tradition to be "the better part of all of us" and history "our greatest well of inspiration." The past was thus nothing less than "the fountain" from which the present flows, and Williams was committed to keeping that flow clear and full in order to ensure the necessary context for individual responses (IAG, 189).

In thus diverging from Emerson, Williams follows a path similar to that traced by William James who, while sharing Emerson's faith in the inviolability of the individual living in the present moment, recognized that individuals must have some sense of tradition and community in which to locate their own acts and beliefs. Though, as with Emerson, there is no clear evidence that Williams ever read James, the unmistakable confluence of their ideas suggests that Williams must have been familiar with James's work in some form. In addition to sharing James's interest in providing a context for Emersonian individualism, Williams incorporated variations on pluralism, radical empiricism, and pragmatism into his work. He believed that each individual contributed a unique perception to the overall picture of human experience; he demanded that any overarching claim about truth or reality be judged according to its consistency with actual experience; and he maintained that no human forms or institutions are ever absolute but are always in the process of evolving. In each case, Williams not only echoes James but reflects those ideas of Emerson's that James had built into his own work. Just as Du Bois applied the lessons of Emerson and James to the question of race, Williams demonstrated their implications for poetry and other forms of creative expression.

The parallels between Williams and James are most evident in *The Embodiment of Knowledge,* a collection of miscellaneous pieces Williams wrote between 1928 and 1930 and offered to his sons as a blueprint for "an American education." Like James, who rejected philosophical systems that sought to impose absolute patterns on individual experience, Williams asserted the priority of the individual to all systems, philosophical, political, and cultural. In this case his aim was to reclaim the field of knowledge from any who would separate it into fixed, hierarchical divisions that were beyond the reach of those whom knowledge was meant to serve (EK, 9). Williams insisted that knowledge was not an absolute entity existing outside the individual's experience but a product of that experience, of the individual's ongoing interaction with the world. Rejecting what he saw as the absolutist and exclusionist tendencies of philosophy and science, Williams asserted: "All knowledge must be conceived as within the scope of human understanding; that is, *any* human understanding . . . its acquirement is a series within the scope of the mind" (EK, 41). Just as James sought to redefine truth as something which was mutable and open to individual variations, Williams presented knowledge as fundamentally defined by its variety and openness to change.

Though *The Embodiment of Knowledge* is by no means a unified work, it nonetheless coheres around a few central principles. Foremost among these is Williams's desire to be through with "the comprehensive pretense" of philosophy and science (EK, 52). In the quest for unity, the disciplines of philosophy and science had claimed to represent, between them, the whole of human knowledge, subsuming many different "branches of understanding" within their static hierarchy. For Williams, the only true unity was a "multiformity," a vision that took into account the variety of ways of knowing and the variety of things to be known (EK, 73). This multiformity, or "multiplicity," demands that any "universal" system of knowledge be held accountable to the experience of each individual: "in the case of any man, the knowledge of each precept of philosophy and so of philosophy [as a whole] must be re-enacted for him before it exist. Each proposition of philosophy is not proven until it has been proven in each case" (EK, 79). This is a clear echo of James, who believed that any system that failed to accommodate the variety of individual perceptions was inherently flawed. Instead of measuring individual experience against predetermined notions of absolute truth—or knowledge—both James and Williams sought to bring "all mean absolutisms" down to the level of individual experience. The defining condition of "everything" is "the pluralism of experience," and this condition presumes decentralization (EK, 149).

Like James, and like Emerson as well, Williams rejected the pretensions of absolutism not only because they tended to suppress individual variations but because they created a false picture of human experience— reality, truth, knowledge, history—as fixed and unchanging. In "Experience" Emerson acknowledged that "our love of the real draws us to permanence," but quickly added that our "sanity of mind" demands variety and change (476). Life is lived most fully in the moment of transition, and to deny those moments is to deny life itself. James, too, emphasized that an awareness of experience as always evolving was the key to understanding that experience: individuals react to truth, which changes the character of truth, which, in turn, alters the nature of future reactions, and the cycle repeats. Williams offered a similar observation in his introduction to *The Wedge*, a volume of poems he published in 1944: "A man isn't a block that remains stationary though the psychologists treat him so. . . . Consistency! He varies . . . if he is to retain his sanity."[28] Consistency, Emerson's "hobgoblin of little minds," was something imposed upon human experience in a manner that denied the variety and mutability that were at its core.

Williams thus sought to break up the static patterns and fixed notions that conspired to inhibit individual expression. He was especially interested in reasserting the creative power of words by "blasting away" the "stultifying" forms which have "denied them their dynamic potentialities by fixing them in meanings which prostitute the intelligence." Just as truth, philosophy, and knowledge are dynamic rather than static, so too must language, as their fundamental building block, remain fresh and unconstrained. Indeed, Williams takes James's effort to dislodge the notion of absolute truths to a deeper level, focusing on the language in which those truths are fixed:

> [B]y breaking up formulas would we not be merely losing sight of fixed truths which we need for our continued intellectual existence, would we not be reverting to nonsense without any compensatory gain—even were it possible to break up language to that extent? No. Language is the key to the mind's escape from bondage to the past. There are no "truths" that can be fixed in language. It is by the breakup of language that the truth can be seen to exist and that it becomes operative again. (EK, 19)

Williams here recalls James's idea that truth exists in a meaningful way only when we surrender the notion that it is fixed. We construct truths, just as we construct knowledge and formulate language, as a direct consequence of our experience; there is no absolute truth to organize or guide that experience.

Both James and Williams recognized that this lack of certainty surrounding our actions and beliefs carried with it an element of risk and danger, the possibility that at any point we might be operating under mistaken assumptions and end up lost in the whirl of confusion. For James, this condition represented the very meaning of life: one must accept the universe as "really dangerous and adventurous" and be "willing to live on a scheme of uncertified possibilities" that is open to change at any time.[29] Williams, too, insisted that we must be willing to live with this uncertainty if our lives are to have any meaning at all: "Man must give himself without complete knowledge in the world—or he will not give himself at all" (EK,

53). As Emerson had claimed from the start, to live was to be always searching and never settled, and Williams clearly agreed: one must "take the chance that he is right" and "proceed with his arguments" until experience points in another direction (EK, 66).

It is at this point that Williams and James split most distinctly from Emerson. As I have suggested, each advocated radically undercutting the authority of the past, of tradition, of all fixed notions of truth and knowledge, and each revelled in the uncertainty that would ensue. However, neither Williams nor James was willing to reject entirely all manifestations of tradition. As James noted in *Pragmatism,* "we can hardly take in an impression at all, in the absence of a preconception of what impressions there may possibly be," and he devoted the bulk of his work not to destroying all preconceptions but to ensuring that they remain flexible (595). Similarly, Williams acknowledged that the endless experimentation advocated by Emerson must take place within some broader context. He quotes with approval from Pasteur: "Nothing can be done without preconceived ideas, only there must be wisdom not to accept their deductions beyond what experiments confirm" (EK, 88). Only when those preconceived ideas became absolute and resistant to change did they need to be dissolved, and the task Williams set for himself was to maintain the "dynamic potentialities" of language, of history, and of tradition, each of which was essential to "our continued intellectual existence."

Williams thus alternates in his work between the process of clearing the ground of accumulated dead traditions and the task of creating new and living ones. As Vera Kutzinski noted, Williams sought coherence rather than unity; he wanted to recognize individual differences without denying what was shared, and to join voices without obscuring their separateness. This dual project—at the same time cultural, social, and political—was at the heart of *Paterson* and animates Williams's statement of the purpose of the poem:

> To make a start,
> out of particulars
> and make them general, rolling
> up the sum, by defective means (3)

Though our individual efforts may be "divided as the dew" and as independent as "the floating mists," they are nonetheless ultimately "regathered into a river that flows / and encircles" and from which other efforts emerge

(5). It was this balance of the particular and the general, the individual voice and the chorus in which those voices are inevitably joined, that Williams deemed essential to any truly American endeavor.

In *Kora in Hell,* Williams offered a particularly compelling metaphor to describe his vision of this balance: "one does not attempt by the ingenuity of the joiner to blend the tones of the oboe with the violin. On the contrary, the perfections of each are emphasized . . . no means is neglected to give each the full color of its perfections" (KH, 19). To reach its fullest expression, the orchestra must reflect the nuances of each individual instrument, allowing each to explore the limits of its range. At the same time, Williams recognized that these instruments must work within some sort of structure or risk cacophony. The ultimate goal, after all, is music, and the oboe must not play its part in a way that obscures the violin and undermines the harmony.

While this metaphor helps to clarify the central component of Williams's project, it also leaves unanswered a number of vexing questions: Who fulfills the role of "joiner"? Who determines, and according to what criteria, when the proper balance has been achieved? At what point does the discipline that harmony requires become one of those narrow and restricting forms that Williams elsewhere sought to discard? Clearly, Williams was not interested in designing a new set of rules to govern the production and reception of culture, yet he also refused to embrace cultural detachment and isolation: his artist was not to be a disaffected outsider. He wanted to open this orchestra to a diverse array of voices, including the screams of a puma, without sacrificing coherence. In fact, as Williams himself recognized, he could give no satisfactory answers to these questions. As suggested in the passage from *Paterson* quoted above, the means by which this balance was to be achieved are by definition "defective." The Passaic River, American culture, and American democracy are forever works in progress that must resist being pinned down. Any predetermined notion of what American culture ought to look like—or sound like, or feel like—violated the very principles of indeterminacy and flux that Williams, following Emerson and James, considered to be fundamental.[30]

Part of Williams's answer to these questions, then, was to say that there should be no fixed criteria governing the interaction of oboe and violin: the balance he envisioned was necessarily imperfect and ever-changing. However, this still leaves the troubling question of the identity and role of the "joiner" in a democracy. Like Emerson, Williams had great faith in the artist's ability to guide the incoherent mass in its quest for expression, yet he also feared that any individual artist might come to enjoy too strong an influence. Eliot was only one of many cautionary examples. Within the terms of Williams's metaphor, it would be risky for even the most American of poets to be trusted with the roles of conductor or composer, given the tendency of the culture to devote considerable attention—and bestow considerable power—upon those positions.

Williams might have avoided this question altogether had he chosen a different musical genre for his metaphor, one which largely eliminated the role of conductor and blurred the lines between composer and performers. He wrote *Kora in Hell,* the source of the oboe-violin passage, in 1920. It was not until later in his life that he came to appreciate jazz as an expression of the kind of American idiom he sought in his poetry. He particularly admired the successful blending of innovation and structure, and the liberation of individual voices accomplished without sacrificing the unity of expression.[31] Wynton Marsalis has recently defined the Americanness of jazz in terms that resonate with Williams's project: "The principle of American democracy is that you have freedom. The question is 'How will you use it?' which is also the central question in jazz. In democracy, as in jazz, you have freedom with restraint. It's not absolute freedom, it's freedom within a structure."[32] What Marsalis calls the "conversation" of jazz, the interplay of improvisation and structure, reflects more completely the vision of culture, and of democracy, that runs through Williams's work, a vision that Allen Ginsberg, one of Williams's young protégés, would incorporate more fully into his own poetry.

Williams knew that his vision of American culture rested on a precarious balance, and that the rugged individualism that grew out of the American worship of "freedom" threatened his efforts. Whereas Marsalis would employ a qualified definition of freedom, Williams located the problem within the idea of freedom itself. Though it was "the commonly accepted and much copied cliché," "freedom" implied a lack of discipline and a regrettable tendency to dispersion, exclusion, and isolation (SE, 208–9). In searching for an alternative Williams concluded that "liberty was the better word" since it represented the enabling condition that Americans have always needed: "not so much liberty for freedom's sake but liberty to partake of, to be included in and to conserve." While freedom is centrifugal and implies a "breaking away," liberty "has the significance of inclusion." Williams continues:

> But to have liberty, one must . . . maintain oneself under adverse weather conditions as still part of the whole. Discipline is implied. . . . The real character of the people is not toward dispersion except as a temporary phase

for the gathering of power, but to unite. To form a union. To work toward a common purpose.

For what? On the principle that only in this way can that which is common, commonly possessed—be preserved among differences. (SE, 209)

This balance—between commonality and difference, freedom and discipline, tradition and innovation, the instrument and the ensemble, the individual and society—was at the core of Williams's work and is the central issue confronting American democracy.[33] The discipline it requires is awesome, as William James noted when he remarked upon the tragic but essential task confronting a modern democratic society: the determination of which part of the "ideal" must "be butchered" in order to further the "social scheme" of life (*Will to Believe*, 202–3). Just as James confronted the unpleasant fact that all individual desires could not be accommodated, so Williams acknowledged the inevitable friction between the terms he sought to balance. The following comes from "The Basis of Faith in Art," written in the midst of the social and political turmoil of the Great Depression:

> There is no conflict between the individual and society—unless the individual offend. None but a fool contends that the function of society is to generate surpassing individuals. That is antiquated reasoning. The truth is nearer and harder, merely that society, *to be served*, must generate individuals to serve it, and cannot do otherwise than to give such individuals full play— *until* or unless their activities prove antisocial. (SE, 193)

The offending, antisocial individual; the oboist who plays out of turn; the jazz soloist who refuses to yield; these are the results of freedom without discipline, of dispersion rather than inclusion. They are peculiarly, if not exclusively, American problems, and the peculiarly American solution is to accept that there is perhaps no final solution at all. In the ongoing conversation of American culture, the sought-after balance between contending forces can never be finally achieved. The terms of the balance and the context in which it is to be struck are always changing; the liberty that Williams sought was of necessity a moving target.

In *Spring and All* Williams described his life's project as "seeking to place a value upon experience and the objects of experience that would satisfy my sense of inclusiveness without redundancy—completeness, lack of frustration with the liberty of choice; the things which the pursuit of 'art' offers" (SA, 115–16). This desire for inclusiveness was rooted in Emerson's powerful faith in the sanctity of individual experience and expression, and incorporated James's vision of a pluralistic universe in which each individual contributed to the production, transmission, and revision of truth—and of culture. It echoed Du Bois's effort to create a place for himself in American culture without sacrificing his own individuality. The object of Williams's quest was also that of Emerson, James, Dewey, and Du Bois: an understanding of what was shared through an exploration and affirmation of what was unique. This, in turn, is nothing less than the ongoing object of American democracy.

EPILOGUE

Emersonian Refractions

The cover of Cornel West's *The American Evasion of Philosophy* depicts a tree with its roots wrapped around an open book. The trunk of the tree is labeled "Emerson," while the branches bear tags labeled "Dewey," "James," "Du Bois," "Peirce," "Niebuhr," "Trilling," "Mills," "Hook," "Rorty," and "Quine." It is unclear from the picture whether this arrangement illustrates the varieties of fruit produced by the Emersonian tree or the proliferation of branches sprouting from an Emersonian trunk. In either case, the image serves as a metaphor of West's "genealogy of Pragmatism" in which succeeding figures, drawing on the common Emersonian source, move on in their own direction, that is, branch out. The key point, for West, is that the intellectual tradition he is tracing be understood as nonlinear: the family line has expanded, mingled with other families, been more productive in some directions while, perhaps, tapering off in others.

West's arboreal metaphor (or that of his publisher's art designer) is provocative, and might serve my purposes as well. On a visit to a glass museum, however, I discovered an exhibit that better illustrates both the basic notion of intellectual tradition that I have been working with and the particular tradition that I have tried to sketch. When a beam of light passes through a prism it is refracted: its direction changes, it can become either more sharply focused or more diffuse, it can even be broken up into two or more constituent beams. Now imagine three prisms—A, B, C—arranged on a flat surface. A beam of light is aimed at prism A, which refracts the light and passes some of it on to B and some to C. Prism B, in turn, passes some light on to C while reflecting some back to A, which then passes some of this light to C, and so on. Add more prisms, and you have more paths, more refractions, more reflections. Some prisms receive the light directly, others only as refractions, and still others in various combinations of direct and refracted light.

What does this have to do with Emerson? As I have suggested throughout this study, there are any number of traditions that have derived from
Emerson. Beginning with the same light source—Emerson's essays, poems,
lectures, letters, and journals—generations of literary critics, industrialists,
artists, social commentators, poets, Rotary Club spokesmen, philosophers,
and historians have responded to that source in a variety of ways. Some
have had direct access to the originating beam, others have confronted only
previous refractions. Some have been willing prisms, others reluctant, resistant, even unaware. In emphasizing one idea or set of ideas over others, in
offering different interpretations of key passages, and in their often competing attempts to put Emerson to use, these figures have cooperated in the
construction of a variety of Emersonian traditions. And, as with light
passing through a collection of variously arranged prisms, some of these
paths intersect while others move in opposite directions.

In the 150 years since his first forays into public expression, Emerson has
been transmitted, and transmuted, along many more paths than have yet
been traced. I have focused my attention primarily on two of these—the
sense of discomfort with Emersonian individualism that ran from Henry
James, Sr. to Yvor Winters and a sort of response to that discomfort that
emerges from the work of William James, John Dewey, W.E.B. Du Bois,
and William Carlos Williams. I end with Williams because he brings a
form of closure to the particular path in which I am interested. That is,
Williams does with poetry and cultural criticism in general what Du Bois
does with racial politics and social criticism in general; each brings to bear
on their own field of work an Emersonian sensibility that is in part received
from Emerson and in part refracted by James and Dewey.

Of course, the sense of closure I claim is artificial. Neither Du Bois
nor Williams are opaque, and each refracts as well as receives. The path
through Du Bois may be traced as it, in turn, passes through and is refracted by Ralph Ellison and Cornel West.[1] The path through James and
Williams enjoys its most recent manifestation in A. R. Ammons's *Garbage,*
a stunning meditation on the mutability of language, truth, and the material culture of everyday life.[2] Two other contemporary refractions of the
Emersonian beam deserve mention, though they are tangential to what I
have pursued in these pages. Coming to Emerson after rediscovering Thoreau, Stanley Cavell has claimed for Emerson a place at the center of modern philosophical inquiry, joining Heidegger, Wittgenstein, Kleist, and,
among other texts, such films as *The Lady Eve* and *You Can't Take It with
You.*[3] Emerson also stands at the head of a tradition of nature writing and

environmental thought that passed through John Burroughs and John Muir on the way to Gary Snyder, Annie Dillard, and Edward Abbey.[4]

These, however, are the subjects for further study. I would like to return, by way of conclusion, to the two particular paths I have traced, these two traditions of responding to Emerson. My argument has been that James, Dewey, Du Bois, and Williams provided an answer to the charge, leveled by the critics I discuss in the first two chapters, that Emerson's easy optimism, his radical individualism, and his mystical idealism contained too little fiber for a twentieth-century diet. T. S. Eliot declared him a burden, Irving Howe found his work thin and pale, Yvor Winters would have him charged with manslaughter. Implicit in these and other charges was the fear of what would happen if Emerson's ideas were taken seriously, if, that is, his claims were applied to political and social life. Critics eagerly pointed to ruthless capitalists, monomaniacal dictators, and self-centered flaunters of social convention as cautions against allowing Emerson too much room in the culture. Clearly, this was too high a price to pay for mere "intellectual independence."

A telling, if rather tame example of this motif of Emersonianism-gone-bad is Charles Ives (1874–1954), the extraordinarily innovative American composer (and life-insurance salesman) whose work remains intimately associated with Emerson and the Transcendentalists.[5] Ives's stubborn adherence to his own genius, his deliberate experimentation and nonconformance with the musical standards of his day, was a direct and acknowledged result of his reading of Emerson. His "Essays before a Sonata," intended as explanatory notes to accompany his four "Concord Sonatas" (titled "Emerson," "Hawthorne," "The Alcotts," and "Thoreau"), is perhaps the best record we have of a particular artist's struggle to articulate the nature of Emerson's influence.[6] As fully as any American artist of his day, Ives answered Emerson's call for originality and independence, and while his music was largely ignored during his own life, current interest in his work points toward his ultimate triumph.

However, as a number of critics have noted, Ives's musical accomplishments contrast sharply with the narrowness of his political and business ideas. His "perversion" of Emerson and the Transcendentalists can be seen in his impatience with political dissent, his fondness for moral absolutes, and his intolerance of ambiguity. In his long essay "The Majority," a rather petulant call for restoring power to "the People," he "corrupt[ed] Emerson's conception of the Over-Soul into the deification of the majority as the literal embodiment of truth, political justice, and God's will." And, in his approach to selling insurance, he "reduced Transcendentalism to a public relations approach to salesmanship and business efficiency." The same Emerson who inspired Ives the artist also, apparently, underwrote Ives the self-satisfied crank.[7]

If Ives represents the kind of Emersonian influence feared by many of the critics I have discussed, his is also the type of Emersonianism against which I have posed my readings of James, Dewey, Du Bois, and Williams. Each of these writers demonstrates that Emerson's affirmation of the importance of individual insight does not necessarily authorize the abandonment of social ties. Each offers an explicit claim that Emerson's validation of the individual—a validation based on a complex blending of freedom and fate, assertiveness and obedience, independence and commitment—is the necessary animating force not only of American culture but of American political and social life as well. Indeed, it is a wide-ranging culture of democracy of which Emerson and the others speak, a culture that entails the perceptions of art, the reflections of philosophy, the observations of science, and the practice of politics. Emerson's insights—and those of his "tribe"—necessarily have political implications because in a democracy the political is intimately bound up with the literary, the philosophical, and the cultural.

This argument was first suggested by Vernon Parrington. Locating Emerson squarely in the progressive Jeffersonian line that animated his *Main Currents in American Thought,* Parrington treated Emerson as an explicitly political thinker who, "in transcendental fashion," ranged himself "on the side of Jefferson, in opposition to a coercive sovereignty."[8] Though aware that his portrayal of Emerson as a political theorist went against the grain of almost all existing criticism, Parrington pressed his point: "Emerson knew very well where his political theory led, and he had no timid compunction about following it through." Drawn into an "analysis of political parties and the nature of the political state" by his "deepening concern over the state of politics in America," Emerson reaffirmed the priority of the individual over the narrow materialism of the modern state (384–85).

In depicting Emerson as a progressive political thinker, Parrington had set himself a rather imposing task. Emerson had simply not inspired many observers to view his work or his life in political terms. Conservatives like Oliver Wendell Holmes, Henry Van Dyke, and Irving Babbitt had applauded Emerson's occasional expressions of distrust in the democratic masses and his apparent appreciation of the need for some form of aristocratic restraint, but they worried that his emphasis on self-reliance and individualism might lead to an erosion of social and political authority. This paradox ultimately discouraged them from claiming Emerson as a political thinker, since whatever politics he professed was too erratic to categorize. On the other hand, liberal critics like Brooks and Frank were equally uncomfortable with Emerson's self-reliant individualism, suspecting that it encouraged a posture of detached indifference toward social reform that was, in effect, antipolitical.

Parrington acknowledged these obstacles but sought to navigate around them. First, he argued that the individualism Emerson espoused was a response to divine edict: "In accepting himself he accepted his fellows, and he accepted God" (382). Rather than encouraging anarchy or detachment, Emersonian individualism promoted community, an awareness of other individuals, and "a common political brotherhood," characteristics readily assimilated by Parrington's liberal-Jeffersonian ideal. Parrington then explained Emerson's occasional contempt for the masses by arguing that what Emerson condemned was not the masses themselves but the low condition to which Hamiltonian materialism had brought them. Emerson

> elaborated what we may call a transcendental theory of politics, a theory closely akin to philosophical anarchism. All the elaborate machinery devised by political thinkers like Montesquieu and John Adams, with their schemes of checks and balances to preserve the status quo, he calmly throws overboard. . . . The single, vital, principle on which the true republic must found itself, he insists, is the principle of good-will. (385)

Emerson's transcendental politics would ensure the formation of good government because it would ensure that those coming together to form that government were willing to cooperate in the pursuit of common well-being. Accordingly, government must justify itself on moral and ethical grounds—along the lines of Jefferson's "Declaration of Independence"—rather than relying on the economic imperatives of the Hamiltonian federalists who sought to secure "rulership by persons of principle and property" (388).

Parrington encounters some difficulty when he moves from his description of Emerson's transcendental political theory to a discussion of that theory's applicability to specific political issues. Thrust by Parrington into the debate between Whigs, Federalists, Republicans and Democrats on the "nature and functions of the ideal republic," Emerson's "political theory" seems not so much overmatched as just out of place. Parrington might have fared better had he pursued his revisionary reading of Emersonian individualism, a task that John Dewey and W.E.B. Du Bois, among others, would accomplish with some éclat. Despite his now widely acknowledged limitations, Parrington nonetheless succeeded in demonstrating the connections between democratic culture and the politics of democracy. In locating Emerson at that particular crossroads he helps to illuminate the Emersonian tradition that I have been tracing.

If Parrington gave the first, shaky expression to this nexus of Emersonian individualism, democratic culture, and political democracy, F. O. Matthiessen and Sherman Paul were its most eloquent and expansive chroniclers. Each found in Emerson affirmation of their own belief that truly American artists (scholars, poets, philosophers) must continuously cultivate a relationship with the wider democratic community. Matthiessen saw this "devotion to the possibilities of democracy" as the "common denominator" linking Emerson, Thoreau, Hawthorne, Melville, and Whitman, each of whom gave voice to "the last struggle of the liberal spirit" against "the rising forces of exploitation." It was their "major desire" that "there should be no split between art and the other functions of the community," and each writer, whatever their differences, strove "to provide a culture commensurate with America's political opportunity." Matthiessen attributes his awareness of this important strain of thought to the architect Louis Sullivan, who declared that the artist "must prove that he is a citizen, not a lackey, a true exponent of democracy, not a tool of the most insidious form of anarchy." These standards, Matthiessen concludes, are "the inevitable and right extension of Emerson's demands in 'The American Scholar,'" and they represent the most significant aspect of Emerson's legacy.[9]

Paul himself was drawn to Emerson while studying with Matthiessen in graduate school, and was particularly inspired by Matthiessen's allusion to the Emerson-Sullivan connection.[10] In particular, Paul found in Sullivan affirmation of an important article of faith: "that art is a social activity and that the communication of creative impulse is a necessity of democratic society."[11] This affirmation had its roots in Emerson, and formed the basis of John Dewey's portrayal of Emerson as the "philosopher of democracy." It also forms the basis of Paul's eclectic "green American tradition," his own tracing of the Emersonian presence in American culture. To this extent, Paul's (and Matthiessen's) claim has also been my own: Rather than capitulating to the siren songs of romantic individualism and the lofty pursuit of art, Emerson and those in his line struggled to reconcile these potentially isolating impulses with the requirements of living within a democratic community.

Paul believes that one of Sullivan's most important contributions was to

rong with America. Rather, Emerson contains within himself
the bad, the genius and the madness, the generosity and the
e communal and the archly independent, with all of it a ready
piration. One finds, in Updike's Emerson, what one is looking
Updike, one is looking for something solid to grab onto, one is
d: "as I read [Emerson], a hundred stimulated thoughts would
, but all in the nature of paint that would not stick" (165). Or, as
es Sr. characterized his friend from Concord: "you man without

swer Updike provides for the question—What can we do with
?—is hardly new. The idea that Emerson could legitimately be
ood to mean almost anything dates back to his own lifetime, and
shared assumption of much of the commentary in the years follow-
death. It is precisely this answer, however, that the boom in Emer-
holarship over the last twenty years has rejected. Richard Poirier
this point with particular reference to Updike:

> he [Emerson] boom does not mean that a single or even consistent image
> f Emerson will emerge. It means only that he cannot any longer be treated
> s anything less than the great and difficult writer he is, as a writer who has
> already anticipated any degree of sophistication that might be brought to
> him. It is no longer permissible to go to him as to some department store that
> might or might not supply your list of household needs, as John Updike did
> in a sulky piece on Emerson that appeared a few years ago in the *New
> Yorker*. . . . Updike is merely negligent.[16]

A similar charge might be leveled against Barrett Wendell, Hamilton
Wright Mabie, Charles William Eliot, and the entire tradition in which
Updike's reading of Emerson stands. Confronted with the difficulty of
Emerson's work, frustrated critics have repeatedly fallen back on anecdotes,
aphorisms, and personality sketches, willing to explore the rather simple
question of "What Ralph Waldo Emerson Means to Me," but reluctant or
unable to consider what Emerson might, in fact, mean.

For Poirier, the key to avoiding this sort of misreading is to expose
and explore the complex, fluid, and fundamentally difficult nature of
Emersonian individualism, an individualism that is alternately indifferent
and antagonistic to our common understanding of individual effort and
achievement. Emerson's is an individualism stripped of all egoism, a condition that makes claims like Updike's difficult to sustain. As Poirier suggests,
Emerson's reputation, the manner by which we will assess his importance,
relates directly to how we understand and make sense of "individualism."

carry the "democratic idealism" rooted in Emerson and the Transcendentalists to "the pragmatism of our own era." J. David Greenstone has made a
similar claim for the importance of Jane Addams.[12] Specifically, Addams
represented a transition in American liberalism and the American reform
tradition from a "politics of interests" to a "politics of standards," from "the
moral certainty and self-reliance of Emerson's Transcendentalism to the
collective action and moral inquiry of Dewey's Pragmatism" (527). While
Greenstone is wrong to characterize Emerson's self-reliance as a form of
moral certitude, and misses Dewey's own testament to Emerson's importance, he does highlight the important links between Emerson and Dewey:

> Both men insisted, though in different ways, on the decisive importance of
> an active, interpreting, human intelligence, and, as a result, the active culti-
> vation of every individual's artistic and cultural faculties. On the other hand,
> Emerson and Dewey also stressed the individual's responsibility to engage in
> practical, ethical action according to standards independent of one's mere
> personal preferences. (544)

It was these shared precepts that Addams helped to keep alive in her own
work, carrying the Emersonian legacy into the harsh realities of modern
political and social life and demonstrating their validity not only to John
Dewey but, Greenstone believes, to the progressive reformers of the New
Deal and the 1960s as well (554).

The political implications of this Emersonian tradition are given their
most forceful expression in the work of political philosopher George Kateb. At the heart of Kateb's project is his effort to affirm the centrality of
rights-based individualism to democracy in the face of growing attacks
from both the Left and the Right. Pointing to the dangerous excesses that
have emerged from America's individualist ethos, liberal communitarians
and reactionary conservatives alike have proposed placing restraints on the
exercise of individual rights. Such proposals, Kateb claims, amount to an
abdication of democracy itself. At the same time, he endeavors to reclaim
his own definition of "democratic individualism" from the narrow clutches
of libertarians, Social Darwinists, and radical free-marketers whose excesses
in pursuit of individual freedom have all too often justified the attacks on
individualism.[13]

The key figure in Kateb's reformulation of individualism is, significantly,
Emerson. While Emerson's influence is decisively individualistic, "democracy helps Emerson and others to deepen the meaning" of that individuality, thereby making it "seem more interconnected and less idiosyncratic"
(153). Seizing on this passage from Emerson's "Politics"—"Governments

have their origin in the moral identity of men"—Kateb formulates his definition of democratic individuality in a manner that bears a striking resemblance to Williams James:

> To live in a democracy is to live in a society in which the most important judgment made about persons is that they are of equal worth just because they are human beings. . . . What is primary is humanness. The political system, insofar as it is democratic, is built on such acceptance. . . . In effect, each is saying to the rest, Whatever you do, however you live your life, provided you accept me and others, I accept you. (155)

Of course, this is a direct challenge to many of Emerson's (and James's, and Dewey's) less tolerant critics, who would either refuse to see this formulation as having anything to do with Emerson, or, granting the connection with Emerson, would see it as precisely the kind of lapse in standards and discrimination to which they were opposed. Such critics, of course, are not contained solely within the group I discussed in the first two chapters. If James, Dewey, Du Bois, and Williams offered a response to the doubts about Emerson, their response is by no means the final word in the debate. Just as the continuation of their efforts can be followed in such later figures as Matthiessen, Paul, Kateb, Kloppenberg, Ammons, or Cavell, the doubts and denunciations of Babbitt, Eliot, and Calverton also enjoy an ongoing history. Though not as shrill as Lewishon or Winters, many contemporary critics still declare the Emersonian tradition to be pale, thin, or dangerous.

I have already discussed a key text in this countertradition, David Marr's *American Worlds since Emerson*. Marr traces our modern day political crisis to the "idealized privatism" of the Emersonian tradition, a tradition that encourages a retreat from the world of public affairs into the private realms of thought. This emerges as the logical outcome of Emersonian individualism, and while finding much to admire in Emerson and those who followed him, Marr concludes that the tradition has done more harm than good. John Diggins has similarly pointed to Emerson's "privatization of virtue" as a source of America's contemporary troubles: "Today, when America seems awash in a 'culture of narcissism' and Emerson's doctrine of 'self-reliance' has dropped from the 'Over-soul' to the underbelly, Tocqueville's fears of 'the passionate and exaggerated love of self' have made the demands of the 'Me' the first priority of politics."[14] While Diggins is willing to grant that Emerson may not be directly responsible for this—that he may simply be the unlucky victim of careless readers—the burden of guilt still falls most squarely on his shoulders. What Diggins and Marr offer

as a tale of damage done w. critics sought to dissociate En. ideas, and more than half a cei their own, different, concerns.

John Updike has given us perh. lingering doubts about Emerson, . concerns of Emerson's earliest critic but affirmative answer to the questio. center of [Emerson's] reputation, som he has left us?" (149). In Updike's read trine of righteous selfishness," giving ini. creed of Rugged Individualism." His ic damned" sentiment of the robber barons moral" ethics of the Yippies (159). Here is ne Emersonianism I have been tracing. For Gr. Jane Addams) informed the politically engage. of the 1960s; for Updike, Emerson's influence achieves fruition in the feckless pursuit of self-gr. the counterculture. One thinks of the question P. two advisors who had offered sharply conflicting re. Vietnam: "You two did visit the same country, didn't.

While Updike echoes the fears of many of Emers. such doctrines as self-reliance might undermine the 1 havior (whether by validating the rapaciousness of Iv. detached narcissism of Generation X), he also gives ne concern about Emerson's influence on American culture. formulation, though Updike's, might just as well have c. Wyck Brooks or Waldo Frank:

> The famous American pragmatism and "can do" optimism were g most ardent expression by Emerson; his encouragements have th elements in the magnificent sprawl we see on all sides—the parking 1 skyscrapers, the voracious tracts of single-family homes, the heaped . market aisles and crowded ribbons of highway: the architectural mani. tions of a nation of individuals.

For Updike, Emerson ultimately authors the same materialistic cu. against which he sought to provide an antidote. He contains within hims. seeds of "the notorious loneliness and callousness and violence of America life" which accompanies that life's "many authentic and, indeed, unprecedented charms" (161–62). It is not that Updike sees Emerson as the source

This is one of the principal points that I have tried to develop in these pages: the complex of interpretations and conditions that surround the idea "individualism" is the crux around which Emerson's readers—academic critics, literary professionals, and casual saunterers alike—have perennially arranged themselves.[17]

A final example should help to illustrate my point. In his penetrating critique of the American mythology of the "imperial self," Quentin Anderson offers the following analysis:

> Individualism, insofar as it stands for the energy, inventiveness, and adaptability of Americans committed to commercial or industrial enterprise, is a name for those personal qualities which foster impersonality in social and economic relations; the individualist is (again, in the very terms of the myth) the man who subjects others to himself through his shrewdness in gauging their appetites or anticipating their needs.[18]

As his study unfolds, it is clear that Anderson locates the origin of this cultural flaw in the work of Emerson. For George Kateb, however, Emerson

> corrects the latency in rights-based individualism to make too much of oneself. The nobility of the Emersonian aspiration lies in transcending the ideal of individualism understood as the cultivation and expression of personality, precisely because Emerson, like his great colleagues Thoreau and Whitman, knows how social, and not individualist, such an ideal is. They all go in the direction of self-abandonment, away from egotism, even away from self-expression, and do so as proponents of individualism. (236)

The difference here is not that Kateb and Anderson have read different Emersons. Rather, each begins with a very different understanding of the scope and meaning of individualism and reads Emerson through that. Anderson is specifically concerned with individualism as it is manifest in economic life and, like many other observers of the American scene, he does not like what he sees. Better to do without Emerson than to suffer such alienation and exploitation. Kateb, on the other hand, considers individualism in a wider context, and while aware of the nefarious tendencies of certain expressions of individualism, upholds Emerson as the key to transcending those tendencies without giving up on individualism itself.

What Kateb implicitly recognizes, through his reading of Emerson, is that American democracy cannot be divorced from its own founding insight: that equal value inheres in each person solely on account of that person's humanness. To be sure, this individualist ethos has underwritten a long history of violence, selfishness, exploitation, and alienation. It is at the root of all sorts of antisocial behavior, and is regularly invoked to justify opposition to even the mildest laws and regulations. But to see Emerson and the individualism he espoused as forming a subtext for William Graham Sumner or the militia movement is, as Poirier would see it, a case of negligent reading. Emersonian individualism is not a blueprint for corporate rapaciousness; nor does it forbid us to distinguish between Martin Luther King Jr. and David Koresh, each of whom, after all, was merely pursuing his own vision of God's plan. What Emerson does do is challenge his readers to struggle with the extraordinarily complex nature of individualism, to see it as something fluid, with different meanings, and different ramifications, in the varying contexts of American life. At its base, as William James so clearly saw, Emersonian individualism is an ethical claim. It imposes responsibilities far more than it undermines them. As Kateb observed, the real task then is not to replace individualism but to rehabilitate it (239).

It was the achievement of Dewey, James, Du Bois, and Williams to recognize and accept this challenge. James did so by stressing that individuals exist only in relation to other individuals, and he demonstrated the philosophical and practical impossibilities of seeing the self as solitary or imperial. While the inner lives of people had serious consequences for their social lives, so too did the reality of social existence have real consequences for individuals. Dewey sought to replace the older individualism with one that was better adapted to the changes in American economic and social life. In the process he argued that the value of individual endeavor was determined solely by the degree to which it was made part of the life of the community. Du Bois recognized the mockery that Emersonian individualism made of America's racial prejudices, while also realizing in his own life the importance of subordinating that individualism to a wider social goal. For his part, Williams sought to negotiate cultural space for a variety of American voices while ensuring that those voices made meaningful music together. In his vision of a democratic culture, he sought to balance the two dominant images of the artist's relationship to society: that of the always-alienated outsider crying in the wilderness, and that of the purveyor of a time-honored and stagnant national tradition. His search for the unity that could be found within difference, and without repressing difference, was Emersonian to the core.

Each of these appropriations of Emerson coheres around a complex understanding of individualism that is anything but rugged and possessive. To discard individualism, to ignore Emerson, is to forfeit any possibility of understanding the "hard mystery" that Robert Frost saw at the heart of

American democracy. When the presidential candidates of both parties can, simultaneously and with no acknowledgment of contradiction or complexity, praise the tradition of American individualism, criticize the ceaseless clamor for rights, and call for a restoration of community values, then the challenging claims of the tribe of Waldo seem very timely indeed.

NOTES

Introduction. An Individualism of Vaporous Spirituality

1. David Reynolds would, no doubt, claim Walt Whitman as at least an equal player in this endeavor, and not merely because Whitman's work was similarly marked by contradiction and paradox. See his *Walt Whitman's America: A Cultural Biography* (New York: Vintage, 1995).

2. *The Inner Ocean: Individualism and Democratic Culture* (Ithaca, N.Y.: Cornell University Press, 1992).

3. *The Emerson Effect: Individualism and Submission in America* (Chicago: University of Chicago Press, 1996), 1.

4. While I do not deal directly with Newfield or Kateb in the following pages, it should become evident that the Emersonian tradition I trace has more in common with Kateb's liberal individualism than Newfield's corporatism.

5. F. O. Matthiessen, *American Renaissance* (New York: Oxford University Press, 1941); Perry Miller, "Jonathan Edwards to Emerson," *The New England Quarterly* 13 (December 1940): 589–617, and "Emersonian Genius and the American Democracy," *New England Quarterly* 26 (March 1953): 27–44; Sherman Paul, *Emerson's Angle of Vision: Man and Nature in American Experience* (Cambridge, Mass.: Harvard University Press, 1952); Stephen Whicher, *Freedom and Fate: An Inner Life of Ralph Waldo Emerson* (Philadelphia: University of Pennsylvania Press, 1953).

6. T. S. Eliot, review of vol. 2 of Trent, Erskine, Sherman, and Van Doren, eds., *Cambridge History of American Literature*, in *Athenaeum* 4643 (25 April 1919): 238. Though Eliot's recorded comments on Emerson are few, a number of critics have made interesting attempts at uncovering an intellectual relationship. See John Clendenning, "Time, Doubt and Vision: Notes on Emerson and T. S. Eliot," *American Scholar* 36 (Winter 1966–67): 125–32; Robert G. Cook, "Emerson's 'Self-Reliance,' Sweeney, and Prufrock," *American Literature* 42 (May 1970): 221–26; and Ronald Bush, "T. S. Eliot: Singing the Emerson Blues," in *Emerson: Prospect and Retrospect*, ed. Joel Porte (Cambridge, Mass.: Harvard University Press, 1982), 179–97. The prospect that Eliot's early career was devoted to consciously evading the force of Emerson's influence is intriguing; see Lyndall Gordon, *Eliot's Early Years* (Oxford: Oxford University Press, 1977).

7. Irving Howe, *A Margin of Hope: An Intellectual Autobiography* (New York: Harcourt, Brace Jovanovich, 1982), 142–43; "An Interview with Irving Howe," *American Literary History* 1.3 (Fall 1989): 556. Howe's major reassessment of Emerson is *American Newness: Culture and Politics in the Age of Emerson* (1986).

8. Emerson himself had taken steps in this direction, though this has often been overlooked. Throughout his work are passages which temper the reputed antisocial tendencies of his ideas, passages which assert the notions of duty and responsibility to a higher source than the simple self as a means of ensuring that the individualism he articulated did not deteriorate into chaotic assertions of base self-interest. A compelling argument to this effect is Lou Ann Lange, *The Riddle of Liberty: Emerson on Alienation, Freedom, and Obedience* (Atlanta, Ga.: Scholar's Press, 1986). Lange wants to correct what she sees as a dominant strain in Emerson criticism which, in failing to acknowledge his argument for the "girding belt," has persisted in seeing Emerson as "endorsing a view of individual freedom so radical and thoroughgoing as to border either on an unhealthy solipsism or on anarchy" (xii). The effort to reclaim Emerson from this view is itself part of a prominent strain in Emerson criticism, and is the premise upon which much of the boom in Emerson studies is based. For related arguments, see Daniel Aaron, *Men of Good Hope: A Story of American Progressives* (New York: Oxford University Press, 1951); Gertrude Reif Hughes, *Emerson's Demanding Optimism* (Baton Rouge: Louisiana State University Press, 1984); Maurice Gonnaud, *An Uneasy Solitude: Individual and Society in the Work of Ralph Waldo Emerson*, trans. Lawrence Rosenwald (Princeton, N.J.: Princeton University Press, 1987); and Robert Richardson, *Emerson: The Mind on Fire* (Berkeley: University of California Press, 1995).

9. Richard Brodhead, *The School of Hawthorne* (New York: Oxford University Press, 1986).

10. *The Green American Tradition: Essays and Poems for Sherman Paul,* ed. H. Daniel Peck (Baton Rouge: Louisiana State University Press, 1989), 2.

11. "Emerson's Essays," in Sherman Paul, *Repossessing and Renewing: Essays in the Green American Tradition* (Baton Rouge: Louisiana State University Press, 1976). This is the best introduction to Paul's work, collecting essays on all the key figures in his Emersonian tradition that supplement his book-length studies of Emerson, Wilson, Sullivan, and Bourne.

12. Christopher Lasch, *The True and Only Heaven: Progress and Its Critics* (New York: Norton, 1991), esp. pp. 546–51. Lasch is certainly not the first to advance this sort of argument about Emerson—Aaron's *Men of Good Hope* and Newton Arvin's "The House of Pain: Emerson and the Tragic Sense," *Hudson Review* 12 (Spring 1959) are only two precursors—but his treatment is noteworthy for its freshness: Lasch admits that it was only late in life that he came to see Emerson as such a crucial figure, and he seems intent on compensating for his earlier blindness.

13. David Marr, *American Worlds since Emerson* (Amherst: University of Massachusetts Press, 1988).

14. Cornel West, *The American Evasion of Philosophy: A Genealogy of Pragmatism* (Madison: University of Wisconsin Press, 1989). West's use of "genealogy" implies a Nietzschean concept of pragmatism as a term which, rather than standing for a relatively fixed body of ideas moving through time, has been continuously and radically revised and redefined by those who have appropriated it. For a trenchant critique of West's argument, see Robert Gooding-Williams, "Evading Narrative Myth, Evading Prophetic Pragmatism: A Review of Cornel West's *The American Evasion of Philosophy,*" *American Philosophical Association*

Newsletter 90.3 (Fall 1991): 12–16. Gooding-Williams claims that West's unfolding of pragmatism relies more on an organic model of exposition than genealogy.

15. West, *The American Evasion*, 212. For an argument that West's "prophetic pragmatism" is no more responsive to the wretched of the earth than the models he seeks to supersede, see Ross Posnock, "The Politics of Pragmatism and the Fortune of the Public Intellectual," *American Literary History* 3.3 (Fall 1991): 566–87. See also Evan Carton, "Two Faces of American Pragmatism," *Raritan* 11.2 (Fall 1991): 115–27, for a shrewd comparison of West and Marr.

16. James T. Kloppenberg, *Uncertain Victory: Social Democracy and Progressivism in European and American Thought, 1870–1920* (New York: Oxford University Press, 1986), 64–65, 73.

17. See ibid., 93, 95–98, 147–50, 160–63, 190–91.

18. The exclusively male lineage of my cast of characters is a function of coincidence rather than design. These four men provide the most compelling alternative to a broad-based dismissal of Emerson that is, in itself, distinctively masculine. The story of the gendered reading of Emersonian individualism—which might include Jane Addams, Kate Chopin, and Emma Goldman, among others—is the subject for another book.

1. The Aroma of Personality and the Dignity of Clean Living

1. George Fredrickson discusses the gradual shedding of some aspects of Emersonianism and the redefinition of others in *The Inner Civil War: Northern Intellectuals and the Crisis of the Union* (New York: Harper & Row, 1965), 172–80. While Fredrickson makes some useful observations about the fate of Emerson's reputation in the years following the Civil War, his suggestion that Emerson himself came to reject much of his earlier work significantly overstates the case.

2. Sara Norton and M. A. DeWolfe Howe, eds., *The Letters of Charles Eliot Norton*, 2 vols. (Boston: Houghton Mifflin, 1913), 1:399.

3. H. L. Kleinfield, "The Structure of Emerson's Death," *Ralph Waldo Emerson: A Profile*, ed. Carl Bode (New York: Hill and Wang, 1968), 187. This is a revised version of the article which originally appeared in the *Bulletin of the New York Public Library* 65 (January 1961): 47–64.

4. In a brief discussion of Emerson's hagiography, Joel Porte suggests that the influence Emerson had on his contemporaries was "more a question of the transcendent aura that appeared to surround him than of the orphic and uplifting nature of his pronouncements," and that after his death he underwent a "quasi-apotheosization as the patron saint of America's spiritual life." *Representative Man: Ralph Waldo Emerson in His Time* (1979; New York: Columbia University Press, 1988), 19–20. My discussion in this chapter builds on Kleinfield's analysis of the tributes to Emerson published between 1882 and 1903, and expands on Porte's suggestion.

5. F. O. Matthiessen, *The James Family* (New York: Knopf, 1947), 43, 436. The first passage comes from a letter James wrote to Emerson early in their acquaintance, the second from the essay "Mr. Emerson," which Matthiessen reprints (434–38). The essay was first published in *The Literary Remains of the Late Henry James*, ed. William James (1884).

6. Henry James Sr., "Emerson," *Atlantic Monthly Magazine* 94 (December 1904): 740. According to the introductory note by William James, this essay was written around 1868 and presented privately, but never before published. It is interesting to note the date of

composition (Emerson had fourteen years left to live) because the essay reads very much like a memorial address. Like Norton a few years later, James must have been convinced that Emerson had nothing left to give.

7. For broad discussion of the interplay between gender and the spheres of intellect and character, see Ann Douglas, *The Feminization of American Culture* (New York: Knopf, 1977) and Nancy F. Cott, *The Bonds of Womanhood: "Woman's Sphere" in New England, 1780–1835* (New Haven, Conn.: Yale University Press, 1977). The feminization of Emerson, coincident with the gradual blurring of his ideas, would make him an enigmatic figure for those writers and critics in the twentieth century who were interested in developing a "stronger," more masculine, and more ideological mode for American literature.

8. Robert E. Burkholder and Joel Myerson argue that Lowell's commentary exercised a great deal of influence on the way Emerson was viewed throughout the rest of the nineteenth century; "Ralph Waldo Emerson," in *The Transcendentalists: A Review of Research and Criticism,* ed. Joel Myerson (New York: Modern Language Association of America, 1984), 143.

9. James Russell Lowell, "Emerson the Lecturer," *The Recognition of Ralph Waldo Emerson,* ed. Milton R. Konvitz (Ann Arbor: University of Michigan Press, 1972), 45. Originally appeared in *Nation,* 12 November 1868, and *My Study Windows* (1871). Lowell's comment gets to the heart of a frequently repeated story concerning Emerson's appeal to his audience. A washerwoman in Concord who always took off early to attend Emerson's lectures was asked if she understood what he was saying. She replied: "Not a word; but I like to go and see him stand up there and look as if he thought every one was as good as he was." The source for this is Edward Waldo Emerson, *Emerson in Concord* (Boston, 1889), 148. Other appearances include Thomas Wentworth Higginson, "The Personality of Emerson," *The Outlook* 74.4 (23 May 1903): 221, and Charles Ives, *Essays before a Sonata* (1920; New York: Norton, 1961), 35. A similar story appears in *A Western Journey with Mr. Emerson* (Boston, 1884), where James B. Thayer describes a newspaper account of one of Emerson's lectures as providing a "meagre outline of the address" but affirming that "all left the church feeling that an elegant tribute had been paid to the creative genius of the Great First Cause, and that a masterly use of the English language had contributed to that end." Among the many reappearances of this story is Oliver Wendell Holmes, *Ralph Waldo Emerson* (Boston: Houghton Mifflin, 1884), 267.

10. It is interesting to note Lowell's assertion of Emerson's masculinity in contrast with Henry James Sr.'s acceptance of Emerson's fundamentally feminine nature. It is also worth noting that Lowell's associating Emerson's significance with his ability to inspire others would be echoed less favorably by later critics who would blame Emerson for the excesses of his "disciples."

11. *Boston Evening Transcript,* 27 April 1882, p. 4, col. 2. This approach to eulogizing recently deceased literary figures was a characteristic of nineteenth-century journalism and criticism in general, and I do not mean to suggest that it was unique to Emerson: Longfellow, Whittier, and Bryant were among those who were mourned as much for the loss of their comforting presence as for the blow this loss struck to American literature. Still, Emerson's case is special in that he was so thoroughly defined by this process. While he received more frequent and more elaborate expressions of affection, he also enjoyed considerably less in the way of attention to what he wrote.

12. *San Francisco Chronicle,* 28 April 1882, p. 2, col. 1; *Daily Picayune* (New Orleans), 28 April 1882, p. 6, col. 1.

13. *Chicago Tribune,* 28 April 1882, p. 3, col. 6; *Atlanta Constitution,* 28 April 1882, p. 5, col. 2, emphasis added.

14. The passage quoted is from the *San Francisco Chronicle.* Similar sentiments were expressed in the New Orleans *Daily Picayune,* the *Chicago Tribune,* and the Washington Post, 28 April 1882, p. 2, col. 2. Of course, any significant figure is subject to reevaluation by the critics of succeeding generations. My point is that in Emerson's case they would have had a precariously thin tradition to reevaluate.

15. *New York Times,* 28 April 1882, p. 1, col. 5.

16. Of course, Edna Pontellier's fate in Chopin's *The Awakening* suggests that Emerson might not have been all that safe for Victorian womanhood after all.

17. William T. Harris, "Ralph Waldo Emerson," *Atlantic Monthly* 50 (August 1882): 245, 242.

18. Characteristic of these personal accounts is Charles J. Woodberry who, as a student at Williams College, met Emerson three or four times. His *Talks With Emerson* (1890; New York: Horizon Press, 1970) concludes with the sentiment that Emerson will be remembered "less as a man of unmatched originality, an unfailing fountain of delightful ideas, a moral genius of extraordinary insight and mastery . . . than as an inheritance of the divine presence" (177). Similar testaments can be found in Moncure D. Conway, *Emerson at Home and Abroad* (1883; New York: Haskell House, 1968); Alexander Ireland, *Ralph Waldo Emerson, His Life, Genius and Writings* (1882; Port Washington, N.Y.: Kennikat Press, 1972); and John Albee, *Remembrances of Emerson* (New York: R. G. Cooke, 1901).

19. Oliver Wendell Holmes, *Ralph Waldo Emerson* (Boston: Houghton Mifflin, 1884). For a discussion of the influence of Holmes's study on subsequent Emerson criticism, see Len Gougeon, *Virtue's Hero: Emerson, Antislavery, and Reform* (Athens: University of Georgia Press, 1990), 1–23. Gougeon argues that Holmes founded a tradition of depicting Emerson as a social and political conservative, with little sympathy for or interest in abolition.

20. Oliver Wendell Holmes, "Address on Emerson" reprinted in Alexander Ireland, *Ralph Waldo Emerson: His Life, Genius, and Writings,* 239.

21. Though by no means the most authoritative, Holmes's biography was probably the most popular account of Emerson until Ralph Rusk's *Life of Ralph Waldo Emerson* appeared in 1949. See Gougeon, *Virtue's Hero.*

22. Arnold struggled with the composition of the essay and was aware that even though he presented himself as a fervent admirer of Emerson, his relatively tame criticisms would provoke angry rebuttals. See R. H. Super, "Critical and Explanatory Notes," in Matthew Arnold, *Philistinism in England and America,* ed. R. H. Super (Ann Arbor: University of Michigan Press, 1974), 506–7.

23. For a discussion of the controversy aroused by the first few occasions of Arnold delivering the address, see Sidney Coulling, *Matthew Arnold and His Critics* (Athens: University of Ohio Press, 1974), 286–89. While the reaction against Arnold was in part due to his being a foreigner, it was also true that he had criticized Emerson in a way that no American critic had yet dared.

24. "Matthew Arnold on Emerson," *Boston Daily Advertiser,* 3 December 1883, p. 4, cols. 3–4; 7 December 1883, p. 4, cols. 4–5.

25. "Arnold and Emerson," *Boston Evening Transcript,* 3 December 1883, p. 4, col. 2.

26. *Literary World* 15 (3 October 1885): 346.

27. Arnold, "Emerson," *Philistinism in England and America,* 168–74.

28. Edwin Percy Whipple, "Emerson as Poet," *North American Review* 135 (July 1882): 1–

26, and Edmund Clarence Stedman, "Emerson," *Century* 25 (April 1883): 872–86, reprinted in *Poets of America* (Boston: Houghton Mifflin, 1885). Both Whipple and Stedman set out to claim Emerson as the great American poet and place him among the leaders in poetry in English. In each case, however, after making this claim, the author proceeds to detail the many instances in which Emerson fails to meet the test. Both Whipple and Stedman conclude by stressing Emerson's beautiful temper. Arnold addresses Stedman's article at the beginning of his lecture, "Emerson," 168–69. Kleinfield ("Structure of Emerson's Death") discusses Whipple, 186.

29. Nina Baym suggests the tenacity of this influence in "Early Histories of American Literature: A Chapter in the Institution of New England," *American Literary History* 1 (1989): 459–88. The influence of these works, as well as the details of their publication, are discussed in Evelyn R. Bibb, "Anthologies of American Literature, 1787–1964" (Ph.D. diss., Columbia University, 1965), 187–237; and Kermit Vanderbilt, *American Literature and the Academy*, (Philadelphia: University of Pennsylvania Press, 1986). The histories were aimed at a wide audience, intended for use as handbooks in both schools and colleges and as guides for the well-informed general reader.

30. Charles F. Richardson, *American Literature, 1607–1885*, 2 vols. (New York: G. P. Putnam and Sons, 1887, 1889).

31. Indeed, Vanderbilt argues that these volumes (he selectively lists close to thirty published between 1886 and 1907) were derived largely from each other in something of a symbiotic orgy of production, *American Literature*, 126–52.

32. Richard Burton, *Literary Leaders of America* (New York: Scribners, 1904), 135, 163.

33. Walter Bronson, *A Short History of American Literature, Designed Primarily for Use in Schools and Colleges* (Boston: D. C. Heath, 1903), 205, 208–9.

34. Barrett Wendell, *A Literary History of America* (1900; New York: Greenwood Press, 1968), 315.

35. "A Packet of Wendell-James Letters," ed. M. A. De Wolfe Howe, *Scribner's Magazine* 84 (December 1928): 677. The letter is dated October 25, 1900.

36. For intellectual background on Wendell, see Vanderbilt, *American Literature*, 123–45, and Robert T. Self, "Introduction" to Barrett Wendell, *Literature, Society, and Politics: Selected Essays*, ed. Robert T. Self (St. Paul: John Colet Press, 1977), x–xii.

37. Henry Van Dyke, "Introduction," *Select Essays of Ralph Waldo Emerson*, ed. Henry Van Dyke (New York: American Book Company, 1907), 18.

38. Stedman was a member of the so-called genteel circle of poets and critics that presided over the New York literary scene in the late nineteenth century. Van Dyke, though twenty years younger, was cast in essentially the same mold. See John Tomsich, *A Genteel Endeavor: American Culture and Politics in the Gilded Age* (Stanford, Calif.: Stanford University Press, 1971).

39. Brander Matthews, *Introduction to American Literature* (New York: American Book Company, 1896).

40. For a discussion of Matthews's notion of strong literature, see Lawrence J. Oliver, "Theodore Roosevelt, Brander Matthews, and the Campaign for Literary Nationalism," *American Quarterly* 41 (March 1989): 93–111.

41. *American Author* 2.6 (May 1903): 174.

42. Le Baron Russell Briggs, "Address," in Social Circle of Concord, *The Centenary of the Birth of Ralph Waldo Emerson* (Cambridge, Mass.: Riverside Press, 1903), 21.

43. Charles Eliot Norton, "Emerson—The Brahmin View," in *Ralph Waldo Emerson: A Profile*, ed. Carl Bode (New York: Hill and Wang, 1968), 140–41. This is reprinted from *The Centenary of the Birth of Ralph Waldo Emerson*.

44. Kleinfield considers George Willis Cooke, "The Emerson Centennial," *New England Magazine*, n.s., 28.3 (May 1903): 255–64; Cooke, "Emerson the Citizen," *The Nation* 76 (28 May 1903): 428–29; Hamilton Wright Mabie, "Ralph Waldo Emerson in 1903," *Harper's Monthly Magazine* 106 (May 1903): 903–8; "Ralph Waldo Emerson," *Outlook* 74 (23 May 1903): 210–13; and Charles William Eliot, "Emerson as Seer," *Atlantic Monthly* 91 (June 1903): 844–55. Emerson was also praised for his commitment to democracy by Theodore Roosevelt, in a telegram reprinted in the *American Author* 2.6 (May 1903): 186; Edwin Wiley, "Emerson's Ideal of Democracy," *The Book Lover* 4.18 (May–June 1903): 105–7; and Bliss Carman, "Emerson," *The Literary World* 34.5 (May 1903): 120.

45. Eliot quotes the "guide and adorn" passage from Emerson's journal; the "evil intellectual effects" is Eliot's own formulation. Edwin Wiley offers a similar appraisal of Emerson's understanding of democracy, noting that his idea of an efficient state was "one that is made up of strong and sincere personalities," a goal Emerson sought to reach by preaching the gospel of great men ("Emerson's Ideal," 105–6).

46. W. Robertson Nicoll, "Ralph Waldo Emerson," *North American Review* 176 (May 1903): 684.

47. John Albee, *Remembrances of Emerson* (New York: R. G. Cooke, 1903), 94.

48. See "The After-Glow of Emerson," *Unity* 9 (16 June 1882): 167–68, and *Unitarian Review* 17 (May 1882): 458–60.

49. George Gordon, "Emerson as a Religious Influence," *Atlantic Monthly* 91 (May 1903): 581–83, 584.

50. James Mudge, "Emerson and His Centennial," *Methodist Quarterly Review* 52.4 (October 1903): 664, 668.

51. D. S. Gregory, "The Apotheosis of Emerson," *Homiletic Review* 46 (July 1903): 73, 77.

52. "The Emasculation of Emerson," *Ethical Record* 4.5 (June–July 1903): 189–90.

53. Edwin D. Mead advances a similar argument, noting that Emerson's quiet subversion of orthodoxy was the logical and desperately needed step in the evolution of the Christian faith. See *The Influence of Emerson* (Boston: American Unitarian Society, 1903), 70–87.

54. John Jay Chapman, "Emerson, Sixty Years After," in *Emerson and Other Essays* (New York: Scribner's, 1898), 35; reprinted from *Atlantic Monthly* 79 (1897).

55. Stow Persons, *The Decline of American Gentility*, (New York: Columbia University Press, 1973); Larzer Ziff, *The American 1890s* (1966; Lincoln: University of Nebraska Press, 1979); Alan Trachtenberg, *The Incorporation of America: Culture and Society in the Gilded Age* (New York: Hill and Wang, 1982); and Henry F. May, *The End of American Innocence* (1959; New York: Oxford University Press, 1979). See also John Tomsich, *A Genteel Endeavor: American Culture and Politics in the Gilded Age* (Stanford, Calif.: Stanford University Press, 1971); Robert P. Falk, "The Literary Criticism of the Genteel Decades, 1870–1900," in *The Development of American Literary Criticism*, ed. Floyd Stovall (Chapel Hill: University of North Carolina Press, 1955); and Ruth Elson Miller, *Guardians of Tradition: American Schoolbooks in the 19th Century* (Lincoln: University of Nebraska Press, 1964).

56. Ziff, *The American 1890s*, 22.

57. William Dean Howells, *My Mark Twain: Reminiscences and Criticisms* (New York: Harper and Brothers, 1910), 59.

2. The Undersexed Valetudinarian

1. See, for example, Malcolm Cowley, "The Revolt against Gentility," in *After the Genteel Tradition: American Writers, 1910–1930,* ed. Malcolm Cowley (1937; Carbondale: Southern Illinois University Press, 1964); Howard Mumford Jones, *The Theory of American Literature* (Ithaca, N.Y.: Cornell University Press, 1948); Frederick J. Hoffman, *The Twenties: American Writing in the Postwar Decade* (New York: Viking Press, 1955); Henry F. May, *The End of American Innocence* (1959; New York: Oxford University Press, 1979); Daniel Aaron, *Writers on the Left: Episodes in American Literary Communism* (New York: Harcourt, Brace and World, 1961); Richard Ruland, *The Rediscovery of American Literature: Premises of Critical Taste, 1900–1940* (Cambridge, Mass.: Harvard University Press, 1967); and Kermit H. Vanderbilt, *American Literature and the Academy* (Philadelphia: University of Pennsylvania Press, 1986).

2. Alfred Kazin, *On Native Grounds: An Interpretation of Modern American Prose Literature* (1942; New York: Harcourt Brace Jovanovich, 1982), xiii–xv.

3. Frederick Carpenter, *Emerson Handbook* (New York: Hendricks House, 1953), 202.

4. This categorization of critics is imprecise but nonetheless useful: while it is not meant to suggest that those identified with a particular group necessarily agreed with one another, they at least followed a shared method. Kazin, May, Ruland, and Vanderbilt use nearly identical variations on this model.

5. "The Influence of Emerson," in Paul Elmer More, *Shelburne Essays, First Series* (New York: G. P. Putnam's Sons, 1904), 72. This is reprinted from *Independent* 55 (21 May 1903).

6. Emile Aquinaldo was the leader of the Philippine Independence Movement, which was crushed by American forces in the wake of the Spanish-American War. More here is taking a shot at members of the Anti-Imperialist League, many of whom championed Aquinaldo as the legitimate ruler of the Philippine people and some of whom (see chapter 1) invoked Emerson to validate their claim.

7. More's "Emerson" appeared in volume 1 of *Cambridge History of American Literature,* ed. William P. Trent, John Erskine, Stuart P. Sherman, and Carl Van Doren (New York: Putnam, 1917). It was revised and reprinted in More's *A New England Group and Others* (Boston: Houghton Mifflin, 1921). My references are to the latter as reprinted in *Paul Elmer More's "Shelburne Essays" on American Literature,* ed. Daniel Aaron (New York: Harcourt, Brace and World, 1963).

8. *Irving Babbitt: Man and Teacher,* ed. Frederick Manchester and Odell Shepard (New York: Putnam, 1941) 258. Babbitt himself makes the connection with Norton. In a letter to his former student, Stuart Pratt Sherman, Babbitt wrote: "I feel forced to agree with much of what C. E. Norton says in the admirable estimate toward the end of the first volume of his correspondence." *Life and Letters of Stuart P. Sherman,* ed. Jacob Zeitlin and Homer Woodbridge, 2 vols. (New York: Farrar and Rinehart, 1929), 2:514. James Truslow Adams makes the same point, admitting that "the Emerson who so evidently stirred me at sixteen leaves me cold to-day at fifty." Adams also echoes More when he observes that "it seems almost the basest of treason to write this essay." See his "Emerson Re-Read," *Atlantic* (October 1930): 484–92.

9. Babbitt's and More's comments on Emerson are discussed in Robert Bloom, "Irving Babbitt's Emerson," *New England Quarterly* 30 (December 1957): 448–73; Francis X. Duggan, "Paul Elmer More and the New England Tradition," *American Literature* 34.4 (January 1963): 542–61; Rene Wellek, "Irving Babbitt, Paul More, and Transcendentalism," in *Tran-*

scendentalism and its Legacy, ed. Myron Simon and Thornton H. Parsons (Ann Arbor: University of Michigan Press, 1966), 185–203.

10. Irving Babbitt, *The Masters of Modern French Criticism* (Boston: Houghton Mifflin, 1912), 23. The title is disingenuous in that, though the majority of critics discussed are indeed French, Babbitt clearly sees the "crisis" to be international in nature, and particularly ominous in the United States.

11. In Babbitt's scheme, the terms insight, intuition, impulse, and spontaneity, on the one hand, and tradition, order, judgment, and unity, on the other, are interchangeable.

12. On Babbitt, More, and New Humanism, see Ruland, *Rediscovery,* 12–56, and J. David Hoeveler Jr., *The New Humanism: A Critique of Modern America, 1900–1940* (Charlottesville: University of Virginia Press, 1977).

13. This distinction is suggested by Ruland, *Rediscovery,* 12.

14. For background on Sherman, see Vanderbilt, *American Literature,* passim, and Ruland, *Rediscovery,* 57–96. Ruland also discusses the Sherman-Mencken debate, pp. 139–65.

15. Sherman's letter and Babbitt's response are included in *Life and Letters of Stuart P. Sherman,* 2:514–15.

16. Stuart Sherman, "The Emersonian Liberation" reprinted in *Americans* (New York: Scribner's, 1924), 64.

17. Stuart Sherman, "The Point of View in American Criticism," in *The Genius of America: Studies in Behalf of the Younger Generation* (New York: Scribner's, 1925), 230–31.

18. Quoted in Ruland, *Rediscovery,* 69. The Jackson referred to is, of course, Andrew, though Emerson did in fact marry a Jackson: Lydian, his second wife.

19. For example, see Mark Krupnick, "Middlebrowism in the Academy," review of *American Literature and the Academy* by Kermit Vanderbilt, *American Quarterly* 40 (June 1988): 229–39, and Ruland, *Rediscovery,* 57–96, 137–66. Ruland acknowledges Sherman's disturbing rejection of Dreiser and other "immigrant" writers, but argues that Sherman was still in the process of evolving away from the New Humanism of Babbitt and More when he died. The letter to Brownell was written the year before Sherman's death, and Ruland is persuasive in arguing that Sherman was on his way to articulating a more generous, inclusive and liberal criticism.

20. "Diagnosis of Our Cultural Malaise," in *H. L. Mencken's Smart Set Criticism,* ed. William H. Nolte (Washington, D.C.: Gateway, 1987), 6. See also "The National Letters," in H. L. Mencken, *The American Scene,* ed. Huntington Cairns (New York: Vintage, 1982), esp. 61–65.

21. Mencken, "William Lyon Phelps and Others," in Nolte, *Smart Set Criticism,* 18. In "Footnote on Criticism," Mencken declares that "the Paul Elmer Mores and Hamilton Wright Mabies are no longer able to purr in peace," *American Scene,* 188–89.

22. Mencken, "Epilogue," in *Smart Set Criticism,* 334.

23. Mencken, "Final Estimate," in *Smart Set Criticism,* p. 184.

24. In H. L. Mencken, *Prejudices: First Series* (New York: Knopf, 1919), 191.

25. Mencken, "Final Estimate," 184.

26. "The Moonstruck Pastor," in *A Mencken Chrestomathy,* ed. H. L. Mencken (1949; New York: Vintage, 1982), 477. The review originally appeared in the *American Mercury,* October 1930.

27. Letter to Harry Leon Wilson, 7 November 1933, in *Letters of H. L. Mencken,* ed. Guy J. Forgue (New York: Knopf, 1961), 370.

28. It is interesting to note that this potential was warmly appreciated by one of Mencken's own heroes, Friedrich Nietzsche.

29. Mencken, "The Blue Nose," in *A Mencken Chrestomathy,* 470; originally published in *Smart Set,* May 1919.

30. "On Creating a Usable Past," *Dial* 64 (11 April 1918): 337–41. On Brooks, see William Wasserstrom, *The Legacy of Van Wyck Brooks: A Study of Maladies and Motives* (Carbondale: Southern Illinois University Press, 1971) and James Hoopes, *Van Wyck Brooks: In Search of American Culture* (Amherst: University of Massachusetts Press, 1977), as well as the discussions in Ruland, *Rediscovery,* May, *American Innocence,* and Kazin, *On Native Grounds.* See also John L. Thomas, "The Uses of Catastrophism: Lewis Mumford, Vernon L. Parrington, Van Wyck Brooks, and the End of American Regionalism," *American Quarterly* 42.2 (June 1990): 223–51, for a different view of Brooks's project during this period.

31. Van Wyck Brooks, *America's Coming-of-Age* (New York: Huebsch, 1915), 7.

32. Christopher Lasch, *The True and Only Heaven: Progress and its Critics* (New York: Norton, 1991), 547.

33. Typical of the transitions Brooks supplies between original passages from Emerson is this description of Emerson's second marriage: "Then suddenly Emerson found himself to be engaged again to be married—to Lydia Jackson of Plymouth." *The Life of Emerson* (New York: Dutton, 1932), 60.

34. The quoted material is from Wasserstrom, *Van Wyck Brooks,* 59. Wasserstrom discusses Brooks breakdown and his work on Emerson on pages 51–59. See also Hoopes, *Van Wyck Brooks,* chapter 7, and Jackson Lears, *No Place of Grace: Antimodernism and the Transformation of American Culture, 1880–1920* (New York: Pantheon, 1981), 251–60.

35. On the "Young Intellectuals," see Casey Blake, *Beloved Community: The Cultural Criticism of Randolph Bourne, Van Wyck Brooks, Waldo Frank, and Lewis Mumford* (Chapel Hill: University of North Carolina Press, 1990) and "The Young Intellectuals and the Culture of Personality," *American Literary History* 1.3 (Fall 1989): 510–34. Blake offers an insightful analysis of the critical milieu that I am discussing.

36. Waldo Frank, *Our America* (New York: Boni and Liveright, 1919).

37. Vanderbilt refers to Marxist and Freudian criticism as "movements in cultural advocacy," and provides a good general discussion, especially in chapters 18 and 19. See also Aaron, *Writers on the Left,* for a thorough account of developments in Marxist criticism.

38. Ludwig Lewishon, *Expression in America* (New York: Harper and Brothers, 1932), xxxi–ii.

39. Lewishon argues that the evolution of the expressive mind can be divided into three stages which, in turn, "happily" correspond to the three stages of civilization: the bard, who represents primitive articulateness and serves reactively to express the thoughts and desires of the tribe; the artificer, who is more refined and sophisticated than the bard but chooses to speak only in a way that pleases or soothes his audience; and the poet, who is motivated simply by his individual consciousness and freely expresses what he sees as the truth (xx–xxv). The artificer, in this extended discussion, comes to include most journalists, school teachers, college professors, and literary critics, and emerges most clearly as the villain in Lewishon's unfolding scheme.

40. True to form, Lewishon fails to offer even anecdotal evidence to support his contention that Emerson had problems in his "love life"; he merely extrapolates from the comments in the journals. Much of this recalls Van Wyck Brooks at his worst in *The Ordeal of Mark Twain* (New York: E. P. Dutton & Co., 1920).

41. Kermit Vanderbilt suggests something of this when he observes that Lewishon was "an economic socialist but the advocate of a personal and moral individualism" (*American Literature,* 366). Vanderbilt fails, however, to consider the possibility that a commitment to socialism in economic matters may in some cases come into conflict with a strong "moral" individualism.

42. Frank's *Our America* and its sequel, *The Re-Discovery of America* (New York: Scribner's, 1929) were both completed before he began his involvement with the communist-organized League of American Writers. Of course, some aspects of his Marxism can be traced to his earlier work. See his "Values of the Revolutionary Writer" in *American Writers' Congress,* ed. Henry Hart (New York: International Publishers, 1935).

43. V. F. Calverton, *The Liberation of American Literature* (New York: Scribner's, 1932), xii–xiii.

44. For background on Hicks, see Aaron, *Writers on the Left;* also see Hicks's "The Dialectics of the Development of Marxist Criticism" in *American Writers' Congress.*

45. Granville Hicks, *The Great Tradition: An Interpretation of American Literature since the Civil War* (1935; New York: Biblo and Tannen, 1967), 4.

46. Hicks moves back and forth rather sloppily between discussing these writers individually and as a group, but it is clear that the "them" always includes Emerson.

47. On the Agrarians, see Paul K. Conkin, *The Southern Agrarians* (Knoxville: University of Tennessee Press, 1988). Vanderbilt offers a useful discussion of the Agrarians in their institutional setting, while Ruland suggests the loose alliance between the Agrarians, New Critics, and other "formalists" (Vanderbilt, *American Literature,* 362–64; Ruland, *Rediscovery,* 197–208). Kazin also saw the Formalist critics as united in opposition to the Marxists of the thirties, but he strongly condemns both camps for obscuring the true meaning of literature (*On Native Grounds,* 426ff.). This loose grouping of figures is repeated in Michael Wood, "Literary Criticism," in *Columbia Literary History of the United States,* Emory Elliott, general editor (New York: Columbia University Press, 1988), 993–1018. After 1940, of course, the New Criticism became entrenched in university literature departments and came to dominate the field of criticism.

48. Winters did not identify himself directly with either the Agrarians or the New Critics, but his work shares much with theirs. See Kazin, *On Native Grounds,* 431–37, and Russell Reising, *The Unusable Past: Theory and the Study of American Literature* (New York: Methuen, 1986), 57–74.

49. Yvor Winters, "Foreword," *In Defense of Reason* (1947; Athens, Ohio: Swallow Press, 1987), 3, 11. This volume collects Winters's first three books, *Primitivism and Decadence: A Study of American Experimental Poetry* (1937), *Maule's Curse: Seven Studies in the History of American Obscurantism* (1938), and *The Anatomy of Nonsense* (1943), as well as his essay "The Significance of *The Bridge* by Hart Crane, or What Are We to Think of Professor X?" (1947). I will identify my references in the text.

50. Winters identifies the didactic, the relativist, and the hedonistic as characteristics of the type of criticism he shuns. See "Foreword," 3–11.

51. Tate's comments can be found in his essay on Emily Dickinson, reprinted in *Reactionary Essays on Poetry and Ideas* (New York: Scribner's, 1936), 7–8.

52. The exception to this judgment is Jones Very, whom Winters seeks to resurrect from what he considers undeserved oblivion.

53. Winters's example is *The Ambassadors.* While James would have us admire Lambert Strether's decision to give up Maria Gostrey so as not to appear to have gotten anything for

himself, Winters believes that this is a "sacrifice of morality to appearances," the moral choice—rooted in "Christian humility"—being Strether's consideration of Miss Gostrey's feelings rather than his own reputation (*In Defense of Reason*, 335).

54. "The Progress of Hart Crane," in *The Uncollected Essays and Reviews of Yvor Winters*, ed. Francis Murphy (Chicago: Swallow Press, 1973), 81. The review first appeared in *Poetry* 36.3 (1930): 153–65. Winters and Crane enjoyed something of a casual friendship that began in 1926 and effectively ended with this review of *The Bridge*. See Thomas Parkinson, *Hart Crane and Yvor Winters: Their Literary Correspondence* (Berkeley: University of California Press, 1978), particularly 152–56, where Parkinson discusses "The Significance of the Bridge" as an act of Winters's exorcising Crane from his consciousness.

55. "Brooks's Life of Emerson," in Newton Arvin, *American Pantheon* ed. Daniel Aaron and Sylvan Schendler (New York: Delacorte Press, 1966), 10.

56. Bliss Perry, *Emerson Today* (Princeton, N.J.: Princeton University Press, 1931), 11, 26; O. W. Firkins, "Has Emerson a Future?" *Modern Language Notes* 45.8 (December 1930): 498.

3. William James and the Varieties of Emerson

1. F. O. Matthiessen, *The James Family: A Group Biography* (New York: Knopf, 1947), 428, 433.

2. Frederic Carpenter, "William James and Emerson," *American Literature* 11 (1939): 40. See also Carpenter, "Points of Comparison between Emerson and William James," *New England Quarterly* 2 (July 1929): 458–74.

3. George Cotkin, "Ralph Waldo Emerson and William James as Public Philosophers," *The Historian* 49.1 (November 1986): 49–63; Frank Lentricchia, "On the Ideologies of Poetic Modernism, 1890–1913: The Example of William James," in *Reconstructing American Literary History*, ed. Sacvan Bercovich (Cambridge, Mass.: Harvard University Press, 1986), 230, 241; Richard Poirier, *The Renewal of Literature: Emersonian Reflections* (New Haven, Conn.: Yale University Press, 1988), 47, 202. Lentricchia has written on James in two other essays, each of which includes substantial portions of this earlier one; see "The Return of William James," *Cultural Critique* 4 (Fall 1986): 5–31, and "Philosophers of Modernism at Harvard, circa 1900," *South Atlantic Quarterly* 89.4 (Fall 1990): 787–834.

4. Lentricchia, "Poetic Modernism," 230. See also his "Philosophers of Modernism," 813.

5. Lentricchia, "The Return of William James," 22.

6. "Address at the Centenary of Ralph Waldo Emerson, May 25, 1903," reprinted in William James, *Writings, 1902–1910* (New York: Library of America, 1987), 1119–25. For the most interesting account of the composition of this address, see James's letters from this period included in *The Letters of William James*, ed. Henry James, 2 vols. (Boston: Little, Brown, 1926), 2:187–97.

7. James, *Letters*, 2:190.

8. In *Writings*, 1119.

9. On this see Ralph Barton Perry, *The Thought and Character of William James*, 2 vols. (Boston: Little, Brown, 1935); Gerald E. Myers, *William James: His Life and Thought* (New Haven, Conn.: Yale University Press, 1986); Howard M. Feinstein, *Becoming William James* (Ithaca, N.Y.: Cornell University Press, 1984); and George Cotkin, *William James, Public Philosopher* (Baltimore: Johns Hopkins University Press, 1990). See also Matthiessen, *The James Family*, 209ff.

10. Len Gougeon summarizes the criticism of Emerson as being insensitive to reform, and

concludes that much of it was overstated; see *Virtue's Hero: Emerson, Antislavery, and Reform* (Athens: University of Georgia Press, 1990).

11. In *Essays and Lectures* (New York: Library of America, 1983), 262–63. Unless noted, all references to Emerson are to this edition.

12. See Thomas Wentworth Higginson, Franklin B. Sanborn, and Moncure D. Conway.

13. The letter is reprinted in Ralph Barton Perry, *The Thought and Character of William James*, briefer version (1947; New York: Harper & Row, 1964), 52–53; a lengthy extract appears in Myers, *William James*, 3–4.

14. Since the following discussion moves rather freely between James's paraphrases of Emerson and his direct quotations, my references to the latter will always be to the original source in Emerson's works.

15. Carpenter, "William James and Emerson," 42.

16. James makes these points in notes he drew up for a series of talks he gave on Emerson in the early 1900s. See William James, *Manuscript Essays and Notes*, ed. Frederick H. Burkhardt (Cambridge, Mass.: Harvard University Press, 1988), 315–19.

17. See William James, "The Religion of Healthy-Mindedness," in *The Varieties of Religious Experience: A Study in Human Nature* in *Writings, 1902–1910* (New York: Library of America, 1987) and James's introductory note to his father's "Emerson" in *Atlantic Monthly Magazine* 94 (December 1904): 740.

18. The same observation describes Emerson's method of reading, and the method of reading he urged on his contemporaries. See especially Robert D. Richardson, *Emerson: The Mind on Fire* (Berkeley: University of California Press, 1995).

19. William James, *The Will to Believe and Other Essays in Popular Philosophy* (1897; New York: Longmans, Green, 1911), xii–xiii.

20. William James, *Talks to Teachers on Psychology; and to Students on Some of Life's Ideals* (1899; New York: Norton, 1958), 19. These talks originated as a lecture series in 1892. James's first book, *The Principles of Psychology*, was written as a college textbook and published in 1890; an abridged version appeared in 1892.

21. In James, *Talks*, 149–69.

22. Letter to Mrs. Glendower Evans in Perry, *Thought and Character*, 222.

23. Emerson, *Essays and Lectures*, 943.

24. My discussion will focus on James's more general exploration of the topic in *The Will to Believe*. For a discussion of the place of radical empiricism in Western philosophy, see John Wild, *The Radical Empiricism of William James* (Garden City, N.Y.: Doubleday, 1969).

25. Quoted in Perry, *Thought and Character*, 385–86.

26. William James, *Pragmatism: A New Name for Some Old Ways of Thinking* (1907) in *Writings*, 481–82; *The Meaning of Truth: A Sequel to Pragmatism* (1909), in *Writings*, 826.

27. See the letter to Edgar Van Winkle discussed above.

28. Dana Brand, "The Escape from Solipsism: William James's Reformulation of Emerson and Whitman," *ESQ* 31 (1985): 38–48. The essays in question were collected and published as *Essays in Radical Empiricism* in 1912.

29. A similar case can be made for James's theory of pragmatism. While he did not begin his formal examination of the subject until 1905, all of the details had been present in his work as early as the 1890s.

30. *The Varieties of Religious Experience: A Study in Human Nature* collected a series of lectures James delivered in Edinburgh in 1901–2.

31. Ralph Waldo Emerson, "Considerations by the Way," *Essays and Lectures*, 1096.

32. Leo Marx suggests one possible explanation for this in noting that Emerson intended the more radical elements of his doctrine of self-reliance to serve as the foundation of creative work only and not as a general social philosophy. See "Irving Howe: The Pathos of the Left in the Reagan Era," in *The Pilot and the Passenger: Essays on Literature, Technology, and Culture* (New York: Oxford University Press, 1988), 337–47.

33. Lentricchia, "Philosophers of Modernism," 817.

34. Cornel West, *The American Evasion of Philosophy: A Genealogy of Pragmatism* (Madison: University of Wisconsin Press, 1989), 54, 56–57, 60. John Diggins similarly claims that James "remained more concerned about the individual and his and her personal freedom and passional volitional nature in a universe where truths clashed rather than converged." See Diggins, *The Promise of Pragmatism: Modernism and the Crisis of Knowledge and Authority* (Chicago: University of Chicago Press, 1994), 157.

35. James T. Kloppenberg, *Uncertain Victory: Social Democracy and Progressivism in European and American Thought, 1870–1920* (New York: Oxford University Press, 1986), 97–98.

36. John Dewey, *The Middle Works*, vol. 9, ed. Jo Ann Boydston (Carbondale: Southern Illinois University Press, 1981), 57. The citation is from Emerson's essay "Education."

37. In addition to Kloppenberg, the most important discussion of Dewey's ideas is Robert B. Westbrook's *John Dewey and American Democracy* (Ithaca, N.Y.: Cornell University Press, 1991). While Westbrook briefly addresses Dewey's relationship with James, he does not mention Dewey's comments on Emerson.

38. John Dewey, "Ralph Waldo Emerson," in *The Philosophy of John Dewey*, ed. John J. McDermott (Chicago: University of Chicago Press, 1981), 25; first published in *International Journal of Ethics* 13 (1903): 405–13. Cornel West's discussion of this essay can be found in *The American Evasion of Philosophy*, 72–76. He concludes that while "Dewey's attempt to read Emerson in his own image remains incisive and revealing," it "fails at the point where Emerson emerges as somehow transcending his class and becomes an exemplary radical plebian democrat in solidarity with peoples struggling against imperialisms" (75). It is difficult to see where Dewey makes such a claim for Emerson.

39. John Dewey, *Freedom and Culture* (1939; Buffalo: Prometheus Books, 1989), 23, 133.

40. John Dewey, "Maeterlinck's Philosophy of Life," in *The Middle Works*, vol. 6, ed. Jo Ann Boydston (Carbondale: Southern Illinois University Press, 1978), 135. This was first published in *Hibbert Journal* 9 (1911).

41. John Dewey, "The Future of Liberalism," in *The Later Works*, vol. 11, ed. Jo Ann Boydston (Carbondale: Southern Illinois University Press, 1987), 294.

42. Dewey, *The Later Works*, vol. 5, ed. Jo Ann Boydston (Carbondale: Southern Illinois University Press, 1984), 76.

43. Dewey, "The Future of Liberalism," 292.

44. Dewey, *The Later Works*, vol. 2, ed. Jo Ann Boydston (Carbondale: Southern Illinois University Press, 1984), 372.

4. W.E.B. Du Bois and the Implications of Pragmatism

1. Arnold Rampersad, *The Art and Imagination of W.E.B. Du Bois* (1976; New York: Schocken, 1990), vi–vii, 1, 7. See also Rampersad's "W.E.B. Du Bois as a Man of Literature," in *Critical Essays on W.E.B. Du Bois*, ed. William L. Andrews (Boston: Hall, 1985); Manning Marable, *W.E.B. Du Bois: Black Radical Democrat* (Boston: Twayne, 1986); Joseph P. De-Marco, *The Social Thought of W.E.B. Du Bois* (Lanham, Md.: University Press of America,

1983); Houston Baker, "The Black Man of Culture: W.E.B. Du Bois and *The Souls of Black Folk*," in *Long Black Song: Essays in Black American Literature and Culture* (Charlottesville: University Press of Virginia, 1972); and Keith E. Byerman, *Seizing the Word: History, Art, and Self in the Work of W.E.B. Du Bois* (Athens: University of Georgia Press). David Levering Lewis was the first scholar to enjoy full access to the various collections of Du Bois's papers; see *W.E.B. Du Bois: Biography of a Race, 1868–1919* (New York: Holt, 1993). Shamoon Zamir has offered the most thorough attempt to place Du Bois in his turn-of-the-century intellectual context, and should be consulted for a reading of Du Bois that differs significantly from my own; see *Dark Voices: W.E.B. Du Bois and American Thought, 1888–1903* (Chicago: University of Chicago Press, 1995).

2. Cornel West, *The American Evasion of Philosophy: A Genealogy of Pragmatism* (Madison: University of Wisconsin Press, 1989), 5. Zamir questions West's reading of Du Bois and his claims for the "positive values of the pluralistic doctrine" (*Dark Voices*, 46).

3. Throughout his book, West uses as essentially interchangeable the terms "pragmatism," "Emersonian theodicy," and variations on "Emersonian culture of individual freedom/radical democracy/creative democracy."

4. Though West intends to offer "genealogy" as a more effective way of describing the ongoing practice of pragmatism than "tradition," he returns to the latter term throughout the book.

5. *Dusk of Dawn: An Essay Toward an Autobiography of a Race Concept,* in W.E.B. Du Bois, *Writings* (New York: Library of America, 1986), 750.

6. The broad definition I intend here is based on West (see note 3) and on James's blending of pragmatism with pluralism and radical empiricism, detailed in chapter 3.

7. Other assessments of Du Bois's pragmatism include Nancy Muller Milligan, "W.E.B. Du Bois' American Pragmatism," *Journal of American Culture* 8 (Summer 1985): 31–37, and H. C. Larue, "W.E.B. Du Bois and the Pragmatic Method of Truth," *Journal of Human Relations* 19 (1971): 76–83. Neither of these offers more than a superficial survey of the subject.

8. Though Du Bois received an A.B. from Fisk in 1888, Harvard would only admit him as a third-year undergraduate. He received his B.A. in philosophy in 1890, an M.A. in political science in 1891, and a Ph.D. in 1895. William's letter to Henry can be found in *The Letters of William James,* ed. Henry James, 2 vols. (Boston: Little, Brown, 1926), 2:196. The other information is drawn from *Dusk of Dawn,* 578–82.

9. Du Bois's recollections can be found in *Dusk of Dawn,* 578, 582.

10. Letter to Ben F. Rogers, 30 December 1939, in *The Correspondence of W.E.B. Du Bois,* ed. Herbert Aptheker, 3 vols. (Amherst: University of Massachusetts Press, 1976), 2:204.

11. On philosophy at Harvard, see Bruce Kuklick, *The Rise of American Philosophy* (New Haven, Conn.: Yale University Press, 1977), and the early chapters of John McDermott, *Streams of Experience: Reflections on the History and Philosophy of American Culture* (Amherst: University of Massachusetts Press, 1986).

12. *The Autobiography of W.E.B. Du Bois: A Soliloquy on Viewing My Life from the Last Decade of Its First Century* (New York: International Publishers, 1968), 132. First published in the United States five years after Du Bois's death, this book was essentially a revision of the earlier *Dusk of Dawn,* with new material covering his experiences in the intervening twenty years.

13. *The Papers of W.E.B. Du Bois,* microfilm edition, W.E.B. Du Bois Library, University of Massachusetts, Amherst, series 10, reel 57, frames 198–232. All rights reserved.

14. *The Papers of W.E.B. Du Bois,* microfilm edition, W.E.B. Du Bois Library, University of Massachusetts, Amherst, series 3, reel 82, frame 1559. All rights reserved.

15. Rampersad, *The Art and Imagination of W.E.B. Du Bois,* 28–32. Lewis gives the fullest account to date of Du Bois's work with James during the Harvard years, but finds claims for James's influence on Du Bois "somewhat unsatisfactory." As a biographer, Lewis is interested in something more definitive than a "plausible nexus" between ideas. See *W.E.B. Du Bois: Biography of a Race,* 86–96, 603n50. Shamoon Zamir has built on Lewis's questioning of the James–Du Bois relationship, and concluded that "neither Du Bois's student writings nor *Souls* reveal an emotional tenor or intellectual orientation that can be termed unproblematically Jamesian" (*Dark Voices,* 11). It is my claim that Du Bois's relationship with James, rather than being unproblematic, is analogous to James's relationship with Emerson: a matter of creative and selective appropriation. Zamir also focuses on a very different aspect of James's work than I do.

16. Du Bois, *Dusk of Dawn,* 574.

17. Ibid., 770–75.

18. Aptheker quoted in Marable, *W.E.B. Du Bois,* ix.

19. "Does Education Pay?" in *Writings of W.E.B. Du Bois in Periodicals Edited by Others,* vol. 1 (1891–1909), ed. Herbert Aptheker (Millwood, N.Y.: Kraus-Thomson, 1981) 2–3.

20. *The Papers of W.E.B. Du Bois,* microfilm edition, W.E.B. Du Bois Library, University of Massachusetts, Amherst, series 10, reel 87, frames 201–202. All rights reserved.

21. In Du Bois, *Writings* (Library of America), 438.

22. Thus Du Bois summarized his philosophy and his career in a 1956 letter to Aptheker. In the same letter he elaborated at some length on James's pragmatic theory of truth, perceptively correcting what he saw to be Aptheker's misconceptions about that theory and describing his own conversion from a belief in "Absolute Truth" to an acceptance of James's proposition that truth was always only partially knowable; *The Correspondence of W.E.B. Du Bois,* 3:394–96.

23. In "The Talented Tenth," published in the same year as *Souls* and so often cited as evidence of his intransigent elitism, Du Bois not only argued for the admission of certain blacks to the halls of intellectual commerce but stressed that, unless the achievements of the talented tenth contributed to the well-being of the race as well, they would be of little value.

24. For a stimulating discussion of Du Bois's efforts to connect the struggle for black self-realization with the common good, see Thomas C. Holt, "The Political Uses of Alienation: W.E.B. Du Bois on Politics, Race, and Culture, 1903–1940," *American Quarterly* 42.2 (June 1990): 301–23.

25. Unpublished in Du Bois's lifetime, the address can be found in the Library of America edition, pp. 811–14. Zamir reads this piece as a satire of Emerson, Carlyle, and the Great Man theory, though the distinct absence of a tone of satire makes such a reading problematic. See *Dark Voices,* 60–67.

26. James, *Talks to Teachers,* 169, 19.

27. Emerson, "Nominalist and Realist," *Essays and Lectures,* 585.

28. *The Gift of Black Folk: The Negroes in the Making of America* (Boston: Stratford, 1924).

29. Du Bois, *Writings* (Library of America), 993–1002. Delivered at the Chicago Conference of the NAACP in 1926 and published in *The Crisis* that October, this essay reworks ideas Du Bois introduced in *The Souls of Black Folk* and *The Gift of Black Folk,* and is the most complete statement of his own aesthetic sense at the time of his deepest involvement in

promoting the work of black artists. See Darwin T. Turner, "W.E.B. Du Bois and the Theory of a Black Aesthetic," in *Critical Essays on W.E.B. Du Bois.*

30. Du Bois, *Writings* (Library of America), 817; first published in 1897 in the *Occasional Papers* of the American Negro Academy.

31. W.E.B. Du Bois, *John Brown* (1909; Millwood, N.Y.: Kraus-Thomson, 1973), 400. The passage I have quoted is part of a lengthy, italicized section that Du Bois evidently added to a 1962 reissue of the book, a section—inserted between portions of the original text—in which he links Brown with certain lessons of Marx and Lenin. I quote from this passage because it accurately reflects Du Bois's original assessment of Brown's legacy as presented in the main body of the text, an assessment he offered before ever reading Marx or hearing of Lenin. It also points to a certain continuity in Du Bois's thought, going back to the 1890 commencement address on Jefferson Davis. That Du Bois could be so undoctrinaire in his Marxism recalls Herbert Aptheker's claim that he was never anything other than "a Du Boisite."

32. Emerson's comments on John Brown can be found in *Miscellanies,* volume 11 of *The Works of Ralph Waldo Emerson* (Cambridge, Mass.: Riverside, 1878).

33. "Individualism, Democracy, and Social Control," *The Papers of W.E.B. Du Bois,* microfilm edition, W.E.B. Du Bois Library, University of Massachusetts, Amherst, series 2, reel 80, frame 867. All rights reserved.

34. W.E.B. Du Bois, "The Revelation of St. Orgne the Damned," in *Writings* (Library of America), 1064; and "Social Medicine" in W.E.B. Du Bois, *Against Racism: Unpublished Essays, Papers, Addresses, 1887–1961,* ed. Herbert Aptheker (Amherst: University of Massachusetts Press, 1985), 267.

35. W.E.B. Du Bois, "The Future of Europe in Africa," in *Against Racism,* 198.

36. Du Bois's social and political writings make a worthy contribution to the "philosophy of the via media," that blend of pragmatism and progressivism that James Kloppenberg examines in *Uncertain Victory.*

37. John Dewey, "Maeterlinck's Philosophy of Life," in *The Middle Works,* 6: 135; and *Freedom and Culture,* 133. I have been unable to locate any commentary by Du Bois on Dewey, though he did own copies of *Art as Experience* and *Freedom and Culture.* Zamir discusses possible connections between Du Bois and Dewey in *Dark Voices,* 119–22.

38. W.E.B. Du Bois, "Of the Ruling of Men" in *Darkwater: Voices from within the Veil* (1920; New York: Schocken, 1969), 144–45.

39. W.E.B. Du Bois, "The Release of Earl Browder," in *Against Racism,* 201.

40. For Emerson, see his essay "Politics"; for James, see *Pragmatism,* especially 559–60 and 613–14; for Dewey, see *The Public and Its Problems* in *The Later Works,* vol. 2, and *Freedom and Culture,* 134.

41. In *Writings of W.E.B. Du Bois in Periodicals Edited by Others,* 1:3.

42. *Pragmatism,* 583–84. As with Du Bois's paraphrase of James in the address on Jefferson Davis, his words here precede the publication of *Pragmatism* by a number of years. Still, Du Bois would recall that he studied with James while the latter was working on the idea of pragmatism, and his notebook for Philosophy IV shows James ranging over a variety of subjects that he would not address in print until later. While it is, of course, possible that James paraphrased Du Bois, the evidence suggests that it worked the other way.

43. Du Bois returns to this phrase, or a variation of it, many times in his later work, including *Souls* (four times), "The Talented Tenth," *Dusk of Dawn,* and "The Negro College" (1933).

44. Emerson, "The American Scholar," 54, 67.

45. W.E.B. Du Bois, "Postgraduate Work in Sociology at Atlanta University," in *Against Racism,* 66–67.

46. For the idea that Du Bois's acceptance of segregation marked a practical rather than an ideological shift, see Rampersad, *The Art and Imagination of W.E.B. Du Bois,* and Marable, *W.E.B. Du Bois.*

47. Du Bois, *Writings 1902–1910* (New York: Library of America, 1987), 842.

48. Ibid., 1015; originally published in *Crisis,* August 1933.

49. See James, "A World of Pure Experience," in *Writings,* 1160.

50. Du Bois, *Souls,* 421, 426.

51. For the Washington–Du Bois debate, see Rampersad, *Art and Imagination* and "Slavery and the Literary Imagination: Du Bois's *The Souls of Black Folk,*" in *Slavery and the Literary Imagination,* ed. Deborah E. McDowell and Arnold Rampersad (Baltimore: Johns Hopkins University Press, 1989); Baker, *Long Black Song* and *Modernism and the Harlem Renaissance* (Chicago: University of Chicago Press, 1987); Lewis, *W.E.B. Du Bois,* especially 248–342; Louis Harlan, *Booker T. Washington: The Wizard of Tuskegee* (New York: Oxford University Press, 1983); and August Meier, *Negro Thought in America, 1880–1915: Racial Ideologies in the Age of Booker T. Washington* (Ann Arbor: University of Michigan Press, 1990).

52. Booker T. Washington, *Up from Slavery: An Autobiography* (New York: Doubleday, 1902), 68–69, 265, 286. Unless indicated, references to Washington are to this edition.

53. Described in Harlan, *Booker T. Washington,* 275–76. In 1894, Mrs. Margaret Washington sent to her husband, who was on one of his frequent fund-raising trips, her regular summary of events at Tuskegee. She included this note: "The Emerson moves on. Not all attend, but we have a pleasant time—and now and then we have a little fruit." See *The Booker T. Washington Papers,* ed. Louis R. Harlan, 14 vols. (Urbana: University of Illinois Press, 1972–), 3:487.

54. *The Booker T. Washington Papers,* 3:154.

55. See Jennings L. Waggoner Jr., "The American Compromise: Charles W. Eliot, Black Education, and the New South,"in *Education and the Rise of the New South,* ed. Ronald K. Goodenow and Arthur O. White (Boston: Hall, 1981), and the exchange of letters between Washington and Eliot, *The Booker T. Washington Papers,* 9:71–72, 96–98.

56. See Emerson, *Nature,* in *Essays and Lectures,* 29; "The American Scholar," ibid., 56–58, 62–63; "Man the Reformer," ibid., 140–42; "New England Reformers," ibid., 595; "Culture," ibid., 1020–21.

57. Chapter 13 in *The Souls of Black Folk,* 521–35.

58. *Emerson in His Journals,* ed. Joel Porte (Cambridge, Mass.: Harvard University Press, 1982), 283.

5. Inclusiveness without Redundancy

1. Robert Coles has written at length on Williams's fiction and his poetry; see *William Carlos Williams: The Knack for Survival in America* (New Brunswick, N.J.: Rutgers University Press, 1975) and the essays collected in *That Red Wheelbarrow: Selected Literary Essays* (Iowa City: University of Iowa Press, 1988), 295–352. James E. B. Breslin looks at Williams's prose and poetry in *William Carlos Williams: An American Artist* (1970; Chicago: University

of Chicago Press, 1985). See also Mike Weaver, *William Carlos Williams: The American Background* (Cambridge: Cambridge University Press, 1971).

2. This "new wave" of Williams scholarship includes Brian Bremen, *William Carlos Williams and the Diagnostics of Culture* (New York: Oxford University Press, 1992); Geoffrey H. Movius, *The Early Prose of William Carlos Williams, 1917–1925* (New York: Garland, 1987); David Frail, *The Early Politics and Poetics of William Carlos Williams* (Ann Arbor: UMI Research Press, 1987); Bryce Conrad, *Refiguring America: A Study of William Carlos Williams' "In the American Grain"* (Urbana: University of Illinois Press, 1990); and Vera Kutzinski, *Against the American Grain: Myth and History in William Carlos Williams, Jay Wright, and Nicolas Guillen* (Baltimore: Johns Hopkins University Press, 1987). Each of these authors rightfully pays homage to Paul Mariani's monumental *William Carlos Williams: A New World Naked* (New York: McGraw-Hill, 1981).

3. Carl Rapp, *William Carlos Williams and Romantic Idealism* (Hanover, N.H.: University Press of New England, 1984), 77; Stephen Tapscott, *American Beauty: William Carlos Williams and the Modernist Whitman* (New York: Columbia University Press, 1984), 40.

4. David Bromwich looks at the Emerson-James-Stevens connection in "Stevens and the Idea of the Hero," *Raritan* 7.1 (Summer 1987): 1–27; Lisa Ruddick links Emerson, James, Stein, and Stevens in "Fluid Symbols in American Modernism: William James, Gertrude Stein, George Santayana, and Wallace Stevens," *Allegory, Myth, and Symbol,* ed. Morton W. Bloomfield (Cambridge, Mass.: Harvard University Press, 1981); Darrel Abel makes a case for a lineup of Emerson, James, and Frost in "Two Philosophical Poets: Frost, Emerson, and Pragmatism," *ESQ* 25 (1979): 119–36; David M. La Guardia also sees the line running from Emerson through James and into Stevens, *Advance on Chaos: The Sanctifying Imagination of Wallace Stevens* (Hanover, N.H.: University Press of New England, 1983). Despite giving Williams equal billing in his title, Jeffrey Thomas treats him mostly in passing in "The Contextualist Metaphysics of American Modernist Poetry: William James's Influence on Robert Frost, William Carlos Williams, Wallace Stevens, and Company" (Ph.D. diss., Ohio State University, 1984).

5. Frank Lentricchia, *Criticism and Social Change* (Chicago: University of Chicago Press, 1983); *Ariel and the Police* (Madison: University of Wisconsin Press, 1988); "Philosophers of Modernism at Harvard, circa 1900," *South Atlantic Quarterly* 89.4 (Fall 1990): 787–834; and "The Return of William James," *Cultural Critique* 4 (Fall 1986): 5–31.

6. Richard Poirier, *Poetry and Pragmatism* (Cambridge, Mass.: Harvard University Press, 1992), 3–5, 21–22; see also *The Renewal of Literature: Emersonian Reflections* (New Haven, Conn.: Yale University Press, 1988).

7. Poirier, *Renewal of Literature,* 41; Poirier, *Poetry and Pragmatism,* 31. To clarify his use of "difficult," Poirier quotes Blake: "That which can be made Explicit to the Idiot is not worth my care."

8. Lentricchia, "Philosophers of Modernism at Harvard," 832. The allusion is to Williams's "The Red Wheelbarrow."

9. William Carlos Williams, "The American Background" in *Selected Essays* (New York: New Directions, 1969), 155. This essay was originally published as a contribution to *America and Alfred Stieglitz,* ed. Waldo Frank, Lewis Mumford, et al. (New York: Doubleday, 1934). The standard New Directions editions of Williams's works are used throughout this chapter, and references will be given in the text according to the following key: A = *The Autobiography* (1951); SE = *Selected Essays;* KH = *Kora in Hell* (1920) in *Imaginations;* SA = *Spring and*

All (1923) in *Imaginations;* GAN = *The Great American Novel* (1923) in *Imaginations;* SL = *Selected Letters;* IAG = *In the American Grain* (1925); EK = *The Embodiment of Knowledge* (circa 1928); P = *Paterson* (1946–58), revised edition, ed. Christopher MacGowan (New York: New Directions, 1992).

10. Bryce Conrad discusses Williams's reading of Brooks and points to some of the parallels between Williams and Emerson, *Refiguring America*, 20–23.

11. Ralph Waldo Emerson, *Essays and Lectures* (New York: Library of America, 1983). All references to Emerson will be from this edition, page numbers in parentheses.

12. E. P. Bollier, "Against the American Grain: William Carlos Williams between Whitman and Poe," *Tulane Studies in English* 23 (1978): 132.

13. In *The Collected Poems of William Carlos Williams, Vol II: 1939–1962,* ed. Christopher MacGowan (New York: New Directions, 1988), 62–65.

14. James K. Guimond, "William Carlos Williams and the Past: Some Clarifications," *Journal of Modern Literature* 1 (May 1971): 497.

15. Emerson's definition of "poet" was not limited to a mere maker of verses, but included anyone who endeavored to translate experience into symbolic form: painters, artisans, sculptors, essayists, and so on.

16. Paul Jay, "American Modernism and the Uses of History: The Case of William Carlos Williams," *New Orleans Review* 9 (1982): 20–21. For more on Williams, history, and *In the American Grain,* see Joseph G. Kronick, *American Poetics of History: From Emerson to the Moderns* (Baton Rouge: Louisiana State University Press, 1984); Paul Mariani, *A Usable Past: Essays on Modern and Contemporary Poetry* (Amherst: University of Massachusetts Press, 1984); Bryce Conrad, *Refiguring America;* and Vera Kutzinski, *Against the American Grain.*

17. On Williams, Dewey, and "localism," see Mariani, *A New World Naked,* 166, 271, 544–45; Frail, *The Early Politics and Poetics,* 131, 151–55; and Tapscott, *American Beauty,* 95–102. Williams acknowledges Dewey's influence in *The Autobiography,* 391, and *Selected Letters,* 224.

18. William Eric Williams, "Forward" to William Carlos Williams, *Yes, Mrs. Williams: A Personal Record of My Mother* (New York: New Directions, 1982), ix. This is a good source for Williams's reflections on his family background. See also Mariani, *A New World Naked.*

19. Kutzinski, *Against the American Grain,* 34.

20. Mariani, *A Usable Past,* 26.

21. Mariani, *A New World Naked,* 376.

22. Waldo Frank, "Values of the Revolutionary Writer," *American Writers' Congress,* ed. Henry Hart (New York: International Publishers, 1935), 71. As Hart notes in the introduction, the congress was called to "provide technical discussion of the literary applications of Marxist philosophy" (11).

23. Kenneth Burke, "Revolutionary Symbolism in America," in *The American Writer's Congress,* ed. Henry Hart, 89–90.

24. The reaction to Burke's speech is recounted in Malcolm Cowley, *The Dream of the Golden Mountains* (New York: Penguin Books, 1980), 272–79. Frank Lentricchia describes the speech as being perceived as "the very discourse of excrement," *Criticism and Social Change,* 22.

25. Kenneth Burke, *Counter-Statement* (1931; Berkeley: University of California Press, 1968), viii.

26. "The American Spirit in Art," *Proceedings of the American Academy of Arts and Letters,* second series, 2 (1952): 51–59; quoted in Weaver, *William Carlos Williams,* 114.

27. In fact, Burke himself acknowledged the critical importance of both Emerson and James, and his work occupies an important if esoteric place in the Emersonian tradition I am tracing. See especially *Attitudes toward History* (1937; Berkeley: University of California Press, 1984), 3–33, and *A Grammar of Motives* (1945; Berkeley: University of California Press, 1969).

28. Author's introduction to *The Wedge*, in *Collected Poems* 2:53.

29. William James, *Pragmatism*, 618.

30. David Frail, *The Early Politics and Poetics of William Carlos Williams*, finds no comfort in Williams's failure to answer these questions. However inspired, the constitution that Williams would write for the country would not have allowed the society to work. Frail's analysis of Williams's politics is trenchant, emphasizing the inadequacy of his small-town individualism to a modern industrial society. Nonetheless, Frail is too quick to dismiss Williams's efforts to strike a balance between the individual and society, and seems unwilling to consider the kind of radical challenge that Williams's notion of pluralistic politics can pose to the industrial order; see especially pp. 10, 196ff.

31. On Williams and jazz, see Mariano, *A New World Naked*, 512–15, 716–17.

32. Tony Sherman, "The Music of Democracy," *Utne Reader* 74 (March–April 1996): 35; reprinted from *American Heritage* (October 1995).

33. Stephen Tapscott has discussed Williams's effort to "discipline" the "freedom" of Whitman's free verse; see *American Beauty*, 119.

Epilogue. Emersonian Refractions

1. On Ralph Waldo Ellison's ambivalent relationship with his namesake, see Alan Nadel, *Invisible Criticism: Ralph Ellison and the American Canon* (Iowa City: University of Iowa Press, 1988). West's call for "prophetic pragmatism" can be found in *The American Evasion of Philosophy*, 211–39.

2. A. R. Ammons, *Garbage* (New York: Norton, 1993). Harold Bloom has made the case for Ammons's and John Ashberry's place in the Emersonian tradition. See *Figures of Capable Imagination* (New York: Seabury Press, 1976).

3. Cavell's first treatment of Emerson is in *The Senses of Walden*, expanded edition (San Francisco: North Point Press, 1981). See also *This New Yet Unapproachable America: Lectures after Emerson after Wittgenstein* (Albuquerque, N.M.: Living Batch Press, 1989); *Conditions Handsome and Unhandsome: The Constitution of Emersonian Perfectionism* (Chicago: University of Chicago Press, 1990); and *Pursuits of Happiness: The Hollywood Comedy of Remarriage* (Cambridge, Mass.: Harvard University Press, 1981).

4. Though his focus is on Thoreau, Lawrence Buell outlines this tradition in *The Environmental Imagination: Thoreau, Nature Writing, and the Formation of American Culture* (Cambridge, Mass: Harvard University Press, 1995). Burroughs and Muir each wrote frequently on Emerson. Abbey's testament to Emerson can be found in "Emerson," *One Life at a Time, Please* (New York: Holt, 1987). Snyder's Emersonianism is discussed in Sherman Paul, "From Lookout to Ashram: The Way of Gary Snyder," in *Repossessing and Renewing*. See also Daniel G. Payne, *Voices in the Wilderness: American Nature Writing and Environmental Politics* (Hanover, N.H.: University Press of New England, 1996).

5. A recent three-day festival at the Brooklyn Academy of Music was dedicated to exploring the relationship between Emerson and Ives. The festival received financial support from the National Endowment for the Humanities.

6. Charles Ives, *Essays before a Sonata, The Majority, and Other Writings,* ed. Howard Boatwright (New York: Norton, 1970).

7. This angle on Ives can be found in Sam B. Girgus, *The Law of the Heart* (Austin: University of Texas Press, 1979), 101–5. A similar claim has been made about Frank Lloyd Wright, whose iconoclastic genius, "honest arrogance," and philandering all had common validation in his understanding of Emerson. See William Cronon, "Inconstant Unity: The Passion of Frank Lloyd Wright," in *Frank Lloyd Wright, Architect,* ed. Terence Riley (New York: Museum of Modern Art, 1994).

8. "Ralph Waldo Emerson: Transcendental Critic," in *Main Currents in American Thought,* Volume 2: *The Romantic Revolution in America, 1800–1860* (New York: Harcourt, Brace and World, 1927), 387.

9. F. O. Matthiessen, *American Renaissance: Art and Expression in the Age of Emerson and Whitman* (New York: Oxford University Press, 1941), ix, xiv–xvi.

10. We thus have another series of refractions roughly analogous to my own: Emerson to Sullivan to Matthiessen to Paul.

11. "Louis Sullivan and Organic Architecture," in Sherman Paul, *Repossessing and Renewing: Essays in the Green American Tradition* (Baton Rouge: Louisiana State University Press, 1976), 129, 117. See also Paul's longer work on Sullivan, *Louis Sullivan: An Architect in American Thought* (Englewood Cliffs, N.J.: Prentice Hall, 1962).

12. J. David Greenstone, "Dorothea Dix and Jane Addams: From Transcendentalism to Pragmatism in American Social Reform," *Social Service Review* (December 1979): 527–59.

13. George Kateb, *The Inner Ocean: Individualism and Democratic Culture* (Ithaca, N.Y.: Cornell University Press, 1992). The most lucid and most important communitarian critique of unrestrained individualism is found in the work of Charles Derber, who focuses on the alienating and destructive results of acquisitive and possessive individualism. Derber takes many of his communitarian colleagues to task for stressing the cultural, rather than the economic perversions of individualism in modern American life, and he suggests that the Emersonian promise is forfeited in a culture so passionately committed to an ethos of "I'll get mine." See *The Pursuit of Attention: Power and Individualism in Everyday Life* (New York: Oxford University Press, 1979); *Money, Murder, and the American Dream: Wilding from Wall Street to Main Street* (Boston: Faber and Faber, 1992); and "Coming Glued: Communitarianism to the Rescue," in *Tikkun* 8.4 (July/August 1993): 27–30, 95–99.

14. John Diggins, *The Lost Soul of American Politics: Virtue, Self-Interest, and the Foundations of Liberalism* (1984; Chicago: University of Chicago Press, 1986), 228–29, 336. Diggins returns to some of these issues in *The Promise of Pragmatism: Modernism and the Crisis of Knowledge and Authority* (Chicago: University of Chicago Press, 1994), where he traces the failures of pragmatism in part to the abandonment of the past authorized by Emerson, James, and Dewey. While Diggins's overall critique of pragmatism is compelling, I believe that this particular concern is overdrawn.

15. John Updike, "Emersonianism," in *Odd Jobs* (New York: Knopf, 1991). First delivered as an address in 1983, the essay was later published in the *New Yorker.*

16. Richard Poirier, "Human, All Too Inhuman," *The New Republic,* 2 February 1987, pp. 29–36. The passage cited is on p. 30.

17. See "Introduction," note 8, above, for reassessments of the nature of Emersonian individualism.

18. Quentin Anderson, *The Imperial Self: An Essay in American Literary and Cultural*

History (New York: Vintage, 1971), 4. Claiming to have taken her cue from Anderson, Joyce Warren accused Emerson of adolescent pettiness, provincialism, narrowness, an obsession with self and a disregard for other people. Her discussion of Emerson is itself a model of narrow reading that rivals Yvor Winters in its petulance. See *The American Narcissus: Individualism and Women in Nineteenth-Century American Fiction* (New Brunswick, N.J.: Rutgers University Press, 1984), 23–53.

INDEX